# CRITICAL INSIGHTS

## Romeo and Juliet

# CRITICAL INSIGHTS

## Romeo and Juliet

Editor

**Robert C. Evans**

*Auburn University, Montgomery*

SALEM PRESS

A Division of EBSCO Information Services, Inc.

Ipswich, Massachusetts

**GREY HOUSE PUBLISHING**

Publisher's Cataloging-In-Publication Data
(Prepared by The Donohue Group, Inc.)

Names: Evans, Robert C., 1955- editor.
Title: Romeo and Juliet / editor, Robert C. Evans, Auburn University,
        Montgomery.
Other Titles: Critical insights.
Description: [First edition]. | Ipswich, Massachusetts : Salem Press, a division
        of EBSCO Information Services, Inc. ; Amenia, NY : Grey
        House Publishing, [2017] | Includes bibliographical references
        and index.
Identifiers: ISBN 978-1-68217-264-3 (hardcover)
Subjects: LCSH: Shakespeare, William, 1564-1616.Romeo and Juliet. |
        Shakespeare, William, 1564-1616--Criticism and interpretation. |
        Imagination in literature.
Classification: LCC PR2831 .E93 2017 | DDC 822.33--dc23

First Printing

PRINTED IN THE UNITED STATES OF AMERICA

# Contents

**Resources**

# About This Volume

Robert C. Evans

The present volume is intended to provide a deliberately diverse set of responses to *Romeo and Juliet*, one of Shakespeare's best-known tragedies. Nevertheless, the essays do share many common interests. Not surprisingly (for instance), the famous "balcony scene" is the subject of much commentary by various essayists. Two essays look at specific sections of that scene from multiple perspectives. In addition, two essays examine filmed versions of Shakespeare's play, while another two other essays examine parodies of his well-known text. Multiple essays are concerned with issues of physical *space* in the play, and various essays explore issues of imagination, artifice, and artificiality in the work. So, the following volume is a collection employing varied points of view but also sharing many of the same concerns.

In the essay that introduces this volume, Bruce Boehrer offers a view of Shakespeare's play "as essentially an adaptive and living being, one that exists in a kind of ecological tension with its sources as well as with certain shifts in relation to time and space consistent with the development of early modern urban life." Boehrer views Shakespeare's text "as a recycled play emerging from a centuries-old story-sequence, a play that revises that story-sequence specifically by changing its relation to the recurring cycles of the traditional church calendar," so that "it gives voice in the process to a fear that the cycle of human generational renewal will fail. Here," Boehrer claims, "the play's relationship to *A Midsummer Night's Dream* appears most manifest." Like many other essays in this volume, this article is keenly interested in topics of intertextuality—of relations between one text and others. But Boehrer also relates Shakespeare's play to issues of Shakespeare's life—a life reviewed briefly in an ensuing biographical overview that follows Boehrer's article.

## Critical Contexts

The "Critical Contexts" section of the book opens with an examination, by Benedict J. Whalen, of the play's presentation of Friar Laurence. Whalen suggests that *Romeo and Juliet* "emphasizes the role of the friar, and of confession, as a potential means for reconciling the 'ancient grudge' between the Capulets and Montagues. However," Whalen continues, "Friar Laurence does not make use of the sacrament, or his spiritual authority, when he tries to solve Verona's manifold troubles; instead, he turns to philosophy and natural science." This decision, Whalen thinks, "suggests a grave problem at the very heart of the community: the mechanism through which political and spiritual reconciliation could have been accomplished has been lost." Whalen believes that "Shakespeare's depiction of the conflict echoes some of the grave effects of the Church of England's abandonment of the sacrament of auricular confession." In this respect, "the play engages with contemporary Reformation debates about the nature of the sacraments and the relationship between spiritual and political authorities in a community."

The next essay in the "Critical Contexts" section is an overview, by Richard Harp, of the play's critical reception. Harp focuses on such major critical voices as Samuel Johnson, Samuel Taylor Coleridge, William Hazlitt, Edward Dowden, A. C. Bradley, and many others. He also explores such key topics as Romeo and Juliet as lovers; issues of love and death; the play's imagery; and its use of various kinds of poetry (such as sonnets, the poetry of marriage, and the poetry of morning awakenings). Harp also discusses such matters as oxymorons, stagecraft, the functions of minor characters, and the roles of Mercutio and Friar Laurence.

Harp's essay is followed by one by Robert C. Evans dealing with the variety of possible theoretical approaches to the play. Using a deliberately "pluralistic" method, Evans examines the first fifty lines of the famous "balcony scene" from nearly twenty different points of view. "Critical pluralism" (Evans explains) is "the idea that no single critical perspective can do full justice to the complexity of any truly complex piece of writing. Instead, multiple perspectives can and should be constantly kept in mind as we read. By thinking about any particular word or phrase in light of *multiple* interpretive possibilities," Evans maintains, "we are less likely to interpret any work simplistically or reduce its richness to monolithic meanings."

Finally, complementing Evans's pluralistic approach is an essay by Eric J. Sterling that discusses the many different ways in which the most famous line of the balcony scene—"O Romeo, Romeo, wherefore art thou Romeo?"—has been performed in various filmed versions of the play. Sterling notes that audiences "wait for [the line] to appear and are curious to see just exactly how it will be performed. Stagings of Juliet's opening words on the balcony typically symbolize the choices made (by actors, directors, and scenic designers) for entire productions." Sterling examines the ways Juliet's line is presented in films directed by George Cukor (1936), Renato Castellani (1954), Franco Zeffirelli (1968), Joan Kemp-Welch (1976), Alvin Rakoff (1978), Baz Luhrmann (1996), Rupert Goold (2010), Carlo Carlei (2013), and Don Ray King (2014).

## Critical Readings

The volume's "Critical Readings" section offers numerous different approaches to Shakespeare's play. It opens with an essay by Maurice Hunt that explores the theme of imagination in the drama as well as the imaginative nature of the text itself. Hunt is interested in the ways Shakespeare "imagines his characters and their speeches," but he is also interested in the ways Romeo and Juliet imagine "their love, its fulfillment, and its consequences." He discusses such topics as metaphors, decorum, language, wordplay, puns, conceits, and reason as well as such figures as Petrarch, Cupid, and numerous characters of the play, including Friar Laurence.

Issues of imagination are also central to Frances Teague's essay. Teague challenges the idea that this drama is a great work because it is realistic: "The idea that *Romeo and Juliet* is great art because it is so universally reflective of life seems to me to be accurate only if you have a taste for melodrama." Instead, Teague admires the play precisely for its artificiality, particularly the way "the speeches play with heightened language, while the plot plays with heightened action." Teague finds the play's use of paradoxes especially appealing, particularly the way Shakespeare personifies Death as a lover. She explores this latter paradox by discussing the play's imagery in light of the visual art of Shakespeare's culture.

Christopher Baker's essay "*Romeo and Juliet* on Film" broadens the focus of Eric Sterling's earlier essay. Rather than concentrating on a particular scene or line, Baker explores the history of modern approaches to filming the play in general. He discusses some of the same productions cited by Sterling but adds others as well, and he provides a helpful overview not only of the films themselves but of scholarship about them. Baker comments on the performances of numerous actors in various roles.

Next, James Hirsh, in an important essay that is part of a much larger scholarly project, examines the ways soliloquies are presented in Shakespeare's plays in general and in *Romeo and Juliet* in particular. Hirsh offers numerous striking arguments, including the claim that "*Romeo and Juliet* marked a major watershed in Shakespeare's employment of the late Renaissance dramatic convention of self-addressed speech. Plentiful evidence demonstrates," Hirsh contends, "that, in the process of writing *Romeo and Juliet*, Shakespeare, like the two main characters, fell madly in love. In his case, what he fell in love with were the exciting dramatic possibilities created by the convention governing soliloquies that he himself had helped to establish."

In an essay on trauma in this work, Robert C. Evans notes that "very little discussion seems to exist of trauma in Shakespeare in general or in *Romeo and Juliet* in particular." He therefore tries to offer "a comprehensive overview of traumatic moments in this play, focusing especially on the scenes involving the deaths of Mercutio and Tybalt as well as the later scenes leading up to and involving Juliet's apparent death in her parents' home." According to Evans, *Romeo and Juliet* "illustrates many points made by recent theorists of trauma, and trauma is central to much of this drama's enduring power." He particularly stresses how the play moves toward more and more intensely traumatic episodes as it develops.

Adam Rzepka's essay begins by intriguingly noting that in *Romeo and Juliet*, "Shakespeare unleashes a blizzard of morbidity, including variations on the words 'death' and 'dead' alone (leaving aside references to 'fate,' 'doom,' the 'end' of life, and an ever-expanding constellation of funereal terms like 'bier,' 'tomb,' 'grave,' and shroud) 126 times—more than in any of his other plays." Rzepka suggests that Romeo and Juliet have a way "of placing themselves in the intimacy of tomblike spaces throughout the play" and that "these spaces take on a metatheatrical cast, as they begin to echo the space shared by the play and its audience. The tomb finds a resonance in the theater, that enclosure where Romeo and Juliet are killed, reincorporated, and reanimated in performance after performance."

Space is also an important issue in Matthew Steggle's provocatively titled essay "Flight and Spaceflight in *Romeo and Juliet*." Steggle proposes that this play is "is far more subversive in its relationship to cosmology than has generally been recognized." Whereas the play is often thought to take for granted Elizabethan ideas of an ordered universe, Steggle proposes that Romeo and Juliet often speak and act as if they can defy gravity. In fact, they "repeatedly figure their activities in terms of altering, and indeed destroying, the heavens." But Steggle also notes that "as the play turns to tragedy, imagery of flight becomes increasingly entangled with imagery of death." Steggle concludes by comparing and contrasting Shakespeare's play with Christopher Marlowe's *Doctor Faustus*.

In another essay also concerned with space and spaces, Lisa Hopkins notes that the famous balcony scene "treats the relationship between house and garden," but she also argues that "that relationship in itself can be mapped onto a wider pattern within the play which contrasts the natural world with the built environment." She notes that we "do hear of the architectural detail for which Italy was famous in Renaissance England (particularly in the shape of balconies and walls), but bodies swarm over that architecture and cross its boundaries, first when Romeo scales the wall and climbs up to the balcony and then later when living bodies violate the funerary architecture of the Capulet tomb." Hopkins suggests that

"*Romeo and Juliet* pits against each other images of growth and life, particularly images of fruit and flowers, with images of death, which the play connects to man-made structures such as tombs and statues." She argues that this pattern of imagery, and the paradoxes it implies, helps explain the particular tragic power of this play.

Matters become less serious in Robert C. Evans' essay on "William Hawley Smith's Parody of *Romeo and Juliet* (and of *Hamlet*)." Evans discusses one of the more successful of surviving stage parodies of Shakespeare—a play that manages to give two of Shakespeare's most famous tragedies happy endings by having Romeo marry Ophelia and by having Hamlet marry Juliet. Evans draws on the pioneering work of Richard Schoch (who studied nineteenth-century *English* parodies of the bard) and finds that many of Schoch's ideas are applicable to Smith's American parody, first staged in Illinois in 1902. In a related essay, Sarah Fredericks surveys numerous parodies of *Romeo and Juliet* that were first published in American newspapers. Newspaper parodies of Shakespeare seem to have been popular in nineteenth- and early twentieth-century America, and Fredericks examines six of them in some detail, showing how they allude to social, political, cultural, ethnic, racial, gender, and economic issues of the day. Fredericks, like Evans, suggests that the sheer popularity of Shakespeare's works made them inviting targets for parodists who were often inspired by (and who appealed to) a widespread love of the Bard.

Concluding sections of the book offer a chronology of Shakespeare's life, a chronological listing of his works in various genres, and a bibliography of editions and books relevant to *Romeo and Juliet*.

# THE BOOK
# AND THE
# AUTHOR

# *Romeo and Juliet*, Recycled_____

Singularly identified with William Shakespeare in the modern
cultural imaginary, the story of Romeo and Juliet already existed in
Shakespeare's own day in many versions, genres, and languages. In
English alone, Shakespeare could choose from the prose version in
William Painter's *Palace of Pleasure* (1567), the narrative verse of
Arthur Brooke's *Romeus and Juliet* (1562), and a now-lost play on
the subject that Brooke had already seen by 1562.[1] In French, there
was the prose of Pierre Boiastuau's *Histoires tragiques* (1559). In
Italian, there were numerous sources, most notably the *Novelle* of
Matteo Bandello (1554), Luigi da Porto's *Istoria . . . di due nobile
amanti* (ca. 1530), and the *Novellino* of Masuccio Salernitano
(published posthumously in 1476). Further back, the contending
houses of Montecchi and Capelletti appear in Dante's *Purgatorio*
(c. 1315 [2:6.106]), while broadly similar tales can be traced at least
to Ovid's treatment of Pyramus and Thisbe in the *Metamorphoses* (8
CE [4.55166]). Shakespeare likely did not know all these versions of
his story, but he surely worked with Brooke's and Painter's. And his
use of the Pyramus and Thisbe tale in Act 5 of *A Midsummer Night's
Dream* (ca. 1596)—one of several points of contrapuntal contact
between this play and *Romeo and Juliet* (ca. 1595)—confirms his
awareness of the broader source background.

But my point here is not to establish just what sources
Shakespeare used for his play. Rather, I am interested in what the
source-record says about the adaptive nature of the Romeo and
Juliet story and the textual economy out of which it evolved, an
economy wherein "iterability, that is, the extent to which the story is
recyclable, rather than originality is the prized quality" (Callaghan
157). Bardolatry may obscure the fact, but by the time the tale of
Romeo and Juliet reached Shakespeare, it had already taken on a life
of its own. Moreover, this life has continued beyond Shakespeare,
both with and without his influence, in the latter instance through

*Romeo and Juliet*, Recycled                                                    3 independent treatments of the same material like Lope de Vega's *Castelvines y Monteses* (ca. 1603) and Jacob Struijs's *Romeo en Juliette* (1634), in the former through countless adaptations of and responses to Shakespeare, from Thomas Otway's *History and Fall of Caius Marius* (1679) to Marc Norman and Tom Stoppard's *Shakespeare in Love* (1998) and beyond. In short, the story of Romeo and Juliet was growing and evolving for centuries before Shakespeare, just as it continues to grow and evolve, in different ways, centuries after him.

To consider the Romeo and Juliet story as a kind of living being—and better yet, one endlessly recreated through a constant process of self-recycling—leads to my broader purpose here, which is to depict Shakespeare's *Romeo and Juliet*, in particular, as a pre- or proto-environmentalist play. To that end, I would argue that the Romeo and Juliet story does what life itself does: it reproduces itself by endlessly reworking its own core matter—its DNA, as it were—while introducing modifications associated with the local circumstances—the environment—of this reproduction. And while it may seem tendentious to describe a text as having its own life, at least in any literal sense, the idea can hardly be called new. One finds a version of it in Ludwig Wittgenstein's declaration that "To imagine a language means to imagine a form of life" (1.19, p. 8). And one encounters it still earlier, in the insistence of Shakespeare's near-contemporary, John Milton, that "Books are not absolutely dead things, but do contain a potency of life in them to be as active as that soul whose progeny they are" (999). In what follows, I consider Shakespeare's *Romeo and Juliet* as just such a living being, existing like all such beings in a state of dynamic equilibrium— an ecology—with its forebears, both literary and human, as well as with its broader organic and inorganic environment.

### *Romeo and Juliet* as a Form of Life
If Shakespeare's *Romeo and Juliet* embodies a form of life, what form of life is it? Richard Kerridge, writing on *Macbeth*, discovers within that play "a deep familiarity with a local natural environment as a communal sensibility" (195), and one might say much the

same of *Romeo and Juliet*: it lends voice to a collective agrarian social ethic invested in seasonal rituals of death and renewal. It is also—unusually for Shakespeare—one of a pair of twins: a play sharing clear affinities of origin and appearance with the comedy Shakespeare composed hard on its heels, *A Midsummer Night's Dream*, but informed by a far darker vision. Thus Shakespeare's Verona has been called "a failed *civitas*" (Liebler, "There is" 1:306) and its failure may be read as an expression of anxiety relative to changes in the environmental experience of Elizabethan London—a city in the process of losing its attachment to traditional cycles of agrarian life—and to changes in the personal experience of the play's author as well.

Considered in its communitarian, ritualistic aspect, Shakespeare's play embodies an ethic of recycling endemic to premodern artistic representation that acquires new environmentalist overtones in the present day. It is the same ethic of representation encountered by any baffled gallery-goer confronting a seemingly endless succession of Renaissance crucifixions alleviated only by an equally endless-seeming sequence of annunciations. Such works are simultaneously unique—no one is quite like the others—and yet repetitive, forming an organic whole through their participation in a tradition wherein the images figure not simply as images but also as objects of meditation and—in the case of altarpieces, for instance— as part of the furniture of formal devotional practice. Here we encounter the premodern cultural order described by Walter Benjamin in his classic essay "The Work of Art in the Age of Mechanical Reproduction," a cultural order in which the "uniqueness of a work of art [what Benjamin later famously calls its "aura"] is inseparable from its being imbedded in the fabric of tradition" (223). For Benjamin, art's placement within tradition is progressively disrupted by the development of reproduction technologies that make it ever harder to locate the "original" of a work—e.g., an original photograph or film print—nor is this, in Benjamin's view, a wholly bad thing, leading as it does to the increasing democratization of art. But for us, this is beside the point. More important are the related insights that: 1) in Benjamin's words, "the first deep crisis which befell" this ritualistic

ritualistic approach to art "developed during the Renaissance" (223) and that 2) this crisis also acquired an ecological dimension.

As to the loss of tradition, recall the intimate relation between the development of printing and the spread of dissenting religious opinion. Within 150 years of Gutenberg, Shakespeare inhabited a world in which the medieval Catholic consensus had yielded to numerous alternative, often contradictory versions of the Bible, in multiple languages, all laying claim to being the one true word of God. As to environmental consequences, recall that the invention of movable type comprised only one aspect of the broader technological expansion of Western society. The rapid spread of information via printing encouraged other parallel innovations, such as the growth of maritime trade routes, the establishment of overseas colonies, and advances in metallurgy, mining, agriculture, the production of firearms, etc. Together, these changes had broad environmental consequences, from depletion of natural resources to increases in urban growth, pollution, and waste.[2] Indeed, James Burbage's Theater, where Shakespeare's *Romeo and Juliet* was likely first performed, could only exist because urban growth had created a local audience large enough to make a permanent playhouse profitable. Meanwhile, archaeological studies of the Elizabethan theaters have found them predictably full of urban rubbish (see for instance Bowsher). Shakespeare's stage itself was enabled by and contributed to the first great expansion of modern London, with all the environmental consequences it entailed.

As for Shakespeare's revisions to the Romeo and Juliet tale, they emphasize the play's urban setting and the disruptions this creates in conventional patterns of life. Consider, for instance, one of the poet's principal changes to the story he received: his modifications to its time-line. In previous sources, the love affair between Romeo and Juliet plays out slowly, over months. In Brooke's *Romeus and Juliet*, for instance, Romeo passes by Juliet's window "a week or two in vain" between the couple's first meeting and their second conversation; another "month or twain" pass between their secret marriage and the death of Tybalt (lines 461, 949). By contrast, Shakespeare compresses the affair into five days. The play's opening brawl occurs on a Sunday morning; Romeo and Juliet meet that evening at the Capulets' feast and arrange to wed secretly the next day; later that Monday (3.4.18), Romeo kills Tybalt and is banished; and in response, Capulet advances the date of Juliet's planned wedding to County Paris from Thursday to Wednesday (4.2.23-37).[3] Thus when Romeo encounters Juliet's seemingly-dead body in the Capulet monument, it is early Thursday morning.

On one hand, this foreshortening lends dramatic immediacy to the action, but on another, it places the lovers and the figures surrounding them in separate worlds, obeying their own chronological imperatives, with the latter forcefully impinging upon and eventually annihilating the former. This is the regime of so-called Shakespearian double time (see, for example, Frye 169-72), as illustrated by Juliet's exclamation, when the Nurse suddenly urges marriage to County Paris,

> Is it more sin to wish me thus forsworn,
> Or to dispraise my lord with that same tongue
> Which she hath prais'd him with beyond compare
> So many thousand times? (3.5.236-239)

One might wonder just how many thousand times the Nurse could possibly have praised Romeo, given that she has only known him for forty-eight hours, and the inconsistency reveals a standard feature of Shakespeare's dramaturgy. As his overall time scheme heightens the rush of events, he slows the pace at key moments (e.g., those involving love relationships) whose internal logic requires more leisure. But this technique also produces another effect: it isolates Romeo and Juliet in their own time zone, so to speak, while placing them under increasing pressure from a surrounding world that seems to be moving at a much more rapid pace.

In creating separate time-registers for his lovers, on the one hand, and the characters surrounding them, on the other, Shakespeare also provides these groups with different calendar associations. Again, this feature of Shakespeare's play differs notably from his sources. Brooke, for instance, presents the feast where Romeo and Juliet meet as a recurring feature of "the Christmas games"—the period of seasonal revelry, running roughly from Christmas to Candlemas (February 2), that supplied a traditional focal point for winter socializing in early modern households (line 155). In Shakespeare, by contrast, the Capulets' gathering becomes "an old accustom'd feast" (1.2.20) with no connection to cycles of seasonal festivity. This change, in turn, becomes necessary because Shakespeare has very different uses in mind for the old liturgical calendar, which provides his Juliet with a very specific birthday: "Even or odd, of all days in the year, / Come Lammas-eve at night she shall be fourteen" (1.3.16-17).

Lammas Eve, July 31, inaugurates the annual feast of first-fruits, the harvest festival for the earliest wheat, and as such, this date has been much noted for its place in a chain of fertility-allusions that include Juliet's age; the heat of the play's mid-July setting; and various textual references, of which the most famous may be Lady Capulet's observation to her daughter, "I was your mother much upon those years / That you are now a maid" (1.3.72-3). To all this we might add that Juliet's birthday, defined as it is by its liturgical associations, participates in the same traditional order Benjamin identifies with the role of art in premodern societies: Lammas Eve is rendered unique "of all days in the year" exactly and paradoxically because of its embedment in recurring calendar cycles. As a result, it contrasts sharply with the rushed succession of weekdays, distinct from one another only by being closer or more distant in time, through which Capulet arranges Juliet's wedding to the County Paris: "get thee to church a' Thursday" (3.5.161); "On Thursday, sir? The time is very short" (4.1.1); "I'll have this knot knit up to-morrow morning" (4.2.24); "No, not till Thursday, there is time enough" (4.2.36); "we'll to church to-morrow" (4.2.37). This contrast then extends as well to other counter-cyclical references to time in the world of Verona, as when the Rosalind-besotted Romeo "Shuts up his windows, locks fair daylight out, / And makes himself an artificial night" (1.1.139-140), or when he foolishly compares his fidelity to the moon:

ROMEO: Lady, by yonder blessed moon I vow,
That tips with silver all these fruit-tree tops—
JULIET: O swear not by the moon, th' inconstant moon,
That monthly changes in her circled orb,
Lest that thy love prove likewise variable. (2.2.107-111)

Once united, Romeo and Juliet seem to measure time in more organic fashion, as in their famous leave-taking: "Wilt thou be gone? It is not yet near day. / It was the nightingale, and not the lark, / That pierc'd the fearful hollow of thine ear" (3.5.1-3). And just as Shakespeare's tragedy divides time into two registers, it does something similar with space. The play's latest Arden editor, René Weis, describes it as "follow[ing] Romeo's progress through the physical spaces in Capulet's house," an enclosure equipped with "halls that can be turned into ballrooms, with kitchens and pantry," until he finally reaches the "inner sanctum [of] Juliet's bedroom" (Weis 7-8). But surrounded as they are by this urban domestic setting, Romeo and Juliet consummate their relationship within a carefully-protected green space: the Capulets' walled orchard. Here they give voice to the play's most sensuous nature-imagery. Romeo "hid[es] himself among these trees" (2.1.30) to hear Juliet praise the sweetness of roses, whatever their name (2.2.43-44), and it is here, where "yonder blessed moon . . . tips with silver all these fruit-tree tops" (2.2.107-8), that Juliet's nightingale "nightly . . . sings on yond pomegranate-tree" (3.5.4). Again, the lovers occupy a world apart, one distinguished by its association with natural cycles of fecundity, lunar movement, and birdsong, a world that cannot long endure within the "stony limits" (2.2.67) of Shakespeare's Verona.

Here it becomes most useful to compare Shakespeare's *Romeo and Juliet* with its companion-play, *A Midsummer Night's Dream*. The latter work stands as perhaps the definitive example of Shakespearean festive comedy: a form of drama tied to "the seasonal feasts" of the liturgical calendar and designed—often through salutary flight from city to country—"to promote the effect of a merry occasion where Nature reigns" (Barber 4, 5). The festive pattern established in *A Midsummer Night's Dream*—civilized repression, restorative escape to the natural world, and a reinvigorated return to the original setting—is flipped inside-out in *Romeo and Juliet*, replaced by an attempted interior escape to an unsustainable region of secret liberty, a space rendered untenable by the city that surrounds it. In this sense, the latter play may be described as a kind of Shakespearean "festive tragedy" (Liebler): a drama grounded in the liturgical feast of Lammastide, but one that frustrates the regenerative energies at the heart of such holidays. Beginning with a riot in Verona's central piazza and ending with a brace of deaths in the Capulets' necropolis, *Romeo and Juliet* unfolds in a world of stone walls and princely death-threats, a world very like the one the lovers of *A Midsummer Night's Dream* must escape in order to thrive. In *Romeo and Juliet*, however, escape is reconfigured as exile: Romeo's brief, solitary excursion not to a sustaining green world but to another city.

Indeed, the kinship between *Romeo and Juliet* and *A Midsummer Night's Dream* extends still further, into a mutually-enabling dynamic of parody and inversion. *A Midsummer Night's Dream*, one might argue, is the play that results if one refuses to accept confinement by the world of *Romeo and Juliet*, whereas *Romeo and Juliet* is what happens if one abandons the possibility of flight to the greenwood. In either case, the rejected opposite term survives on the level of burlesque: just as the final act of *A Midsummer Night's Dream* recasts *Romeo and Juliet* as "a tedious brief scene of young Pyramus / And his love Thisby" (5.1.56-7), so *Romeo and Juliet* anticipates the fairy-world of *A Midsummer Night's Dream*, reducing it to the "vain fantasy" of Mercutio's Queen Mab speech (1.5.53-103). In this relation, again, we discover a pattern of twinning and recycling comparable to that encountered in *Romeo and Juliet*'s modifications to its source material and its reappropriation of the liturgical calendar.

## Shakespeare's Personal Relationship to *Romeo and Juliet*

So far, I have urged a view of Shakespeare's *Romeo and Juliet* as essentially an adaptive and living being, one that exists in a kind of ecological tension with its sources as well as with certain shifts in relation to time and space consistent with the development of early modern urban life. But should this view not extend as well to the personal experience of the play's author? Insofar as the play registers anxieties about early modern urban life and the concomitant loss of traditional, cyclical relationships to the natural world, should these anxieties not be visible within the playwright's biography, too? If so, how might Shakespeare's relationship to *Romeo and Juliet* cast light on the ecological determinants of the poet's own consciousness?

Such questions prove difficult in the case of an author as personally reserved as Shakespeare—an author who so seldom seems to address his audience in his own voice. But even so, there remains evidence that Shakespeare understood himself to be a geographically rooted writer: a poet whose creativity existed in special relation to his Warwickshire origins and who carried those origins with him as he migrated to London. This case has been made in persuasive detail by Jonathan Bate, who describes Shakespeare as "a provincial outsider" to London society, afflicted by a typical newcomer's "insecurity in the capital" (33). Thus, especially during the 1590s, he became "unique among the dramatists of his age in locating scenes in Warwickshire and Gloucestershire," compensating perhaps for his insecurity by rooting his work in "the social and natural ecology of rural Warwickshire" (Bate 24, 33) Likewise, and unlike such colleagues as Edward Alleyn and Philip Henslowe, Shakespeare "did not accumulate property and influence near London," preferring to invest his earnings in the Stratford area (Bate 33). As it happens, *Romeo and Juliet* must have been composed sometime between late 1594, when Will Kempe, who was cast as Peter, joined the Lord Chamberlain's Men (see 4.5.101 s.d. in the second quarto text), and early 1597, when the play was first printed in quarto. This places it among plays like *The Taming of the Shrew* (1593–4) and *1 Henry IV* (1596–7)—both of which make very specific use of Warwickshire geography and settings (*Taming* introduction 2.17-22; *1 Henry IV* 4.2)—and during the first ten years of Shakespeare's career in London.

These would have been stressful years for Shakespeare under any circumstances, as he left his family in Stratford, settled in London, and pursued an acting career, while also finding time to write a dozen plays, two narrative poems, and numerous sonnets. The stress factors affecting Shakespeare's life at this time included both environmental and personal events. From late 1592 to early 1594 the city's theaters remained closed by an unusually severe outbreak of plague, closure that forced Shakespeare into his one period of sustained non-dramatic literary output, presumably to compensate for lost box-office income. On this occasion, as typically, plague-related deaths decreased during winter only to return with warmer weather, culminating in peak mortality in summer 1593, when Bartholomew Fair was canceled because of the infection (Stow 1274). The experience of confinement within London's walls during these sultry and unhealthful months arguably leaves its imprint on Shakespeare's Verona, where "the day is hot," "the mad blood stirring," and Mercutio's death falls on Capulet and Montague alike as "a plague a' both houses" (3.1.2, 4, 91). (By contrast Friar John, whose charitable associations with "infectious pestilence" [5.3.10] prevent him from carrying mail to Mantua, reaches Shakespeare from his sources.)

Indeed, flight to the country—the standard response to plague among early modern city-dwellers of means—must have appealed to Shakespeare as a course of self-preservation at this time, but if he made it back to Warwickshire at all during 1593, he would have returned to a rural space beset with problems of its own. That year marked the first in a series of five consecutive bad harvests, dearths produced in part by the unseasonably cold and wet weather-patterns of the Little Ice Age, which together sent grain prices skyrocketing while ensuring that those poor people lucky enough to escape the plague would experience the alternative miseries of famine (Stratton and Brown 44). And again, these conditions arguably found their way into the poet's work, perhaps coloring Titania's complaint about the weather in *A Midsummer Night's Dream*: "The ox hath therefore stretch'd his yoke in vain,/ The ploughman lost his sweat, and the green corn/ Hath rotted ere his youth attain'd a beard" (2.1.93-5). Similar notes may be heard in *Romeo and Juliet*, too, as when Mercutio maligns the "inconstant . . . wind, who woos / Even now [in July] the frozen bosom of the north" (1.4.99-100), or when Capulet laments his daughter's apparent demise: "Death lies on her like an untimely frost / Upon the sweetest flower of all the field" (4.5.28-9).

But amidst these weather-related anxieties, Shakespeare would have recognized more personal concerns as well. By 1595, the poet would have been over thirty years old, living in a city whose mean life expectancy lay "between 30 and 35 years in the wealthier central parishes" (Finlay 100). The complaint of his second sonnet—likely written around this time—which imagines "forty winters" digging "deep trenches" in the beauty of its addressee (2.1-2), confirms Shakespeare's troubled awareness of the passage of time at this stage of his life. And surviving life-records from the mid-1590s confirm that this period marked a notable set of life-passages for Shakespeare and his family. Thus, as the poet began to achieve success in London, he reached out to claim the markers of prosperity in his personal life: in 1596, he successfully renewed his father's lapsed efforts to secure a coat of arms for the family, and the next year, he purchased New Place, the second-largest house in Stratford-upon-Avon and a home with noteworthy historical associations (Boehrer 86-91).

Yet just as Shakespeare's family began to acquire new wealth and status, it also came under new pressure from the age-old imperative to reproduce. "The world must be peopled," declares Benedict in *Much Ado about Nothing* (1598–99; 2.3.242), some three years after the composition of *Romeo and Juliet*. But by that time, the chance of peopling it with direct male descendants of William Shakespeare had already disappeared. Shakespeare's only son, Hamnet, had been buried in August of 1596, guaranteeing that the poet's lineage would continue only through the distaff side. As for his three brothers, they too lacked children at this point, and all would eventually die without legitimate male issue. In 1595, as Shakespeare likely composed his *Romeo and Juliet*, this unhappy outcome still remained in the future; yet Shakespeare himself, demonstrably concerned at this time with the elevation of his family's status and the establishment of a grand family home, would have had every reason to worry, too, about the posterity he hoped would one day inhabit New Place.

In May 1595, Shakespeare's elder daughter, Susanna, turned twelve; his second daughter, Judith, and her male twin, Hamnet, turned ten in February. By both contemporary and current standards, all three were far too young to think of matrimony. In the late 1500s, the median age for marriage among the landed classes in England was about twenty for women, about twenty-two for men, and below the aristocracy, this rose still further, to about twenty-five and twenty-seven, respectively (Stone 40-44). But Shakespeare's Juliet, by contrast, is "a fortnight and odd days" shy of fourteen (1.3.15)—an age Shakespeare deliberately reduces from that given by Arthur Brooke (who makes her sixteen) and William Painter (who follows earlier sources in making her eighteen [Marrapodi 12]). This age-reduction, in turn, carries with it two long-noted effects: first, it makes Juliet little more than a child, essentially of the same cohort as Shakespeare's own children; second, it widens the generational gap separating Shakespeare's lovers from their elders. The result is a play very much about the conflict between young and old, a conflict figured primarily through efforts to control the younger characters' reproductivity.

The elder Capulets, in particular, worry about offspring. Not only does Lady Capulet chide Juliet, "I was your mother much upon these years / That you are now a maid" (1.3.72-3); "younger than you," she insists, "Here in Verona, ladies of esteem,/ Are now made mothers" (1.3.69-71). As County Paris elsewhere observes of Juliet, "Younger than she are happy mothers made" (1.2.12). For his part, Capulet responds to his daughter's reluctance to wed County Paris by exclaiming,

> Wife, we scarce thought us blest
> That God had lent us but this only child,
> But now I see this one is one too much,
> And that we have a curse in having her. (3.5.164-7)

But in a gentler mood, Capulet supplies the most poignant such lines in the play, observing of Juliet, "Earth hath swallowed all my hopes but she; / She's the hopeful lady of my earth" (1.2.14-15). This remark leaves it unclear whether the Capulets have lost other children or whether Shakespeare understands Juliet to be an "only child" (3.5.165) with no erstwhile siblings. But this detail remains relatively unimportant; Shakespeare's obvious concern in these passages is to emphasize the Capulets' fear of the failure of their lineage—the very fear their play is designed to enact.

Hence one of the more curious features of Shakespeare's *Romeo and Juliet*: a recycled play emerging from a centuries-old story-sequence, a play that revises that story-sequence specifically by changing its relation to the recurring cycles of the traditional church calendar, it gives voice in the process to a fear that the cycle of human generational renewal will fail. Here the play's relationship to *A Midsummer Night's Dream* appears most manifest. The comedy enacts generational conflict in ways that favor the young, ending as three pairs of newlyweds celebrate their wedding-night and tutelary spirits guarantee the health and fortune of "the issue the[y] create" (5.1.405). The tragedy, by contrast, ends in a tomb with the triumph of "parents' rage" (prologue.10) over their children's "bud of love" (2.2.121). On the classical festive model, *A Midsummer Night's Dream* enacts rebirth; *Romeo and Juliet* instead functions as a dramatic ritual of failed fertility. Herein lies its distinctive character as a proto-environmentalist play.

## The Play's Ecology

So Shakespeare's *Romeo and Juliet* works from the environmentalist standpoint to register anxiety about the decline of agrarian and communal ways of life associated with the cycles of the old church calendar and threatened by the rise of urban experience. Its principal fear is that something durable in human nature—some "ancient grudge" (prologue.3), "pernicious rage" (1.1.84), or "cank'red hate" (1.1.95)—threatens to disrupt the process whereby generations renew themselves. In this respect, Shakespeare's play substantially revises the moral of earlier *Romeo and Juliet*s, which cast themselves as cautionary tales about "the shameful and wretched ends of such as have yielded their liberty thrall to foul desires" (Brooke, "To the Reader" lxv). Yet Shakespeare's play cannot be credited with voicing a modern ecological sensibility, for it presents humanity's threat to itself not as a problem with the management of natural resources, nor as a product of processes and laws to be understood by modern science (which, after all, did not yet exist in Shakespeare's day), but rather as a failure of moral qualities: civic obedience, self-restraint, forgiveness, and tolerance.

However, modern science—or at least something like it— does make one appearance in Shakespeare's tragedy, in a form that deserves some final scrutiny. It comes into view toward the play's end, in the second of two vignettes that together function as framing devices for the play's main action: Friar Laurence's initial appearance in Act 2 and its distorted echo in Romeo's Act 5 encounter with the nameless, impoverished apothecary who sells him poison. As if to point their kinship, the two scenes open the same way: just as Friar Laurence appears in his monastic herbarium, "fill[ing] this osier cage of ours / With baleful weeds and precious-juiced flowers" (2.3.7-8), so Romeo first spies the apothecary "In tatt'red weeds, with overwhelming brows, / Culling of simples" (5.1.39-40). From there, however, the two tableaux diverge.

Friar Laurence, for his part, remains within his garden, where he delivers a conventional eulogy on the paradoxical properties of natural medicine:

> The earth that's nature's mother is her tomb;
> What is her burying grave, that is her womb;
> And from her womb, children of diverse kind
> We sucking on her natural bosom find:
> . . .
> For nought so vile that on the earth doth live
> But to the earth some special good doth give;
> Nor ought so good but, strain'd from that fair use,
> Revolts from true birth, stumbling on abuse. (2.3.9-12, 17-20)

Note the circular recurrences distinguishing these lines: as womb becomes tomb, so poison becomes medicine, all in accordance with the governing cycles of nature. This is conventional wisdom such as might appear in any medieval herbal or bestiary. Likewise, Friar Laurence remains for Shakespeare a conventional and virtuous medieval monastic, one Chaucer might depict with approval. (Brooke, for his part, admires the friar less, describing him as "superstitious" and a "naturally fit instrument . . . of unchastity" [Brooke, "To the Reader" lxvi]).

In contrast to Friar Laurence, Romeo places the poor apothecary indoors, in his shop, whose furnishings oddly register both his vocation and his penury:

> [I]n his needy shop a tortoise hung,
> An alligator stuff'd, and other skins
> Of ill-shap'd fishes, and about his shelves
> A beggarly account of empty boxes,
> Green earthen pots, bladders, and musty seeds,
> Remnants of packthread, and old cakes of roses,
> Were thinly scattered, to make up a show. (5.1.42-8)

The boxes and packthread and stale rose-cakes all signify poverty, which, of course, is essential to the apothecary's role. But the stuffed animals point in another direction, toward the novel, specialized, and expensive gear of the apothecary's trade. Taxidermy in its modern form—as the mounting of animal-skins for display—dates only to the mid-1500s, with Pierre Belon publishing the first European description of the process barely forty years before Shakespeare's play (8). As for the apothecary's stuffed alligator, it speaks not of privation but of the exotic. One encounters something similar in the earliest surviving illustration of a Renaissance curiosity cabinet, the two-page frontispiece to Ferrante Imperato's *Historia naturale* of 1599 (Fig. 1). Here a massive, ceiling-mounted stuffed crocodile dominates Imperato's personal collection of *naturalia*, among the grandest of its day, housed in Naples' Palazzo Gravina.

Wonder cabinets like Imperato's were a new development in the sixteenth century. While the impulse to collect marvelous things can be traced to earliest antiquity, the 1500s gave it a new form to accommodate the new and wondrous spoils of exploration and discovery: essentially the beginnings of the modern museum, brought to life by aristocratic and professional collectors, many of the latter apothecaries, like Imperato himself. These apothecaries, too, while of ancient lineage, enjoyed a period of enhanced prestige and professionalization beginning in the 1500s. (Hence the Worshipful Society of Apothecaries separated from the Grocers' Company to become its own free-standing London livery company in 1617.) Where Friar Laurence remains rooted in an agrarian past of cyclical fertility, the nameless apothecary inhabits a darker, less fecund urban future. Toward this future, Shakespeare steers his tragedy.

Fig. 1: Frontispiece to Ferrante Imperato, *Dell'historia naturale* (Naples, 1599), depicting Imperato's cabinet of curiosities. Reproduced from the second edition (Venice, 1672). Courtesy Universität Erlangen-Nürnberg.

## Notes

1.  For the lost play, see Brooke (1908), "To the Reader," p. lxvi.
2.  For the environmental impact of changes in early modern European society, see Merchant; for the environmental consequences of urban growth in early modern London, see Boehrer.
3.  All references to Shakespeare's works are to *The Riverside Shakespeare*, edited by G. Blakemore Evans et al.

# Works Cited

Boiastuau, Pierre. *Histoires tragiques*, 1559.

Brooke, Arthur. *Brooke's 'Romeus and Juliet'*, edited by J. J. Munro, Chatto and Windus, 1908.

_____. *Romeus and Juliet*, 1562.

[Bandello, Matteo]. *Novelle*, 1554.

Barber, C. L. *Shakespeare's Festive Comedy: A Study of Dramatic Form and Its Relation to Social Custom*. Princeton UP, 1959.

Bate, Jonathan. *Soul of the Age: A Biography of the Mind of William Shakespeare*, Random House, 2009.

Belon, Pierre. *L'histoire de la nature des oyseaux*, 1555.

Benjamin, Walter. "The Work of Art in the Age of Mechanical Reproduction." *Illuminations: Essays and Reflections*. Translated by Harry Zohn, Schocken, 1968, p. 223.

Boehrer, Bruce. *Environmental Degradation in Jacobean Drama*. Cambridge UP, 2013.

Bowsher, Julian. "Provisioning Shakespeare's Audiences: Food and Drink in the London Playhouses of the Sixteenth and Seventeenth Centuries." *Food and Drink in Archaeology 4*, edited by Wendy Howard, Kirsten Bedigan, and Ben Jervi, Prospect Books, 2010, pp. 134-6.

Callaghan, Dympna, editor. *Romeo and Juliet: Texts and Contexts*. Bedford/St. Martin's, 2003.

da Porto, Luigi. *Istoria . . . di due nobile amanti*. c. 1530.

Dante Alighieri. *Commedia*, edited by Giorgio Petrocchi, vol. 2, Mondadori, 1966-7, p. 6.106. 3 vols.

Finlay, Roger. *Population and Metropolis: The Demography of London 1580–1650*. Cambridge UP, 1981.

Frye, Roland Mushat. *Shakespeare: The Art of the Dramatist*. Houghton Mifflin, 1970.

Kerridge, Richard. "An Ecocritic's *Macbeth*." *Ecocritical Shakespeare*, edited by Lynne Bruckner and Dan Brayton, Ashgate, 2011.

Liebler, Noami. *Shakespeare's Festive Tragedy: The Ritual Foundations of Genre*. Routledge, 1995.

_____. "'There is no world without Verona walls': The City in *Romeo and Juliet*." *A Companion to Shakespeare's Works*, edited by Richard Dutton and Jean E. Howard, vol. 1, Blackwell, 2003, p. 306. 4 vols.

Marrapodi, Michele. "Introduction: Shakespearean Subversions." *Shakespeare and the Italian Renaissance: Appropriation, Transformation, Opposition*, edited by Michele Marrapodi Routledge, 2016, p. 12.

Merchant, Carolyn. *The Death of Nature: Women, Ecology and the Scientific Revolution*. HarperSanFrancisco, 1983.

Milton, John. *Areopagitica*. *The Riverside Milton*, edited by Ray Flannagan, Houghton Mifflin, 1998.

Norman, Marc, and Tom Stoppard. *Shakespeare In Love*, dir. John Madden, Universal, 1998.

Otway, Thomas. *The History and Fall of Caius Marius* , 1692.

Ovid. *Metamorphoses*. Translated by Frank Justus Miller, vol. 4, Harvard UP, 1977), pp. 55-166.

Painter, William. *The second tome of the Palace of Pleasure*, 1567.

Salernitano, Masuccio. *Novellino* (Naples, 1476), thirty-third novella.

Shakespeare, William. *The Riverside Shakespeare*, edited by G. Blakemore Evans et al., Houghton Mifflin, 1997.

Stone, Lawrence. *The Family, Sex and Marriage in England 1500–1800*, Harper and Row, 1979.

Stow, John. *The annales of England*, 1600.

Stratton, J. M., and Jack Houghton Brown, *Agricultural Records A.D. 220–1977*. John Baker, 1978.

Weis, René. "Introduction." *Romeo and Juliet*. Bloomsbury, 2012.

Wittgenstein, Ludwig. *Philosophical Investigations*. Translated by G. E. M. Anscombe, Basil Blackwell, 1958.

# Biography of William Shakespeare

Robert C. Evans

William Shakespeare, who has become perhaps the world's most celebrated writer, was born sometime in late April 1564, in the small market town of Stratford-upon-Avon, about a hundred miles northwest of England's capital city of London. He was christened on April 26 in the local parish church, and it is customary to assume that he was born three days earlier, on April 23. This is not only the exact day on which he would die fifty-two years later; it is also the day devoted to the celebration of Saint George, England's patron saint. (These facts, like most of the others in this essay, are drawn from the splendid chronology of Shakespeare's life and times compiled by G. Blakemore Evans with the assistance of J. J. M. Tobin. Evans's edition of Shakespeare's works contains, especially in its appendices, massive documentation of practically every aspect of the playwright's life.)

William's parents were John and Mary Shakespeare; they had married in 1557, when John was already one of Stratford's four constables. They eventually had eight children in all (the first was born in 1558). William was their first son. Local records indicate that John, a successful glove-maker, was elected and/or appointed to various civic offices in 1559, 1561, 1562, 1565, 1568, and 1571. His selection in 1568 as Bailiff meant that he occupied the town's key office. William, then, was born into a prominent, respected middle-class family.

Shakespeare probably attended the local grammar school, where he would have received a solid education emphasizing mastery of the Latin language and Latin classical literature. Stratford was also a town sometimes visited by traveling theatrical troupes patronized by various aristocrats. Such visits occurred, for instance, in 1568, 1572, 1574, 1576, 1578, 1579, 1580, 1581, 1582, 1583, 1586, and so on. Thus, although Stratford was somewhat distant from London geographically (four days by foot; two days by horseback), it did have some experience of the growing interest in dramatic performance that was becoming increasingly popular in the English capital in the late sixteenth century. In 1576, James Burbage built "The Theatre," London's "first regular playhouse" (Greenblatt 3371), and in 1577, "The Curtain Theatre" also opened in the capital. Other theaters soon followed. By 1581, drama and theaters had become so important that the government issued a decree to make sure they were regulated.

Meanwhile, on November 27, 1582, a license was issued for the marriage of William Shakespeare and Anne Hathaway, the daughter of a prominent local farmer. Shakespeare was eighteen (and thus legally a minor) at the time; his bride was eight years older and was already pregnant. Their first child (Susanna) was christened on May 26, 1583. 1585 saw the birth of two more children: the twins Hamnet and Judith (who were christened on February 2). In that same year, Shakespeare's father was fined for not attending church. His financial fortunes had begun to decline in 1577, when he began increasingly to be "cited for various debts" (Evans 1990). In 1578, Shakespeare's mother had had to pawn various properties to help raise money. Her husband's attempt, in 1580, to redeem the pawned property was unsuccessful. In 1587, John was "ejected by the Stratford Corporation as an alderman for failing, for some years, to attend . . . officially called meetings" (Evans 1996). Thus, as William entered official adulthood, his family's status was no longer as secure as it had been when he was born.

Sometime in 1586 (or 1585), Shakespeare may have left Stratford, perhaps to become a schoolmaster somewhere. (Recent theories assume that he may have taken a position, as tutor and amateur actor, with a prominent Catholic family in Lancashire.) Evans suggests that sometime around 1589 he became associated with a prominent troupe of actors and may have written his first play (Part One of *Henry VI* [later revised]). In ensuing years, he may have written or contributed to other works, such as Part Two of *Henry VI* (1590–91?). (Suggested dates of composition of Shakespeare's writings are often highly conjectural; for alternative datings, which sometimes vary greatly, see the chronology of his works at the end of this volume.) In 1592, Shakespeare had become prominent enough on the London literary scene to be attacked by another professional writer, Robert Greene, who seems to have been bothered by the success of this so-called "vpstart Crow" (Evans 1959). Meanwhile, back in Stratford, Shakespeare's father was "cited [in 1592] for failing to attend monthly church services, as the law required, for fear of being arrested for debt" (Evans 1998). Thus, as the son's fortunes were rising, the father's were in even greater decline.

Shakespeare now became an increasingly prolific and successful writer. Evans attributes his great play *Richard III* to the years 1592–93, years that also saw the composition of his immensely popular narrative poem *Venus and Adonis*, which he dedicated to the Earl of Southampton in 1593. In these early years of the new decade, he may also have been working on *The Comedy of Errors*, his *Sonnets*, a narrative poem titled *The Rape of Lucrece*, the bloody tragedy titled *Titus Andronicus*, and his inventive comedy *The Taming of the Shrew*. Evans dates all these works—so varied in genre—as being composed between 1592 and 1594. Shakespeare's 1594 dedication of *Lucrece* to the Earl of Southampton suggests, again, that he was making valuable contacts among the English aristocracy.

In the middle years of the 1590s, the flood of new works (at least according to Evans's datings) continued: the comedy *The Two Gentlemen of Verona* (1594); the comedy *Love's Labor's Lost* (1594–95); and the history play *King John* (1594–96). In 1595, Shakespeare was paid "for the performance of two comedies at [the royal] court" in late December 1594 (Evans 2002). By 1595, he also seems to have become a "sharer" (or investor) in his acting company, the Lord Chamberlain's Men (so called because their official patron was one of the chief figures of the court). It was as a "sharer" that Shakespeare earned the money that would eventually make him a rich man. Writing plays was not especially lucrative, but owning a right to part of the profits of ticket sales definitely was.

Evans dates the composition of the history play *Richard II* to 1595. He dates both *Romeo and Juliet* and *A Midsummer Night's Dream* to 1595–96. He dates *The Merchant of Venice* to 1596–97 and the First Part of *Henry IV* to that same period. But 1596 also, unfortunately, saw the death of Shakespeare's young son Hamnet, at age eleven. During this period, Shakespeare was also involved in various minor legal troubles. But he continued to write. Evans dates the comedy *The Merry Wives of Windsor* to 1597. (This was the year Shakespeare purchased a substantial home in Stratford called "New Place.") Evans notes that Shakespeare was listed as a comic actor in 1598, and he reports that twelve of Shakespeare's plays were commended by Francis Meres in that same year—a year which also saw the composition of the Second Part of *Henry IV* and (in 1598–99) the composition of the comedy *Much Ado about Nothing*. Evans dates three plays to 1599: *Henry V*, *Julius Caesar*, and *As You Like It*. It was also in 1599 that the almost circular-shaped Globe Theatre—the famous structure so long associated with the glories of the period's drama—was opened in Southwark, on the southern bank of the River Thames.

Evans dates Shakespeare's most famous play—*Hamlet*—to the years 1600–01. In was in the early autumn of 1601 that Shakespeare's father died (perhaps as a Catholic during a time when England was officially a Protestant country). Evans dates the poem "The Phoenix and the Turtle" to around 1601 and dates both *Twelfth Night* and *Troilus and Cressida* to 1601–02. He dates *All's Well That Ends Well* to 1602–03. It was in late March of 1603 that Queen Elizabeth I finally died after forty-five years as one of the most successful monarchs in English history. She was succeeded by King James VI of Scotland, who now also became King James I of England. James's intense interest in literature led him to take over the patronage of Shakespeare's acting company, which now became known as "the King's Men."

During the new "Jacobean" period, Shakespeare produced some of his greatest works, and his plays were now increasingly performed at the royal court. Evans dates the composition of both *Measure for Measure* and *Othello* to 1604, the composition of *King Lear* to 1605, and the composition of *Macbeth* to 1606. He dates the composition of *Antony and Cleopatra* to 1606–07 and the composition of three other plays to 1607–08: *Coriolanus*, *Timon of Athens*, and *Pericles*. In 1607, Shakespeare's daughter Susanna married a man named John Hall, and Evans notes the intriguing fact that in that same year both *Hamlet* and *Richard II* were "acted on board Captain William Keeling's ship, the *Dragon*, off Sierra Leone [Africa], 'which I permit to keepe my people from idlenes [*sic*] and vnlawful games, or sleepe.'" Evans reports that *Hamlet* was performed again on the *Dragon* in March 1608.

In the autumn of 1608, Shakespeare's mother died, but the same year saw some good fortune as well: he now became a "sharer" in an indoor, more elite theater opened within the city of London itself. The year 1609 saw the unauthorized publication of his *Sonnets*, and Evans dates the composition of the play *Cymbeline* to 1609–10. He also suggests that it was in around 1610 that "Shakespeare is believed to have returned to Stratford to live" (2012). Evans dates the composition of *The Winter's Tale* to 1610–11, and he notes that *The Tempest*—often considered Shakespeare's last great play— was acted at court on November 1, 1611, the presumed year of its composition. Evans dates the composition of *Henry VIII* (cowritten with John Fletcher) to 1612–13, the same years during which Shakespeare seems to have cowritten (with Fletcher) a now-lost play called *Cardenio*. The year 1613 also saw the composition, with Fletcher, of the play *The Two Noble Kinsmen*.

But 1613 also witnessed the accidental burning and destruction of The Globe Theatre. Its thatched roof caught fire during a performance of *Henry VIII*. According to a contemporary source, special pyrotechnic effects designed to enhance the authenticity of the performance "did light on the thatch, where being thought at first but an idle smoak, and their eyes more attentive to the show, it kindled inwardly, and ran round like a train, consuming within less then [*sic*] an hour the whole house to the very grounds" (Evans 1968). Although the famous playhouse was quickly rebuilt and the new version opened in 1614, an era had ended. Soon the Globe's beloved chief playwright would also be gone.

In February 1616, Shakespeare's daughter Judith married a man named Thomas Quiney. Judith gave birth, in November 1617, to a son whom she and her husband named "Shaksper." Unfortunately, his namesake, the great dramatist, had already passed away. Having redrawn his will on March 25, 1616, William Shakespeare died less than a month later, on April 23. This, supposedly, was the very day on which he had been born fifty-two years earlier. He was buried, on April 25, in the same church in which he had long ago been christened. In a life that lasted little more than half a century, he had produced some of the greatest literature ever written. Most of his texts were eventually collected and published in 1623 (the same year his widow died) in a massive "folio" (or large-sized) edition compiled by friends and former colleagues. It is a beautifully fitting monument to the treasures it contains.

## Works Cited

Evans, G. Blakemore, editor. *The Riverside Shakespeare*. 2nd ed., Houghton Mifflin, 1997.

Greenblatt, Stephen, editor. *The Norton Shakespeare: Based on the Oxford Edition*. Norton, 1997.

# CRITICAL
# CONTEXTS

# Friar Laurence and Sacramental Confession in *Romeo and Juliet*

Benedict J. Whalen

Arthur Brooke's *Tragical History of Romeus and Juliet*, Shakespeare's direct source for *Romeo and Juliet*, was published in 1562 and begins with an interesting prefatory note "To the Reader." This brief note argues that all human actions, both good and evil, serve and honor God. Brooke writes, "by sundry means the good man's example biddeth men to be good, and the evil man's mischief warneth men not to be evil" (n.p.). Remarkably, Brooke then uses the latter point to explain and justify his tale; Romeo and Juliet are, to his mind, exemplars of evil people doing evil deeds and suffering proper mischief as a result. Indeed, cataloging the evils of his story, Brooke describes his subject as:

> a couple of unfortunate lovers, thralling themselves to unhonest desire; neglecting the authority and advice of parents and friends; conferring their principal counsels with drunken gossips and superstitious friars (the naturally fit instruments of unchastity); attempting all adventures of peril for th' attaining of their wished lust; using auricular confession (the key of whoredom, and treason) for furtherance of their purpose; abusing the honorable name of lawful marriage to cloak the shame of stolen contracts; finally by all means of unhonest life hasting to most unhappy death. (n.p.)

The severity of Brooke's condemnation of Romeo and Juliet may surprise readers who are primarily familiar with the story in Shakespeare's play, in which we find lovers who are "star-crossed"[1] and, perhaps, foolish but not epitomes of evil. More surprisingly, Brooke's ensuing narrative does not, in fact, present Romeo and Juliet in as bad a light as his moralizing prefatory note leads one to expect, and some readers might even find Brooke's narrator's tone sympathetic towards the lovers. But aside from this suggestive conflict in tone or intention within Brooke's work, it is noteworthy that Shakespeare drew his pitiable and at least somewhat sympathetic characters from a work that was supposedly presenting them as negative exemplars.

In addition to his damning judgment of Romeo and Juliet, Brooke's treatment of Friar Laurence might surprise the modern reader. However, to call friars "superstitious" and "fit instruments of unchastity" constituted a fairly typical medieval caricature of friars, and it persisted as a very common anti-Catholic, anti-friar polemic in Elizabethan and Jacobean literature. Friars were often presented not merely as Catholics adhering to an incorrect theology, but as particularly sexually promiscuous and corrupt. They were, supposedly, unscrupulous, and regularly abused their social authority and sacramental powers. Indeed, the Catholic sacrament of confession—a sacrament that was rejected by Protestant reformers— was often depicted as an exceptionally effective tool that served the malicious ends of the evil friars. A classic, pre-Reformation example of such a portrayal occurs in Chaucer's *Canterbury Tales*. Chaucer's narrator describes the pilgrim Friar as speaking with so "muchel of daliaunce and fair langage" (line 211) that "he hadde maad ful many a marriage / of yonge women, at his owne cost" (lines 211, 212-13), suggesting that he had seduced them and then had to arrange marriages for them in order to cover up the natural consequences of his amours. Furthermore, Chaucer's friar "ful sweetly herde he confessioun, / And plesaunt was his absolucioun" (lines 221-222), so long as he could expect "men moot yeve silver to the povre freres" (line 231, page 8). Not only was the Friar unchaste, but the authority to hear confession and absolve sins was, for him, a means of manipulating people and enriching himself.

A later, Reformation-era example of a representation of a friar's abuse of the sacrament of confession appears in Thomas Dekker's *The Ravens Almanacke* (Dekker was a playwright contemporaneous with Shakespeare). This farcical almanac contains several short stories, along with bits of advice and astrological predictions of plague and civil war. One of the stories relates that a certain Friar Pedro, though lustful and possessing "better skill in composing an amorous sonnet then in sowing solemn dirges" (n.p.), had such an appearance of holiness that he was appointed the confessor of a convent full of young nuns. Seducing one fairly willing nun after another through his "counsel" in the confessional, he eventually was so successful in his amorous designs that, "under the color of auricular confession, shadowing his villainy, [. . .] of twenty nuns, fifteen were with child." A fit instrument of unchastity indeed! Dekker's Friar Pedro differs from Chaucer's friar and Arthur Brooke's Friar Laurence in so far as Friar Pedro uses the confessional as the means of seducing women for himself, but each author clearly portrays auricular confession as the especially effective tool of friars' seductions and corruptions. Hence, when Brooke describes confession as "the key of whoredom, and treason," he is being no more novel than when he describes friars as the instigators of unchaste behavior.

But what does this show us about Shakespeare's *Romeo and Juliet*? Surely, Shakespeare's Friar Laurence is no obvious villain and is not obviously or intentionally promoting unchaste behavior. Again, according to Brooke, Romeo and Juliet's very use of confession is itself one of those examples of evil behavior that the author holds up as a warning to readers. But Shakespeare's play does not, at least in any obvious way, present this negative view of auricular confession and a friar's counsel. The play undoubtedly depicts evil actions and grave errors, and Friar Laurence is decidedly inadequate to his aims, but none of this is illustrated for us with the broad strokes of a morality tale depicting readily apparent evil and its consequences. If Shakespeare is not writing a morality tale, though, what does his play suggest about Friar Laurence, auricular confession, and the political and spiritual condition of the community in Verona? As the remainder of this essay will show, Shakespeare's play explores certain aspects of the Protestant Reformation and its possible effects upon individuals and society. Shakespeare's *Romeo and Juliet* emphasizes the role of the Friar, and of confession, as a potential means for reconciling the "ancient grudge" between the Capulets and Montagues. However, Friar Laurence does not make use of the sacrament, or his spiritual authority, when he tries to solve Verona's manifold troubles; instead, he turns to philosophy and natural science.[2] This suggests a grave problem at the very heart of the community: the mechanism through which political and spiritual reconciliation could have been accomplished has been lost. Shakespeare's depiction of the conflict echoes some of the grave effects of the Church of England's abandonment of the sacrament of auricular confession, and in this respect, the play engages with contemporary Reformation debates about the nature of the sacraments and the relationship between spiritual and political authorities in a community.

## Escalus and Benvolio

The "Prologue" of Shakespeare's *Romeo and Juliet* immediately presents the audience with the essential problem of the play: two households "from ancient grudge break to new mutiny" (Prologue 6) and are killing each other in the streets of Verona. This situation raises several serious questions: is there no political authority capable of restraining this violence? Shakespeare emphasizes the political effect of the enmity between these families: "civil blood makes civil hands unclean" (4). The conflict is not simply a private quarrel; it disturbs civil society, and would naturally demand restraint from the political authority in Verona. A second question accompanies the first: is there no religious or spiritual authority capable of ending this violence by fostering forgivingness, charity, and peace? Why has the ancient grudge—so clearly opposed to all Christian teaching—been allowed to fester? The "Prologue" then proceeds to inform the audience that the way this essential problem will be solved is through the sacrifice of the two families' children, and the important point is that this sacrifice is the *only* way in which peace can be accomplished. Shakespeare writes, "the continuance of their parents' rage— / Which, but their children's end, naught could remove— / Is now the two hours' traffic of our stage" (10-12). Nothing else but the children's deaths could remove the enduring rage of their parents. This bleak statement underscores the absence of an effective political or spiritual authority doing what each ought to do.

The implied inadequacies of the political and spiritual authorities in the Prologue's description are quickly confirmed, as both elements are presented as deeply problematic in the very first

---

scene of *Romeo and Juliet*. Two Capulets, Samson and Gregory, pick a fight with Abraham and another Montague servingman. None of these are significant characters, which emphasizes the corrupting nature of the "ancient grudge": it infects everyone, even the lesser members of the two households and the civil community. Not only do Samson and Gregory provoke a brawl, but they do so with evident contempt for the laws of the city. Samson tells Gregory, "Let us take the law of our sides; let them begin" (1.1.35). Law, here, is something to be manipulated for one's advantage, and Gregory reiterates this view when, having bitten his thumb at Abraham and been confronted about the fact, he asks Gregory in an aside, "Is the law of our side if I say 'Ay'?" (1.1.43). Law does not command respect and is not taken as a rule for behavior.[3] This disregard for the laws of the city turns out to be quite understandable, for when Prince Escalus enters to quell the violence, his own words betray his weakness and inability to establish peace and restrain civil violence. The prince has a hard time even getting the combatants to cease fighting at that moment, and when they eventually do cease, Escalus recounts that "Three civil brawls, bred of an airy word . . . have thrice disturbed the quiet of our streets" (1.1.84-86). Repeated, unrestrained violence between citizens who hold the law in contempt indicates a gravely inadequate political authority. Law is not taken seriously, and the fractures within the community are allowed to deepen with continual provocation that is not adequately punished. Indeed, though Escalus appears to be taking a firm stance in this instance, with the edict that "If ever you disturb our streets again, / Your lives shall pay the forfeit of the peace" (1.1.91-2), we find that this new law is disregarded in the very next brawl, and the punishment is lightened to banishment. Escalus does not enforce his laws, and hence it comes as little surprise that they are ignored. His unwillingness to enforce his edict of capital punishment is emphasized when he concludes this speech by ordering "Once more, on pain of death, all men depart!" (1.1.98). He is immediately ignored, as Montague, Benvolio, and Montague's wife all remain in place. The political authority does not enforce its injunctions and allows the ancient grudge to wrack the state of Verona with civil conflict.

If the opening scene of *Romeo and Juliet* emphasizes the external disorder of the state, and the absence of a political authority adequate to secure the peace, the scene also presents an internal disorder on the part of several of the characters. Benvolio, responding to Montague's wife's inquiry after Romeo, states that in the pre-dawn morning, "A troubled mind [drove] me to walk abroad / Where, underneath the grove of sycamore . . . So early walking did I see your son" (1.1.115-118). Benvolio's "troubled mind" leaves him unable to sleep, but finding Romeo also abroad at that early hour is no relief. Romeo avoids Benvolio, who admits to Romeo's parents, "I, measuring his affections by my own, / Which then most sought where most might not be found, / Being one too many by my weary self . . . gladly shunned who gladly fled from me" (1.1.121-125). We never learn what it is that troubles Benvolio, though his sleeplessness, weariness with himself, and restless desire for isolation make it seem that his "troubled mind" is more than just a passing or trivial mood. It is suggestive that the character in *Romeo and Juliet* who is named after "good will" is himself deeply vexed with a troubled mind. Though at this point Benvolio does not know what is distressing Romeo, he does recognize their shared desire for solitude. In a scene that had just depicted great civil strife, this internal disorder experienced by several characters is noteworthy and indicates problems in Verona that are more than political in nature. Indeed, Montague then describes Romeo's behavior by emphasizing both his separation from human society and his desire for darkness, saying that he "private in his chamber pens himself, / Shuts up his windows, locks fair daylight out, / And makes himself an artificial night" (1.1.133-135). Romeo's behavior is clearly disordered, inverting day and night, and rejecting society. In fact, Romeo's attempt to lock out the light and pen himself in isolated darkness is grimly foreboding of his final suicide within a tomb, where he comments that darkness and death reign and where he determines to lie down on a "pallet of dim night" (5.3.107). Romeo's behavior does not, after all, appear to change very much over the course of the play. Indeed, as Montague concludes in his initial description of Romeo, "Black and portentous must this humor prove, / Unless good counsel may the cause remove" (1.1.135-6). This, as it turns out, is precisely correct, and Montague is sadly prophetic: Romeo does not receive "good counsel," and his black, ungoverned humors culminate in the deaths of Paris, himself, and Juliet. Montague's worry in this opening scene identifies the second part of Verona's deep problem: there is no spiritual authority that provides "good counsel" and that can rectify the internal disorder that troubles several of the characters.

Shakespeare makes it quite clear that at least one manner of correcting this internal disorder would be through confession. Montague laments that Romeo is "to himself so secret and so close" (1.1.144) that his parents cannot discover what troubles him, and he vows that "Could we but learn from whence his sorrows grow, / We would as willingly give cure as know" (1.1.149-150). At that moment, Romeo enters, and Benvolio urges the Montagues to leave, promising to discover the source of the problem. Departing, Montague states, "I would thou wert so happy by thy stay / To hear true shrift" (1.1.153-154). "Shrift" was a common word at the time, referring to confession, and while sometimes, as here, it was used in a non-religious context, its general sense was explicitly in reference to the Roman Catholic sacrament of auricular confession (*Oxford English Dictionary*). Montague's wish that Benvolio might "hear true shrift" suggests that, at least in one sense, Benvolio will be attempting to fill the role of the confessor in relation to the troubled Romeo. Of course, it is perfectly in keeping with the offices of a good friend to listen to another's difficulties and to attempt to offer good counsel, but Montague's pointed words, "to hear true shrift," encourage the audience to consider the other, priestly office that might hear a confession, offer absolution, and give counsel. Surprisingly, despite Montague's avowal that Romeo is "so secret and so close," Benvolio easily and immediately succeeds in procuring a confession from him. Romeo readily tells his friend that he is in love but that his beloved does not share the passion. Benvolio, in keeping with his promise to Romeo's parents, attempts to fulfill his role as Romeo's confessor, urging his friend, "Be ruled by me: forget to think of her" (1.1.220). Echoing Prince Escalus' ineffective attempt to assert his political authority to end the feud, Benvolio makes an ineffective attempt to rule Romeo's troubled mind. Not being a priest, he cannot, after all, "hear true shrift," and even the counsel he does offer is immediately ridiculed and rejected by Romeo: "Thou canst not teach me to forget" (1.1.232).

## Confession and the Reformation

Romeo, despite his reluctance to hear friendly counsel, does have a confessor, as we learn in Act 2. But before examining Friar Laurence and his use of his own spiritual authority, some immediate historical context surrounding "shrift" in Shakespeare's England should be considered. Repentance, and the Roman Catholic sacrament of confession, were hotly contested topics during the Reformation. According to the Catholic Church, penance was one of the seven sacraments, and it consisted of three parts: contrition, confession, and satisfaction. While the penitential sinner is essential for the sacrament—he is, after all, the one who supplies the *matter* of the sacrament (the penitence)—the standard Catholic position holds that the sacrament's *form* is the priest's statement, "I absolve thee."[4] Thus, the priest, listening to the confession and then absolving the repentant sinner, plays a necessary role in the completion of the sacrament. These elements of the sacrament of penance constituted the means for receiving absolving grace from God, which restores the sinner's soul to a state of grace. However, in the late medieval and early modern Catholic Church, penance also played an important role in the Church as an integral part of human communities. The social function of confession has been described as "a discipline for the restoration of sinners to the privileges of membership in the Church" (*Medieval Handbooks* 15). One important aspect of these privileges is that, after having gone to confession, the penitent sinner was prepared to receive communion at Mass. As Eamon Duffy writes, "Receiving communion at Easter was called 'taking one's rights,' a revealing phrase, indicating that to take communion was to claim one's place in the adult community. Exclusion was a mark of social ostracism" (Duffy 94; see also Bossy, "The Mass"). Confession, then, was not merely the sacrament for regaining the state of grace in one's soul, but it also served an important social role within communities. It functioned in part as a social mechanism to resolve community disputes, ill will, and conflict (see Beckwith 34-56). These political effects were, to be sure, accidental benefits to the proper end of confession, which was to restore the sinner to the state of grace, but their accidental quality made them no less real or important for the function of medieval and early modern Catholic communities.[5]

Protestant reformers, including Luther and Calvin, vigorously attacked confession as inefficacious or insufficient and rejected the sacrament entirely. In England, sacramental confession persisted, at least in official forms, until the Thirty-Nine Articles of 1563, a good while longer than in many other parts of Protestant Europe. Nevertheless, it was condemned by influential English Church leaders much earlier than that, including William Tyndale in the 1520s in his *Obedience of a Christian Man* and Thomas Cranmer in the 1530s and following.[6] By 1563, however, and persisting through the 1590s, when Shakespeare wrote *Romeo and Juliet*, the official position of the Church of England regarding repentance and confession was neatly stated in the Elizabethan *Book of Homilies*, a collection of officially endorsed sermons that were required by law to be read in English churches. One of those sermons, the three-part "An Homilie of Repentance, and of True Reconciliation unto God," clarifies that while repentance is necessary for salvation, it is not a sacrament, and that auricular confession to a priest, and the priest's dispensation of absolution, are clearly not a part of repentance (*Certaine Sermons* 256-74). In the 1559 *Book of Common Prayer*, repentance is frequently mentioned, and the priest even states that for those with troubled consciences, "he may receive comfort and the benefit of absolution, to the quieting of his conscience, and avoiding of all scruple and doubtfulness" (*Book of Common Prayer* 257). However, here too, the absolution is not sacramental, not a means of obtaining particular graces, but instead of satisfying scruples, and in fact, anyone who is a "discreet and learned minister of God's word" (257) is able to dispense such absolution. The English Church rejected sacramental confession, and priests did not possess the power to hear shrift or actually absolve sins. In fact, surveying English Protestant devotional documents from the period, Heather Hirschfeld finds, "a persistent, insistent need to reiterate the solifidian credentials of Protestant repentance in order to guard its difference from Catholic penance and to reinforce its connection to principles of justification by faith and the utter depravity of the human will."[7] By the time Shakespeare wrote *Romeo and Juliet*, auricular confession had been denounced for decades, and it was more commonly described in pejorative terms, as, for instance, the "key of whoredom, and treason," than as a sacrament.

## Friar Laurence

This Reformation context is important for our interpretation of *Romeo and Juliet* because here we encounter a friar who is continually mentioned and depicted in association with sacramental confession. However, instead of using the sacramental power he possesses, he relies upon philosophy and his knowledge of herbs in a well-meant but disastrous attempt to help Romeo, Juliet, and the community in Verona. At the end of the famous balcony scene with Juliet, Romeo offers us the first reference to Friar Laurence in the play, resolving, "Hence will I to my ghostly friar's close cell / His help to crave and my dear hap to tell" (2.1.230-1). Seeking good counsel at this juncture is an understandable, even judicious, resolution on Romeo's part, as he attempts to navigate the "ancient grudge" that divides the two lovers' families. However, an attentive audience would already also wonder about this "ghostly friar" and how effective he is going to be, given that Romeo had such a troubled mind at the opening of the play and given that it was Benvolio, and not this friar, who originally sought to correct Romeo's disordered spirit. The following scene introduces Friar Laurence, gathering "baleful weeds and precious-juiced flowers" (2.2.8) at dawn, and he exclaims, "mickle is the powerful grace that lies / In plants, herbs, stones" (2.2.15-16). Significantly, the Friar is not at prayer, celebrating Mass, but instead gathering herbs, in which he finds a "powerful grace"; as we will see, Friar Laurence ultimately fails the lovers by turning to this "powerful grace" rather than to his own spiritual power to dispense absolving grace.

If our first glimpse of Friar Laurence reveals his significant knowledge of herbs, his opening speech has also been called "a hymn to power and to the uses and abuses to which it can be put" (Brenner 51). Friar Laurence states, "Virtue itself turns vice, being misapplied, / And vice sometime by action dignified" (2.2.21-22), an odd claim about vice that seems to suggest that the end justifies the means (see Brenner 51). Hearing Romeo cryptically state that, instead of sleeping, "the sweeter rest was mine" (2.2.44), Friar Laurence exclaims, "God pardon sin! Wast thou with Rosaline?" (2.2.44). This is the Friar's first reference to God, and in the context of pardoning sin, it brings to mind Benvolio's attempt to "hear true shrift" (1.1.154), as both friend and priest think of sin in direct association with Romeo's woes. After several more vague comments from Romeo about love, Friar Laurence again emphasizes sin and shrift with the rebuke, "Be plain, good son, and homely in thy drift; / Riddling confession finds but riddling shrift" (2.2.55-56). He speaks with the tone and authority of Romeo's spiritual confessor, one used to hear Romeo's confessions. But, after scoffing at Romeo's inconstancy, chiding him for the suddenness of his new passion, and questioning whether it was actually love or doting that Romeo felt (2.2.65-84), Friar Laurence startlingly reverses course and promises to aid Romeo: "In one respect I'll thy assistant be, / For this alliance may so happy prove / To turn your households' rancor to pure love" (2.2.90-92). Rather than addressing himself to the clearly diagnosed and disordered habits in Romeo, some of which have a clear spiritual component, the Friar aims at the much broader end of reconciling the two families. Does the Friar think his noble end may justify his doubtful means? His "action"—to turn the households' enmity to love—may "dignify" the misconduct of secretly marrying extremely young people without the consent of their parents (an action that was forbidden by the Church's canon law [see Stevenson 32 and Bryant 346-47]). As it turns out, of course, this project fails, and the failure is partly due to Romeo's disordered abandonment to his passions, a fault never corrected by his confessor. Instead of even just "riddling shrift," Romeo finds a spiritual authority willing to facilitate the current of his impetuous, troubled mind for the sake of a larger, "dignified" end. The primary failure, here, is that of the confessor, who does not restrain, counsel, or absolve the young man who sought his help.

The ensuing scenes move quickly, continually returning to Friar Laurence and his ability to hear shrift, but they never present the priest in a devotional, spiritual light, and, perhaps surprisingly, sacramental confession is never apparently performed. Arranging their clandestine marriage, Romeo tells Juliet's nurse, "Bid her devise some means to come to shrift this afternoon, / And there she shall, at Friar Laurence' cell, / Be shrived and married" (2.3.164-166). As they wait for Juliet's arrival, Friar Laurence cautions Romeo that "these violent delights have violent ends" (2.5.9), and yet, while recognizing this, he proceeds with the marriage. Juliet enters, saying, "Good even to my ghostly confessor" (2.5.21), emphasizing his official role as her spiritual counsellor, and he interrupts the lovers' embrace, saying, "Come, come with me, and we will make short work. / For, by your leaves, you shall not stay alone / Till holy church incorporate two in one" (2.5.35-37). Despite the fact that he has repeatedly cautioned against haste and "violent delights," he hastens them to their marriage with no mention of shrift beforehand. Later, when Romeo is hiding in the Friar's cell after having killed Tybalt, he laments the news that he is banished, and the Friar rebukes this lament as a "deadly sin" (3.3.24). Romeo pointedly responds:

> "Banished"?
> O Friar, the damned use that word in hell;
> Howling attends it. How hast thou the heart,
> Being a divine, a ghostly confessor,
> A sin-absolver, and my friend professed,
> To mangle me with that word "banished"? (3.3.47-52)

Again stressing Friar Lawrence's role as confessor, Romeo's despair reveals that this "friend professed," who facilitated rather than forestalled the marriage, has utterly failed in correcting Romeo's "deadly" sinful passions. Romeo invokes Friar Laurence as a "sin-absolver," but the Friar does not use that sacramental power, instead offering "adversity's sweet milk, philosophy, / To comfort thee, though thou art banished" (3.3.56-57). When, shortly afterwards, Romeo attempts to kill himself and the Friar rebukes him, we rightly suspect that this philosophy, which Romeo rejects exclaiming "Hang up philosophy!" (3.3.58), will not be adequate to temper Romeo's wild passions. Friar Lawrence speaks eloquently, even prophetically at times—"Take heed, take heed, for such die miserable" (3.3.145)—but he does not exercise his authority as Romeo's confessor; he offers philosophy and further schemes, rather than spiritual care and sacramental grace, to the desperate youth.

Juliet, too, seeks Friar Laurence in distress, and like Romeo, she does so in the explicit context of confession. Having angered her father by refusing to marry Paris, Juliet tells her nurse she will go "to Laurence' cell / To make confession and to be absolved" (3.5.233-234). When she arrives and finds Paris with Friar Laurence, he asks her, "Come you to make confession to this father?" (4.1.22). But despite these continual reminders of Friar Laurence's position as confessor and spiritual authority, he does not act in that capacity. Indeed, Juliet offers to kill herself, just as Romeo had, and as before, Friar Laurence chooses not to address this suicidal wish in light of his spiritual authority; instead, he depends upon his scientific, herbological knowledge for a solution. When Romeo wants kill himself, the Friar offers him philosophy, and when Juliet points a knife at her breast, the Friar turns to the "powerful grace that lies / In plants, herbs, stones" (2.2.15-16). Friar Laurence's scheme for Juliet is clearly an imitation of Christ's resurrection, even down to the amount of time Juliet and Jesus spent in the tomb (see Weinberger 366). But Juliet's resurrection will be effected not with divine grace, but with the Friar's potions. The whole plan, through its very boldness in imitating the central mystery of the Christian faith, conspicuously lacks any element of the divine or of the spiritual. Instead, it coopts the appearance of the spiritual for other ends, not only in taking Christ's resurrection as a model, but also in having Juliet pretend that the confession at Friar Laurence's cell had convinced her of her error. The nurse observes, "she comes from shrift with merry look" (4.2.15), and Juliet tells her parents:

I have learnt me to repent the sin
Of disobedient opposition
To you and your behests, and am enjoined
By holy Laurence to fall prostrate here
To beg your pardon. (4.2.17-21)

This is a lie that Friar Laurence encouraged her to tell (4.1.89-90). Knowing that instead of shrift and absolution, she received a potent vial from the Friar, the audience can appreciate Shakespeare's emphasis upon the lack of any real repentance.

It is, finally, a simple but important point that the Friar's "good counsel" (3.3.160), as the nurse calls it, utterly fails in curbing the suicidal impulses of the impetuous youths who seek his help. But, as importantly, we must note that this "good counsel" does not consist of his exercising his spiritual authority, or ever clearly hearing shrift. The continual references to shrift, confession, absolution, and sin throughout *Romeo and Juliet* make conspicuous the absence of any actual confession being performed in the play. Instead, philosophy, herbal potions, and wild schemes are substituted, and the end is disastrous. As Gerry Brenner observes, "the Friar's herbological interests align him with the play's other drugmaker, the apothecary who commits the outlawed act of selling poison to Romeo" (Brenner 53). The Friar and the apothecary both dispense drugs, one of which kills, and the other simulates death. Neither rectifies the disordered, self-destructive desires of Romeo and Juliet. The Friar, then, utterly fails in caring for the spiritual condition of the young lovers, fails as their "ghostly father." We should also consider, however, whether he succeeded in his larger aim of reconciling the houses and ending the "ancient grudge." In the closing couplets of the play, the Prince announces the arrival of a "glooming peace" (5.3.305) and declares, "Some shall be pardoned, and some punished" (5.3.308). These statements are, on the one hand, hopeful, but they should also remind the audience of the Prince's declarations in the opening scene of the play, in which he commanded peace and threatened future punishment. It was not effective then; will it be effective now? The feuding families are ostensibly reconciled, but the manner in which this reconciliation is expressed suggests that all is not as well as the Prince fondly hopes. The parents intend to erect statues of gold to honor their children, but as Marjorie Garber observes, "the play's references to gold are frequently negative and debasing" (212). Gold is, after all, what Romeo used to purchase his poison from the apothecary, saying, "There is thy gold—worse poison to men's souls, / Doing more murder in this loathsome world, / Than these poor compounds that thou mayst not sell" (5.1.80-82). If the play's closing symbol of future peace is composed of such a "poison to men's souls," we should be skeptical of the lasting nature of Verona's peace.[7]

Shakespeare's presentation of Friar Laurence is, in light of all of this, both in keeping with certain aspects of traditional caricatures of friars, and, in other respects, strikingly different. Friar Laurence fits the stereotype in that he is meddling and a failed spiritual leader, but, notably, he does not abuse the confessional. In fact, the play suggests that things would be much better had he properly exercised his spiritual authority, had he heard shrift and given good counsel, and had he focused primarily upon the spiritual ills of those seeking his help. Instead of witnessing confession abused by the meddling friar, we find that it is never used, but only spoken of. Indeed, we never behold Friar Laurence, or any other character in the play, at prayer at all. Rather than showing auricular confession as the "key of whoredom, and treason," as Shakespeare's source would have it, Shakespeare depicts a clergy that abandons the confessional, with destructive consequences to both the spiritual and communal conditions of Verona. In this last respect, *Romeo and Juliet* is suggestive about Shakespeare's own Reformation-era England, which had also abandoned sacramental confession. Certainly, *Romeo and Juliet* does not definitively show what shrift might have accomplished in Verona, but it also does not let the audience forget the conspicuous absence of shrift either. It is, perhaps, in the absent but continuously mentioned forum of the confessional that the "ancient grudge" could have been healed, turning old "rancor to pure love" (2.2.92).[8]

## Notes

1. All quotations are from *The Norton Shakespeare*, edited by Stephen Greenblatt et al.

2. James C. Bryant observes this same connection in Shakespeare's partial use of the stereotypically nefarious friar, writing that despite Friar Laurence's good intentions, "It is quite possible that Shakespeare retains something of the comical friar tradition by implying a disparity between the cleric's holy commitment and his actual behavior" (343).

3. D. Scott Broyles observes, "Given the sorry state of Verona's political landscape, one should not be surprised to find that the eleven references to "the law" throughout the play are mocking and deprecating. None is respectful or deferential to the dignity or higher purposes of the rule of law" (81).

4. See Thomas Aquinas, *Summa Theologica* III, Q. 84, Art. 3. The importance of the priest in the sacrament is derived from John 20:23.

5. For further discussion, see Bossy, *Christianity* (35-75). He writes, "the sacrament [confession] represented a moment of critical transition: for the community and for the individual, a passage from a baptized but sinful condition into a supernatural state of 'grace', a passage from particularity towards membership of the whole body of Christ, a reconciliation to God and the neighbor" (46).

6. See Null (116-156) for a helpful discussion of Cranmer's sustained rejection of sacramental confession.

7. *The End of Satisfaction*; see pp. 16-38 for a helpful overview of various positions on penance in England at the time.

7. Garber encourages us to "approach with great caution and many reservations the final scheme of reconciliation put forward by the Montagues and the Capulets. . . . At the close of the play, at the end of the tragedy, the final tragedy would seem to be that no one left alive onstage has understood the play" (211-212). D. Scott Broyles is also suspicious of the closing peace: "there is nothing in the uncertain peace that assures us that the underlying causes of Verona's political

ills—its factional discord and absence of civic virtue and patriotism—
have been dealt with" (113-114).

## Works Cited

Aquinas, Thomas. *Summa Theologica*. Translated by Fathers of the English Dominican Province, 5 vols., Christian Classics, 1948.

Beckwith, Sarah. *Shakespeare and the Grammar of Forgiveness*. Cornell UP, 2011.

*The Book of Common Prayer: 1559 The Elizabethan Prayer Book*, edited by John Booty, U of Virginia P, 2005.

Bossy, John. *Christianity in the West 1400–1700*. Oxford UP, 1985.

_____. "The Mass as a Social Institution 1200–1700." *Past &Present*, vol. 100, 1983, pp. 29-61.

Brenner, Gerry. "Shakespeare's Politically Ambitious Friar." *Shakespeare Studies*, vol. 13, 1980, pp. 47-58.

Brooke, Arthur. *Tragical History of Romeus and Juliet*. 1562. *Early English Books Online*, 10 Aug. 2016. Accessed 21 Feb. 2017.

Broyles, D. Scott. "Shakespeare's Reflections on Love and Law in *Romeo and Juliet*." *Journal Jurisprudence*, vol. 18, 2013, pp. 75-115.

Bryant, James C. "The Problematic Friar in *Romeo and Juliet*." *English Studies*, vol. 55, 1974, pp. 340-350.

*Certaine Sermons or Homilies Appointed to be Read in Churches In the Time of Queen Elizabeth I*. A Facsimile Reproduction, edited by Mary Ellen Rickey and Thomas B. Stroup, Scholars' Facsimiles & Reprints, 1968.

Chaucer, Geoffrey. *Canterbury Tales: Fifteen Tales and the General Prologue*, edited by V. A. Kolve and Glending Olson, W. W. Norton, 2005. Norton Critical Edition.

Dekker, Thomas. *The Ravens Almanacke*. 1609. *Early English Books Online*, 12 Aug. 2016. Accessed 21 Feb. 2017.

Duffy, Eamon. *The Stripping of the Altars: Traditional Religion in England c. 1400–1580*. Yale UP, 1992.

Garber, Marjorie. *Shakespeare After All*. Pantheon Books, 2004.

Hirschfeld, Heather. *The End of Satisfaction: Drama and Repentance in the Age of Shakespeare*. Cornell UP, 2014.

*Medieval Handbooks of Penance: A Translation of the Principal* Libri Poenitentiales. Translated by John T. McNeill and Helena M. Gamer, Columbia UP, 1990.

Null, Ashley. *Thomas Cranmer's Doctrine of Repentance: Renewing the Power to Love*. Oxford UP, 2000.

*OED Online*, 2017, oed.com/. Accessed 21 Feb. 2017.

Shakespeare, William. *The Norton Shakespeare*, edited by Stephen Greenblatt et al., 3rd ed., W. W. Norton, 2016.

Stevenson, Robert. *Shakespeare's Religious Frontier*. M. Nijhoff, 1958.

Weinberger, Jerry. "Pious Princes and Red-Hot Lovers: The Politics of Shakespeare's *Romeo and Juliet*." *The Journal of Politics*, vol. 65, no. 2, 2003, pp. 350-375.

# The Critical Reception of *Romeo and Juliet*

Richard Harp

## Early Criticism

Substantive criticism on *Romeo and Juliet* began with Samuel Johnson's famous preface to his 1765 edition of Shakespeare's works. Johnson there praised Shakespeare's drama as "mirror of life" allowing a hermit to imitate the "transactions of the world and a confessor [to] predict the progress of the passions." This seemed particularly true for *Romeo and Juliet*, which Johnson considered especially pleasing. He called its scenes "busy and various, the incidents numerous and important, [and] the catastrophe irresistibly affecting" (124-25). Commenting on his early disappearance from the play, Johnson remarked that "Mercutio's wit, gaiety, and courage, will always procure him friends that wish him a longer life; but his death is not precipitated, he has lived out the time allotted him" in the construction of the play (see Bloom and Marson 48). Juliet's Nurse was the other character Johnson especially praised. He thought her a character who delighted Shakespeare himself, for he had "with great subtilty [sic] of distinction, drawn her at once loquacious and secret, obsequious and insolent, trusty and dishonest" (see Bloom and Marson 48).

Johnson also perceptively noted Shakespeare's abilities in both tragedy and comedy, saying that "his tragedy seems to be skill, his comedy to be instinct" (128). Although a tragedy, *Romeo and Juliet* contains several notable early comic passages. In the very first scene, Montague and Capulet family servants engage in rudely and ridiculously aggressive banter. The play is generally considered to have been written in the mid-1590's, about the same time as the comedy *A Midsummer Night's Dream*. This may partly explain how easily Shakespeare moves back-and-forth between the two genres in *Romeo and Juliet*. Johnson considered the comic scenes "happily wrought" but thought the play's "pathetic strains are always polluted with some unexpected depravations" (see Bloom and Marson 48).

The next great Shakespearean critic was the Romantic author Samuel Taylor Coleridge, who praised the play's opening events for presenting "a lively picture" of all the play's "impulses," showing "the laughable absurdity of the evil," since its "contagion" reaches even "the servants, who have so little to do with it." He also highlighted the excellence of this whole first scene: the intense arc of the Montague/Capulet feud leads from the servants' absurdities through the families and their relatives and friends to the Prince of Verona himself—"a motley dance of all ranks and ages to one tune" (see Bloom and Marson 62).

Coleridge also commented upon the love story: Shakespeare shows fine "insight into the nature of the passions." Romeo's first love "Rosaline was a mere creation of his fancy. Romeo shows "boastful positiveness" in a love of his own making, which is never shown where love is really near the heart" (see Bloom and Marson 62-63). In contrast, Romeo's genuine love for Juliet causes "an anxiety for the safety of the object, a disinterestedness, by which it is distinguished" from counterfeit affection (Coleridge 228). Coleridge also compares Juliet to Prospero's daughter Miranda in *The Tempest,* who had spent most of her young life isolated from young men until one fortuitously washed ashore on the desert island where she lived in exile with her father: "There seems more passion in the one, and more dignity in the other; yet you feel that the sweet girlish lingering and busy movement of Juliet, and the calmer and more maidenly fondness of Miranda, might easily pass into each other" (229).

Coleridge considered Mercutio's death, and its circumstances, crucial to the play's development: on his death "the whole catastrophe depends; . . . . Had not Mercutio been rendered so amiable and so interesting, we could not have felt so strongly the necessity for Romeo's interference [in the sword fight with Tybalt] connecting it immediately, and passionately, with the [lover's] future fortunes." Like Johnson, Coleridge found Mercutio highly attractive: he had "all the elements of a poet . . . . combined with the manners and feelings of a perfect gentleman" (in Taylor and Loughrey 35).

Coleridge's contemporary William Hazlitt was also a fine judge of the play. He observed that "Romeo and Juliet are in love but they are not love-sick." Romeo had of course been love-sick when he spoke about Rosaline, but this tone was quickly abandoned when he went to Capulet's ball and first glimpsed Juliet's beauty. Their courtship, Hazlitt says, does not feature "an insipid interchange of sentiments lip-deep, learnt at second-hand from poems and plays" (see Bloom and Marson 55). Instead, critics more frequently noticed the extraordinary maturity of Juliet as a heroine (especially given her age as a very young teenager. Indeed, in Hazlitt's age some "Bowdlerizers" (named after Thomas Bowdler, whose *Family Shakespeare* omitted "words and expressions . . . which cannot with propriety be read aloud in a family" [title page, vol. 10]) objected to Juliet's candid eroticism. "Such critics," Hazlitt retorted, "do not perceive that the feelings of the heart sanctify, without disguising, the impulses of nature. Without refinement themselves, they confound modesty with hypocrisy" (253). Juliet's character, Hazlitt continued, combines "warmth of imagination and tenderness of heart with the most voluptuous sensibility" (254).

Comparatively little discussion of the play occurred in the Victorian period, although the Irishman Edward Dowden in his *Shakespeare: A Critical Study of His Mind and Art* (1875), responded to Hazlitt's idea that Romeo is "Hamlet in love" (see Bloom and Marson 59). Dowden also noticed a similarity: in each, he says, "the will . . . is sapped," although for different reasons: Romeo's incapacity is his bad luck—"the stars are inauspicious to him"— while Hamlet's "disease of soul" paralyzes his ability to act (see Bloom and Marson 86). The comparison is apt, although Hamlet, like Romeo and Juliet, is also deeply affected by circumstances not of his own making—Romeo is, as Hamlet says to Horatio, "benetted round with villainies" (5.2.29).

Dowden also showed critical prescience in comparing men to women in Shakespeare's plays. Although the dramatist was interested in both sexes, "the chief problems of life seemed to lurk for Shakespeare in the souls and in the lives of men," as his greatest tragedies were about them. Shakespeare's women, Dowden continues, "have almost always the advantage of his men," as they "are in the highest degree direct in feeling and efficient in action" (see Bloom and Marson 91). Prominent Victorian critics such as Dowden and A. C. Bradley wrote more copiously about Shakespeare's tragedies (although Bradley hardly discussed *Romeo and Juliet* at all in his famous work *Shakespearean Tragedy*) than his comedies, where women are often the plays' major heroes. This is one reason among many that *Romeo and Juliet* is so interesting: it is a love tragedy with Juliet as principal protagonist. Even Dowden admits this; Juliet is "all and entire in each act of her soul," he says, whereas Romeo, "on the contrary, is as yet but half delivered from self-consciousness" (see Bloom and Marson 91).

## Twentieth and Twenty-First Century Criticism

## Romeo and Juliet as Lovers

Modern criticism has naturally continued this interest in the couple's love affair. Act 2, Scene 2 (where Romeo overhears Juliet on her balcony confess her love for him) is one of the most famous scenes in world drama. It presents a transformed Petrarchan model of a man worshipping (to no avail) a woman from afar and being pained/ confused/contented (the latter because it allowed him to continue being pained and confused) into the companionable dialogue of two very young lovers speaking their minds without artifice. As Geoffrey Hutchings says: "Romeo is learning a new dimension to himself, skillfully guided by Juliet's instincts. In the balcony scene he is still tied to the rhetoric of love, and Juliet has to school him beyond the mere conventions" (104). But it is not only tepid Petrarchan conventionalities that Romeo must overcome; the crude sexual language and innuendo of his peers is another teenage custom to be abandoned. Aristotle famously defined virtue as a mean between two extremes, and Juliet guides Romeo to a love neither artificial and oblique nor rude and offensive: "Juliet's directness is magnificent. It is she who proposes marriage. But since she is neither brazen nor falsely modest, she has no need of bawdry" (Hutchings103-04). Thomas Honegger also notices this new approach to lovemaking. Shakespeare departs from the way his source material (Arthur

---

Brooke's *The Tragicall History of Romeus and Juliet)* portrayed a protracted relationship between a "reluctant and aloof lady and patiently suffering lover." Instead, Shakespeare introduced "new interactional complexities . . . by making Juliet a much more active protagonist" than Brooke's heroine. While Romeo continues his immature "exploration of Petrarchan imagery," Juliet "gets down to the reality of love and the problems that such a liaison creates, whereas Romeo is still busy searching for new oxymorons and metaphors" (Honneger 76). Honegger says Juliet "increasingly gains a voice of her own," which reaches its full development in her later marriage song (84).

The quality of verse throughout the balcony scene is superb. Jill Levenson, for example, remarks that in various Shakespeare plays from the 1590s "the more sensual and genuine the feelings, the more original and lyric their expression." But in *Romeo and Juliet*, he "fuses these qualities in verse at times so wonderful that it seems to embody the emotion itself: the garden and balcony passages express transcendent love in transcendent poetry" (8). Daniel Burt voices similar praise: "In some of the most impassioned, lyrical, and famous verses Shakespeare ever wrote, the lovers' dialogue perfectly captures the ecstasy of love and love's capacity to remake the world" (277).

## Love and Death

But some critics have found the lovers not just in love with each other but also with the darkness cloaking their passion. The German philosopher G. W. F. Hegel thought that however much one sorrowed over the "pathetic transiency of such a beautiful love," it is nonetheless "a kind of *unhappy blessedness* in misfortune" (see Taylor and Loughrey 38). One modern source for this discussion is Denis de Rougemont's *Love in the Western World* (1939), which argued that adulterous love affairs where marriage was impossible (as between the medieval lovers Tristan and Isolde) ultimately sought consummation in death. But Geoffrey Hutchings disputes any application of this idea to Shakespeare's play: "Romeo and Juliet are brought to passionate life in their love. Their marriage is consummated, and the consummation [is] symbolized in the beautiful poetry of the scene in the wedding-bed." If that bed finally becomes a "sacrificial altar," the transformation results from the "cankered hate in society" (105-06).

Still, if Romeo and Juliet are neither adulterers nor in love with death, critics have objected to their love for other reasons. Joseph Pearce makes an especially strong case against them in what he considers an appropriately Catholic interpretation. "Providence," he writes, "has outwitted and outmaneuvered the hatred of the families and the disordered eros of the lovers, punishing the sinners for their transgressions," making "the play's denouement . . . not a meaningless mess . . . but a revelation of God's hand at work" (129). There is nothing heroic about the couple's love, as it leads to their suicides. The "death of the lovers [is] a warning bell . . . of the mortality of the body and the immortality of the soul" (127). Ronald Bond agrees. He regards the couple's love as a "compressed version of the *gradus amoris*, the steps towards illicit love which requires a succession of senses." Such a sequence begins with sight, "the religion of the eye," then proceeds to conversation, touching, kissing, and ultimately intercourse. There is no "ethereal love" here, says Bond, but rather "lovers rapturously devoted to the flesh" (25).

Other critics differ. Noting that Shakespeare inherited from Brooke "a cautionary narrative against unruly yielding to sexual passion, in the homiletic vein of Puritan preachers," David Bevington suggests that Shakespeare created sympathy "with the perils of young lovers whose desires are unappreciated by an unfeeling world" (461). Paul Siegel believes that the sexual nature of their love comports with Christian tradition—it is a "manifestation of the all-pervading love of God, through which the universe is governed"—and Siegel even thinks "their death converts the evil and hate of the world into the social harmony of love in the 'death' of the feud" (see Evans 14-15).

## Imagery

The play's imagery of day and night, light and dark has been of especial interest to critics since Caroline Spurgeon's landmark book

*Shakespeare's Imagery* (1935). The scenes of violence and feuding, from the opening street fighting to the incendiary duel where Tybalt kills Mercutio just as Romeo attempts to end their conflict, occurs in the hot July daytime, while the various scenes of lovemaking take place at night. But light imagery is still applied to Romeo and Juliet; it is, in fact, a quality each notices about the other, from Romeo's comparing Juliet to the bright torches to her later impatiently saying, "Come, night. Come Romeo. Come, thou day in night" (3.2.17), to his saying about his apparently dead, entombed bride, "her beauty makes / This vault a feasting presence full of light" (5.3.85-86).

Yet the lovers cannot completely transform the gloomy, foreboding darkness hovering over their union. Indeed, the play's "principal tragic effect" resembles a "lightning flash against the night," said the poet and critic Mark Van Doren in 1939: "Night is the medium through which the play is felt and in which the lovers are most at home—night, together with certain fires that blaze in its depths for contrast and romance" (54). More recently, Marjorie Garber has agreed, saying that night is the play's "interior world," a "middle world of transformation and dream sharply contrasted to the harsh daylight world of law, civil war, and banishment" (195).

## Sonnet

The play's formal aspects—its use, for example, of the sonnet, the epithalamion, the aubade, and figures of speech such as oxymoron—has also drawn much attention. Sonnets were, especially in Shakespeare's era, a form in which male speakers expressed devotion or complaint to their lovers. Many famous sonnet sequences were written by men, such as Sir Philip Sidney or Shakespeare himself, but in this play, Shakespeare transforms this and other well-worn literary genres. He introduces dramatic dialogue into the form as Romeo and Juliet alternate addressing one another when they first meet. The love sonnet derives from the Middle Ages, when courtly love made familiar the metaphorical comparison of "lover is to lady as pilgrim is to shrine or saint"—the trope with which Romeo begins the sonnet to Juliet. But here, the religious language is not merely conventional but "strangely appropriate, for if it is hyperbolic, it is also the aptest language for the sacramental quality" of the couple's burgeoning love-relationship (Watts 72-73).

Marjorie Garber notes that love at first sight is not "something to distrust" in Shakespeare, where it is a "common phenomenon" in the plays. Hence, Romeo and Juliet's sonnet "ends sonneteering for the rest of the play" (Garber 193). The "sonnet tradition of unattainable or unrequited love is turned inside out, and the artifice of conventional language goes with it. This is love at first sonnet" (194).

## Epithalamion

The "Epithalamion," or wedding song, is a venerable form, usually sung by a man (as in Edmund Spenser's famous "Epithalamion"); it was "a joyful song," says Francis Fergusson, with which "wedding guests were supposed to accompany the ceremonious progress of bride and groom to their nuptial chamber. But Juliet must sing hers alone, in her child's voice; and as we listen we know [as she does not] that her Romeo is banished already" (see Bloom and Marson 211). But here, too, Shakespeare transforms a genre. Juliet is very young but as she speaks the wedding song (3.2), awaiting Romeo's coming to her bedroom on their wedding night, her verses are exceptionally memorable. She does show youthful impatience for the coming of night, but her innocence combines flawlessly with an ardent sensuality that betrays a maturity beyond her years. Caroline Spurgeon (65) notes how Juliet speaks of contrasting colors as she awaits her husband, saying he will "lie upon the wings of night / Whiter than snow upon a raven's back" (lines18-19), and Harold Bloom well summarizes the overall effect: "we are reminded once again that [Juliet's] love is an ennobling one and that she, in contrast to her immoral nurse and the debauched perspective of Mercutio, has kept her virginity for her wedding night. . . . Juliet proves herself a faithful wife as yet inexperienced, who will hold her marriage vows sacred" (Bloom and Marson 26).

## Aubade

The aubade (or dawn song) also derived from the medieval courtly love tradition and "usually describe[s] the regret of two lovers at their imminent separation" (Drabble 49). In *Romeo and Juliet*, this occurs at 3.5, the morning after their wedding night. Juliet, noticing Romeo's preparing to leave, says "Wilt thou be gone? It is not yet near day," saying that it was not the lark, the herald of the new day that Romeo had heard but rather the nightingale. Shakespeare revitalizes this poetic form, which conventionally has lovers quarrel about the time of day, by having them quickly change their minds and oppose the arguments they initially made. Romeo decides not to insist that it is indeed the dawn, only to have Juliet respond—out of concern for her husband—that it is. Their love once again triumphs over a conventional poetic formula. Harold Bloom thinks this scene symbolizes the entire play. He calls the couple's aubade "disturbing precisely because they are not courtly love sophisticates working through a stylized ritual." The play's "subtle outrageousness" derives not just from the fact that the sun has ended the pair's exceptionally brief honeymoon. Instead, "everything is against the lovers: their families and the state, the indifference of nature, the vagaries of time, and the regressive movement of the cosmological contraries of love and strife" (Bloom 102).

Francis Fergusson also finds ominous overtones in the aubade (see Bloom and Marson 211). Although Romeo and Juliet speak movingly and tenderly of both their desire (and concern) for each other, Fergusson suggests that in aubades "love is always amoral, all-powerful, and so wonderful it can be fulfilled only in or through death." And indeed the next time Romeo and Juliet see each other is in the gloomy Capulet tomb where they take their own lives. Fergusson concludes that Shakespeare saw "something terrifying . . . in their absolute (and too literal and impatient) obedience" (see Bloom and Marson 212) to love.

## Oxymoron

The oxymoron (an adjective modifying a noun that is its opposite) is used (to excess) by Romeo in complaining about his unrequited love for Rosaline ("O brawling love, O loving hate . . . Feather of lead, bright smoke, cold fire, sick health" (1.1.176, 180), but these paradoxical conjunctions, says David Bevington, express "a conflict in humankind, as in the universe itself" (462). The early stacking up of oxymorons, however, is Shakespeare's intentional stylistic excess; it shows the gulf between language and genuine passion—Romeo is not in love with the real person Rosaline but only with his own image of her. And there is equal artificiality in the feud's absurd formalities ("Do you bite your thumb at us, sir?" a Montague servant demands [1.1.44]), where nearly any gesture or word may lead to violence. In such situations, language has no reasonable reference to reality. As Marjorie Garber remarks, "artificiality in language [is] a sign of lack of self-knowledge, a failure to acknowledge what is wrong in Verona—all the way to the County Paris's final and futile rhyming speech at Juliet's tomb" (190). But ultimately, puns, oxymorons and other wordplays serve an important purpose, according to M. M. Mahood: poetry's prerogative is "to give effect and value to incompatible meanings" by means of "paradox, the recurrent image, the juxtaposition of old and young" so that "we are both absorbed by and aloof from the lovers' feelings." Such phrasing, Mahood argues, allows us to experience "a tragic equilibrium which includes and transcends" both feelings of sorrow at the tragic waste and of satisfaction as "if the play were a simple expression of the *Liebestod* ["love in death"] theme" (see Taylor and Loughrey 166).

## Stagecraft

Giorgio Melchiori interestingly discusses the play's use of the Elizabethan theatre's practice of doubling, or having the same actor play two different parts: Shakespeare's doubling suggests "parallelisms in the roles played by different characters" (790). Thus, the same actor plays both Benvolio and Balthasar; in the last act, Balthasar fulfills "the role of confidant that had been Benvolio's" earlier. It is "dramatically correct that the two characters with the same function should be identified with each other" (788). Doubling was a practical necessity in small Shakespearean acting companies, but Melchiori's suggestion that the Bard makes a virtue of necessity

---

by using the technique to add thematic richness to the play could also be useful to modern producers.

Neville Coghill remarks, too, how imaginative staging can also highlight a scene's significance. Coghill, who was both a director and noted scholar, thinks Romeo's first declaration of love for Juliet would have been spoken "downstage, out on the apron," where Juliet would have been brought by the masquerade dance and where the lovers would have kissed after they had spoken their shared sonnet. Coghill thinks the lovers' kiss ("the oldest, the most beautiful, the easiest symbol in the art of theatre"), occurring immediately after "Tybalt's rage juxtaposed images of the two great passions that power the play, and which in the end destroy one another. It is a meaning that can be *seen*" (30-31). Arthur Kinney finds particularly affecting another piece of stagecraft: the moving final tableau where the bodies of Romeo and Juliet lie "as silent emblems of authority and responsibility . . . . Now that Romeo and Juliet appear with all the others for the first time, their silent presence judges everyone else" (see Bloom 83).

## Minor Characters

### Nurse

*Romeo and Juliet* excels in subordinate characters, including Juliet's Nurse, a favorite among critics since Johnson. Barbara Everett superbly analyzes the passage in which the Nurse discusses weaning Juliet (at the time of the "earthquake now eleven years" ago) by laying "wormwood to my dug / Sitting in the sun under the dovehouse wall" (1.3.24, 27-28). The dovehouse, Everett notes, symbolizes "mildness and peace and affectionate love" and the Nurse sitting there while weaning a child is "framed as in some piece of very early genre painting." Hence, the "most domestic and trivial event, personal and simply human as it is, is set beside the violently alien and impersonal earthquake," and only the Nurse's "wandering mind" would think to relate them. Because they do "relate, they interpenetrate" (see Taylor and Loughrey 172). Similarly, then, Romeo and Juliet's very natural love is overshadowed by the earthquake-like feud of their families. In addition, Juliet's weaning also foreshadows her ultimate dismissing of the Nurse when she counsels Juliet to marry Paris even after knowing that she was already married to Romeo (3.5.237-244). Of the relation of this scene to the ultimately tragic fate of the lovers, Everett says: "A weaning is a stage, from milk to the stronger meat of existence; so also with love and death, if we take it that it is the death of eros in agape, and of youth in manhood which is in question" (see Taylor and Loughrey 138).

Marjorie Garber says the Nurse's opening speeches show her "earthiness and practicality, as well as her frankness in sexual matters [and] offer a welcome antidote to the artifice, false idealism, and even prissiness embodied in Lady Capulet's advocacy of Paris." She is, Garber believes, a "forthright descendant of [Chaucer's] Wife of Bath." But like various other critics, Garber finds the Nurse diminished later when she advises Juliet to commit bigamy by marrying Paris: this "is wholly inadequate for Juliet's needs and for the needs of tragedy" (197). Comparing the Nurse to another important secondary character, Friar Laurence, Garber says the Friar is "all authority and no experience, the Nurse all experience and no authority" (198). Looked at as a dramatic part, says Cedric Watts, the Nurse is a "celebrated theatrical 'cameo role'" because "though the part is not a lengthy or dominating one, it is vivid, distinctive, and provides an easy opportunity for a veteran actress to display engaging and even scene-stealing traits of character" (84-85).

## Mercutio

Barbara Everett says that as Romeo and Juliet are really "two romantic children" it is vital for the tragedy's success that Shakespeare find ways to make us take them completely seriously. Thus the importance of the Nurse and Mercutio, who are equally foolish and whose foolishness helps preserve a dignified respect for the two impetuous teenagers (see Taylor and Loughrey 131). David Bevington makes the same point more specifically: "Mercutio and the Nurse are among Shakespeare's bawdiest characters. Their wry and salacious view of love contrasts with the nobly innocent and yet physically passionate love of Romeo and Juliet" (161).

Johnson's and Coleridge's discussions of Mercutio's early death have already been noted; Harold Bloom provides a logical addendum by remarking that Mercutio becomes "irrelevant once Juliet and Romeo fall profoundly in love. What place, Bloom wonders, has Mercutio once the play "becomes dominated by Juliet's magnificent avowal of her love's infinitude" (see Bloom and Marson 291). Bloom is thinking of her declaration to Romeo that her love is as deep as the sea (2.2.133-35). Mercutio's dying words to Romeo—"A plague o' both your houses" (3.1.90), says Bloom in *Shakespeare: The Invention of the Human*, "is what in his death Mercutio becomes, a plague upon both Romeo of the Montagues and Juliet of the Capulets, since henceforward the tragedy speeds on to its final double catastrophe" (96). Bloom thinks Mercutio dies "without knowing what *Romeo and Juliet* is all about: the tragedy of authentic romantic love" (97).

But Mercutio is many-sided. He is, says Coleridge, "a man possessing all the elements of a poet . . . . utterly unconscious of his powers" (see Taylor and Loughrey 35). His final speech displays poised gravitas. Finally, Susan Snyder acutely remarks that with Mercutio's death, "Shakespeare makes the birth of tragedy coincide exactly with the symbolic death of comedy," as the play then loses its "element of freedom and play" (see Taylor and Loughrey 172) as well as losing, as Marjorie Garber adds, "the voice of imagination and moderation and perspective," so that "we stop laughing" (205).

## Friar Laurence

No secondary character, though, has been as controversial as Friar Laurence—although to call him a "secondary" character may be a misnomer, as he speaks more lines than anyone else except Romeo and Juliet. Some critics find little if anything good in the Friar; Gerry Brenner, for example, says that while all the authority figures (the Prince, Old Capulet, and Friar Laurence) act out of self-interest, the Friar is the worst of all. In secretly marrying the lovers and doing other things without consent from their parents or the Prince, the Friar aims at being ultimately lauded as "Verona's miracle worker, its true leader" (Brenner 54). Jill Kriegel says the Friar's error involves trusting overmuch to natural science and magic potions—both formidable influences upon Renaissance thought—such as he gives Juliet to save her from marrying Paris. "Here he assumes the irreverent and, as the plot soon reveals, unwise role of Magus" (Kriegel 141). If Juliet erred in taking Romeo as the "god of my idolatry" (2.3.114), the Friar, too, comes uncomfortably close to "placing himself on par with God" (140).

David Bergeron is more sympathetic to the Friar's dabbling in herbal lore. The Friar finds in herbs a metaphor for human nature: "Two . . . opposed kings encamp" in "man as well as herbs—grace and rude will" (2.3.27-28); and there is a logical relationship, says Bergeron, between the Friar's interest in natural philosophy and his spiritual vocation: hence, when Romeo asks him to perform his marriage with Juliet, the Friar, "who understands the medicinal power of herbs is now called on for spiritual medicine, and indeed he hopes to turn the family rancor into love. He understands the potential for a universal spiritual cure" (see Nardo 98).

Bertrand Evans' 1950 essay offers extended sympathy for Laurence. Evans focuses on the Friar's concluding forty-line speech, which rehearses the events leading up to the tragic ending. Audiences have found this recital tedious (it is often cut in productions) and all too characteristic of his often pointless rhetorical flourishes. But Evans argues that all the characters still alive are together for the first time here and become aware only then exactly how the tragedy occurred. Only the audience, Evans points out, had previously known these details:

> When those through whose acts Fate worked are shown the connections between their actions and the catastrophe, the audience, which until then has borne alone and inexpressibly the mounting agony of knowing all, experiences relief. In this relief lies something, I think, of the pleasure that belongs to the full experience of the tragedy. (864)

Yet, Evans continues, pain is also part of the experience of tragedy and the Friar's speech makes that clear: "Pain of a kind proper to tragedy lies in our reflection that of the four (Tybalt, Romeo, Juliet,

Paris) whose bodies are here none died aware of the situation as it really was. Add to these Mercutio, whose body is elsewhere, and all five youths, one may say, died 'not knowing'" (865). The poignancy of none of the characters' ever having had the clarity about events that the Friar manifests is part of the pathos of the tragic conclusion.

Jay Halio also thinks Shakespeare makes the Friar more sympathetic than his counterpart Brooke: there he is presented "contemptuously" (32), an assessment corroborated by David Bevington, who says that Shakespeare has "tidied up the Friar's immorality and deleted [Brooke's] antipapal tone" (461). Paul Voss compares Shakespeare's Friar with friars depicted by Marlowe, Greene, and Chapman and finds that in "almost every play except Shakespeare's, friars are lecherous villains, comic buffoons, or black magicians" (135).

Finally, one might add to Evans' comments about the dramatic impact of this most affecting tragedy. Mark Van Doren remarked insightfully that "Few other plays, even by Shakespeare" involve their spectators "so intimately," as the dramatist handles the "hearts of his hearers" with "the greatest human respect." The pain of the lovers' fate is made endurable by "the simplicity with which sorrow is made lyric." This is especially true, says Van Doren (59-60), in the "five short words" Romeo utters at Juliet's bier—"O my love! My wife!" which "make up for all of Romeo's young errors"—as well as in the already-wedded-to-Romeo Juliet's exclamation after her father cholerically insists upon her marrying Paris: "Is there no pity sitting in the clouds / That sees into the bottom of my grief?" (3.5.198-99)

## Works Cited

Bergeron, David M. "Sickness in *Romeo and Juliet*." *CLA Journal*, vol. 20, no. 3, 1977, pp. 92-99.

Bevington, David, editor. *The Necessary Shakespeare*. 4th ed., Pearson/ Longman, 2014.

Bloom, Harold. *Shakespeare: the Invention of the Human*. Riverhead Books, 1998.

_____, editor. *William Shakespeare's "Romeo and Juliet."* Bloom's Literary Criticism, 2010.

_____ and Janyce Marson, editors. *Romeo and Juliet.* Bloom's Literary Criticism, 2008.

Bond, Ronald B. "Love and Lust in Romeo and Juliet." *Wascana Review of Contemporary Poetry and Short Fiction*, vol. 15, no. 2, Fall 1980, pp. 22-31.

Bowlder, Thomas, editor. *The Family Shakespeare.* Longman, et al., 1818. 10 vols.

Brenner, Gary. "Shakespeare's Politically Ambitious Friar." *Shakespeare Studies*, vol. 13, 1980, pp. 47-58.

Burt, Daniel S. *The Drama 100: A Ranking of the Greatest Plays of All Time.* Facts On File, Inc., 2008.

Coghill, Neville. *Shakespeare's Professional Skills.* Cambridge UP, 1965.

Coleridge, Samuel Taylor. *Coleridge's Literary Criticism.* Oxford UP, 1908.

de Rougemont, Denis. *L'Amour et l'Occident.* 1939. [Translated as *Love in the Western World.*] Pantheon, 1956.

Dowden, Edward. *Shakespeare: A Critical Study of His Mind and Art.* King, 1872.

Drabble, Margaret, editor. *The Oxford Companion to English Literature.* 5th ed., Oxford UP, 1985.

Evans, Bertrand. "The Brevity of Friar Laurence," *PMLA*, vol. 65, 1950, pp. 841-65.

Everett, Barbara. "*Romeo and Juliet*: The Nurse's Story." *Critical Quarterly*, vol. 14, 1972, pp. 129-39.

Garber, Marjorie. *Shakespeare After All.* Pantheon, 2004.

Halio, Jay L. *"Romeo and Juliet": A Guide to the Play.* Greenwood, 1998.

Hazlitt, William. *The Round Table; Characters of Shakespeare's Plays.* Dent, 1964.

Honegger, Thomas. "'Wouldst thou withdraw Love' Faithful Vow?': The Negotiation of Love in the Orchard Scene." *Journal of Historical Pragmatics*, vol. 7, no. 1, 2006, pp. 73-88.

Hutchings, Geoffrey. "Love and Grace in Romeo and Juliet." *English Studies in Africa: A Journal of the Humanities*, vol. 20, 1977, pp. 95-106.

Johnson, Samuel. *Samuel Johnson on Shakespeare*, edited with an introduction and notes by H. R. Woudhuysen, Penguin Books, 1989.

Kinney, Arthur F. "Authority in *Romeo and Juliet*." *William Shakespeare's "Romeo and Juliet,"* edited by Harold Bloom, Bloom's Literary Criticism, 2010, pp. 77-84.

Kriegel, Jill. "A Case against Natural Magic: Shakespeare's Friar Laurence as Romeo and Juliet's Near-Tragic Hero." *Logos: A Journal of Catholic Thought and Culture*, vol.13, no. 1, Winter 2010, pp. 132-45.

Levenson, Jill L. *Romeo and Juliet*. Manchester UP, 1987.

Mahood, M. M. *Wordplay in Romeo and Juliet* (London, 1957). *Shakespeare's Early Tragedies: "Richard III," "Titus Andronicus" and "Romeo and Juliet": A Casebook*, edited by Neil Taylor and Bryan Loughrey, Macmillan, 1990, pp. 152-66.

Melchiori, Giorgio. "Peter, Balthasar, and Shakespeare's Art of Doubling," *Modern Language Review*, vol. 78, 1983, pp. 777-92.

Nardo, Don, editor. *Readings on Romeo and Juliet*. Greenhaven Press, 1998.

Pearce, Joseph. *Shakespeare on Love: Seeing the Catholic Presence in Romeo and Juliet*. Ignatius Press, 2013.

Siegel, Paul. "Christianity and the religion of love in *Romeo and Juliet*." *Shakespeare Quarterly*, vol. 12, 1961, pp. 383-92.

Snyder, Susan. *The Comic Matrix of Shakespeare's Tragedies. Shakespeare's Early Tragedies: "Richard III," "Titus Andronicus" and "Romeo and Juliet": A Casebook*, edited by Neil Taylor and Bryan Loughrey, Macmillan, 1990, pp. 168-78.

Spurgeon, Caroline. *Shakespeare's Imagery, and What It Tells Us*. Cambridge UP, 1935.

Taylor, Neil, and Bryan Loughrey, editors. *Shakespeare's Early Tragedies: "Richard III," "Titus Andronicus" and "Romeo and Juliet": A Casebook*. Macmillan, 1990.

Van Doren, Mark. *Shakespeare*. Doubleday, 1953.

Voss, Paul J. "'My Ghostly Father': Teaching the Friar in *Romeo and Juliet*." *Approaches to Teaching Shakespeare's Romeo and Juliet*, edited by Maurice Hunt, The Modern Language Association of America, 2000, pp. 131-36.

Watts, Cedric. *Romeo and Juliet*. Twayne Publishers, 1991. Twayne's New
   Critical Introductions to Shakespeare.

# Critical Pluralism and the Opening of the Balcony Scene in Shakespeare's *Romeo and Juliet*

Robert C. Evans

*Romeo and Juliet* has long been one of Shakespeare's most popular plays, and the famous "balcony scene" has long been one of the most beloved and most frequently examined sections of the work as a whole. Most scholars who discuss the tragedy typically focus much attention on this scene. Thus it seems worthwhile here to suggest how truly variously the scene (and, by implication, the entire play, or any literary work) can be approached. Rather than looking at the balcony episode by using just one critical perspective, this essay will adopt an approach known as "critical pluralism"—the idea that no single critical perspective can do full justice to the complexity of any truly complex piece of writing. Instead, multiple perspectives can and should be constantly kept in mind as we read. By thinking about any particular word or phrase in light of *multiple* interpretive possibilities, we are less likely to interpret any work simplistically or reduce its richness to monolithic meanings.[1]

Take, for example, the opening line of this scene. Mercutio has just been mocking Romeo's love-sickness. In response, Romeo privately declares, "He jests at scars that never felt a wound" (2.2.1). This single line can be variously interpreted. **Aristotle**, **Horace**, and twentieth-century **formalists**, for instance, all stress the importance of keeping characters consistent. Consistency contributes to a work's "complex unity" (a favorite formalist phrase) and shows the author's skilled craftsmanship. Romeo's words about Mercutio definitely contribute to our sense of *both* characters' consistency: jesting is one of Mercutio's most typical traits, whereas Romeo is typically far more serious. This contrast in their personalities will be especially relevant later, when Mercutio's habit of mocking others results in his own death. This, of course, is a death that the typically more serious Romeo tries to prevent. **Formalists**, who value irony because it contributes to a work's complex unity, would therefore especially admire the ironic foreshadowing latent in Romeo's opening line in the balcony scene. Anyone who knows the rest of the play will immediately realize that Mercutio will later be wounded quite literally and fatally.

Even now, though, the potential ways of responding to Romeo's opening line are far from exhausted. Thus **Horace** (who valued a work's ability to appeal to the widest possible audience) might admire the line's simple, plain phrasing; **thematic** critics (who emphasize a work's key motifs) would note how this line fits the play's overall emphasis on connections between love and death; while **traditional historical critics** might note that the line perfectly exemplifies the growing importance of iambic pentameter rhythm in the development of English Renaissance dramatic verse. **Psychoanalytic** critics, who stress the tensions in human minds between reason and emotion, might note that Romeo is actually the more emotional character here: he is driven by the impulses of his irrational "id," whereas Mercutio is more firmly in touch with his rational "ego." **Archetypal** critics, however—who (like Horace) stress the importance of stereotypical characters, situations, and themes—might see Romeo as the archetypal young person consumed by passion and Mercutio as the archetypal young person given to playfulness.

**Structuralist** critics, who emphasize the ways literary works are structured in terms of a systematic pattern of binary oppositions, would see Romeo here as personifying emotion and Mercutio as personifying reason, although **deconstructors** (who stress the difficulties of making any such clear distinctions) would suggest that Romeo could just as easily be seen as the reasonable character here, with Mercutio as the character least in control of his emotions. For deconstructors, any simple binaries would be dissolved. Binaries would be replaced instead with ambiguities and irresolvable paradoxes. Some **feminists** might suggest that Mercutio is typically male in his blatant sexism (expressed in lines that precede Romeo's response) and that even Romeo is motivated less by genuine love than by the kind of erotic desire that makes a woman's beauty more important than her character. After all, Romeo has suddenly lost his earlier interest in Rosaline now that he has witnessed the greater beauty of Juliet. Typically, as a male, he is free to walk the streets by himself at night, and it is he, as a male, who takes the initiative of seeking out Juliet at home. **Reader-response critics**, who stress the importance of individual reactions to any detail of a work, might suggest that anyone who has ever felt the kind of passion Romeo feels would be able to relate to his statement here, while **dialogical critics** (interested in the ways texts reflect diverse "voices") might see Romeo's statement as reflecting a whole long tradition in Western literature of men claiming they have been wounded by a woman's beauty. Romeo, in other words, simultaneously speaks for himself and echoes countless previous male lovers in the Western literary tradition.

**New historicist critics**, who stress various kinds of power struggles (whether between individuals or groups), might see this line as typifying the struggle and tensions that exist between Romeo and Mercutio throughout the play, while **Marxist critics** might see both young men, despite their obvious differences, as members of the same privileged class—wealthy, well educated, and well connected. We never see them actually doing any *work*, not even on behalf of their already rich families. They are (**multicultural critics** might note), privileged in other ways as well: they are white, male, young, able-bodied, and heterosexual, and thanks to these advantages, they enjoy greater power than other characters in the play, such as the Nurse. (She, along with the other servants, would simultaneously interest Marxists, new historicists, and multicultural critics). **Postmodernists**, who emphasize freedom and impulsiveness of various sorts, might admire Romeo's willingness to break rules and take risks by surreptitiously entering Juliet's family's garden, while **ecocritics** (who stress the significance of humans' relations with nature) might see the garden as an appropriate symbolic setting for the young couple's ensuing expressions of romantic love. Finally, **Darwinian critics** might consider Romeo's expression of love-stricken pain as reflecting the kind of fundamental sexual desire humans have inherited during their long course of evolution on this planet.

Of course, no reader—and especially no member of a theatrical audience—could have *all* these different possible perspectives simultaneously in mind when reading or watching the play. Human brains simply do not work that way (as any **cognitive critic**, interested in how real brains realistically operate, would be quick to point out). There remains much value, however, in constantly realizing that *any* detail of *any* work is open to an enormous variety of possible interpretations. Many such interpretations do not necessarily conflict; some, in fact, reinforce one another. Sometimes, however, the same detail can be interpreted in exactly *opposite* ways, and it is precisely this fact that lends some credence to the **deconstructive** view that there *are* no final, correct, indisputable interpretations of any word, phrase, sentence, or text. Opponents of deconstruction would argue that this sort of extreme skepticism is unwarranted—that deconstructors set the interpretive bar too high. In fact (opponents of deconstruction might say), we usually have little trouble making basic sense of most words we encounter. (Deconstructors, after all, assume that their own texts can be understood.) One value of **critical pluralism**, then, is that it encourages us to be alive to the possibility of a whole diverse range of possible meanings *without* assuming that interpreting meaning is fundamentally impossible. And one further advantage of pluralism for any interpreter who *does* have a particular kind of argument to make is this: pluralism keeps interpreters constantly aware of potential *counter*-arguments. Thus, as an interpreter develops his or her own reading of a word, line, or passage, s/he remains continually alert to potential objections to (or shortcomings of) his or her particular kind of reading.

## Pluralism in Practice

Pluralists would note (as they always note) that the ensuing lines of Romeo's speech can be interpreted in many different ways. Thus his very next line—"But soft, what light through yonder window breaks?"—might be interpreted by **Horace** (that rare critic who was also a professional writer) as evidence that Shakespeare was a professional dramatist who constantly had to keep in mind that he was writing for the stage, including props, stage business, and actors moving about an actual wooden platform. **Aristotle**, **formalists**, **thematic critics**, and **structuralists** might note how this line contributes to the play's pervasive imagery of light vs. darkness. Such imagery is used again in Romeo's very next line ("It is the East, and Juliet is the sun"). This line introduces a comparison that Shakespeare, demonstrating the kind of literary talent that **Aristotle** and **formalists** would especially appreciate, then proceeds to develop over the course of several further lines. Thus, Romeo (out of Juliet's hearing) calls her a "fair sun" and urges her to

> kill the envious moon
> Who is already sick and pale with grief
> That thou, her maid, art far more fair than she.
> Be not her maid since she is envious
> Her vestal livery is but sick and green,
> And none but fools do wear it. Cast it off.

This kind of extended metaphor was known in Shakespeare's time (as **traditional historical critics** might explain) as a "conceit." In fact, the ability to craft such lengthy comparisons was a talent especially prized by the **formalist critics** of Shakespeare's era. Readers with formalist interests (a **traditional historical critic** might report) abounded during the Renaissance, even though "formalism" as a term was not then used. Readers interested in poetic skill, however, would not be the only readers interested in these lines, with their artful use of personification. **Archetypal** critics might note that the sun has traditionally been associated with male power and the moon with female beauty—associations Shakespeare reverses here. Some **feminist** critics, meanwhile, might appreciate how Juliet is linked with power, although they might also note that her power is associated with her physical beauty. This kind of female power over an excited male would not, of course, surprise **Darwinian** critics, with their interest in the physical attractiveness of both sexes. **Psychoanalytic** critics influenced by Jacques Lacan might note that

Juliet here resembles many women in being subject to a desiring male "gaze."

This passage would naturally also interest modern **Marxist** critics. After all, these lines allude to the whole economic power structure of the Renaissance, which emphasized masters (or mistresses) and servants and which required servants (like those seen earlier and later in the play) to wear particular kinds of "livery." Special clothing marked their obligatory allegiance to the powerful people who controlled their lives. **Formalist** and **thematic** critics might note the irony of Romeo's reference to Juliet killing the moon, since the only murder Juliet will really commit will occur when she later kills herself. **Psychoanalytic** critics, interested in all things sexual, might hear some hint of erotic desire in Romeo's wish that Juliet should "Cast . . . off" her metaphorical clothing. Finally, **traditional historical critics** might note that the word "envious," in Shakespeare's time, could imply not only jealousy but also hatefulness. Therefore, **thematic** and **structuralist** critics might suggest that "envious" reiterates the theme of hate vs. love that runs all throughout this play.

Romeo's next two lines—"It is my lady. O, it is my love! / O, that she knew she were!"—would interest various critics for various reasons. **Formalists**, fascinated by details of language, might note the repetition and balance in the first line as well as that line's use of alliteration and its heavy metrical emphasis on the alliterated words "lady" and "love." **Psychoanalytic** critics might suggest that Romeo's emotional "id" is here dominating his thinking, as the repeated "O's" and accompanying exclamation marks imply. Some **feminists** might conceivably be bothered by his double use of the possessive adjective "my," while both **Darwinists** and **archetypal** critics might both say that such language is simply typical of people of either sex who feel deep attraction to another person. **Horace**, with his concern to make sure that any work would appeal to the broadest possible audience, might admire Shakespeare's phrasing not only here but throughout this scene: that phrasing is clever but clear, artful but rarely if ever obscure.

Both **formalists** and **dialogical** critics might be interested in Romeo's next lines: "She speaks, yet she says nothing. What of that? / Her eye discourses; I will answer it." Formalists, with their interest in skillful phrasing, might note the paradox of speaking but saying nothing, just as they might also note the clever punning on "eye" and "I." Formalists might also comment on the metaphor implied in the words "Her eye discourses," as well as the ways this phrase contributes to this scene's heavy emphasis on eye imagery. Meanwhile, dialogical critics, with their interest in varied tones and voices, might note Romeo's literal dialogue with himself in the first line here. **Psychoanalytic** critics might note how he tries to check his emotional id when he tells himself "I am too bold," while **formalists** might note the continuing development (in the ensuing lines) of images of eyes, imagery of light and darkness, and imagery of heavenly bodies. All these repeated images contribute to major **thematic** patterns of the play. Some **feminists**, however, might be disturbed by Romeo's (and Shakespeare's) continuing focus on Juliet's mere physical beauty—the way she is "objectified" here and throughout the play. **Ecocritics**, interested in relations between humans and the immediate natural environment, might note the reference to "birds" in line 22 (suddenly we are back down on earth rather than in the heavens), while **formalists** might note that the bird imagery here anticipates later, similar imagery, especially in the scene where Romeo takes his leave of Juliet after their marriage (3.5.1-7). Meanwhile, **dialogical** critics, interested in the ways one text can echo others, might note how Romeo's language often draws on phrasing used in poetry written and influenced by the fourteenth-century Italian poet Francesco Petrarca ("Petrarch" in English). **Traditional historical** critics would note the immense influence of Petrarch's love poetry throughout Europe, especially during Shakespeare's era.

**Psychoanalytic** critics, who emphasize emotions (especially erotic emotions), might note the force of Romeo's ensuing exclamation when Juliet "leans her cheek upon her hand": "O, that I were a glove upon that hand, / That I might touch that cheek!" His exclaimed "O" implies the force of his id, and **Darwinian** critics would also note the importance of sexual attraction to the lives of numerous species: by desiring physical contact with Juliet, Romeo expresses impulses that guide the behaviors of many creatures. These impulses help ensure that genes are passed from one generation to the next. Yet Romeo's phrasing here is fairly restrained, as indeed it is throughout the play. Little in this work would seem so shockingly sexual that it would have offended most members of Shakespeare's original audience. **Horace**, who stressed that writers needed, above all, to please their immediate readers or listeners, would therefore commend Shakespeare for having dealt sensibly with a subject (erotic attraction) that could easily have bothered some of his contemporaries. Indeed, **traditional historical** critics would note that attitudes toward sexual expression, like attitudes toward most subjects, usually reflect a given era's prevailing values: language that might seem tame during one period might seem offensive during another and vice versa. The "proper" use of "appropriate" language is therefore an especially common cause of political and social tension, and whenever there are struggles for power and the need to negotiate solutions to those struggles, **new historicist** critics are interested. Most "solutions," of course, are merely temporary. New historicists believe that cultures are constantly in political, social, and economic flux. Negotiated solutions have to be constantly *re-negotiated*, and sometimes violence replaces negotiated compromise (as when the theaters in England, and performances of plays like *Romeo and Juliet*, were forcibly shut down during the English Civil Wars that began in 1642). Puritans of Shakespeare's time were sometimes offended even by plays (such as this one) that today strike most people as acceptably restrained. For **new historicists**, as for **traditional historical critics**, the words of an influential recent **Marxist** critic (Frederick Jameson) are key: "Always historicize!" Always, that is, place any matter being investigated in its various historical contexts.

The balcony scene is famous partly because of the eloquence of the woman who speaks from the balcony. Yet that "woman" (various kinds of critics would note) was not a woman at all. **Traditional historical** critics would explain that women's roles on the Elizabethan stage were played by boys *dressed* as women. **New historicist** and **feminist** critics would note that in Shakespeare's England, the idea of letting actual women *play* women on public stages was simply too controversial—almost inconceivable, in fact. At the royal court, in theatrical productions known as "masques," women in fact did appear as women, a fact that would interest both **new historicists** and **Marxists**. When the public theaters reopened after the 1660 "Restoration" of the monarchy, women were now allowed to play women, proving once again (**traditional historicists**, **new historicists**, and **Marxists** would claim) the importance of knowing history in order to properly interpret any text.

Deconstructors, with their interest in fluidity, instability, and the breakdown of rigid categories, might note that Juliet and the other women in this play were simultaneously women *and* not-women. Similarly, **postmodernists**, with their interest in violating neat categories of proper decorum, might consider the Elizabethan habit of having boys play women liberatingly postmodernist, although **deconstructors** might argue that this habit could be seen as both freeing *and* restrictive, both liberating (since males pretended to be females) *and* non-liberating (since real females could *not* appear as females). **Multiculturalists**, with their interest in the *varied* kinds of identities that constitute any culture, might find it interesting that in Elizabethan public theaters, men could impersonate women, relatively poor persons could impersonate the rich and powerful, Englishmen could impersonate "foreigners," Protestants could impersonate Catholics (and vice versa), and so on. On the Elizabethan stage, actors could inhabit multiple identities while still, in some senses, remaining themselves.

## Juliet Speaks Two Words

When Juliet finally speaks in the balcony scene, she manages to emit just two words—"Ay me"—before Romeo again takes over. Those two words, of course, would instantly interest **psychoanalytic** critics because they imply some sort of emotion (and perhaps even some sort of conflict between the id and the superego). In any case, **formalists**, with their interest in a work's careful construction, would note how

Shakespeare's decision to give her just two words contributes to this moment's suspense: what will she actually say when she finally *does* get to speak at length? For the moment, it is Romeo who again takes center stage. His lofty language here and throughout the play (as when he calls Juliet a "bright angel" and compares her to a "wingèd messenger of heaven") would interest the ancient Greek theorist **Longinus**, who believed great works should not only express the writer's noble soul but also help enoble the souls his audience. Romeo's language throughout the first part of the balcony scene is precisely the sort Longinus would have admired: in phrasing, tone, and substance, it is both elevated and elevating. This is one reason it has been so widely admired for expressing lofty ideals of genuine love. **Multiculturalists** would note that Romeo's phrasing here implies that he is a Christian, although both **multiculturalists** and **historicist** critics would note that Christianity, during Shakespeare's era, had now subdivided into Catholicism and numerous Protestant versions of the same basic faith. All Christians agreed that angels existed, but the play later raises highly controversial religious issues (such as the proper behavior of priests and proper attitudes toward suicide).

In any case, **formalists**, **multiculturalists**, and **thematic** critics might note how Romeo's language here has shifted from his language earlier: previously he had referred to the heavens in non-religious terms, but now his phrasing seems explicitly Christian. **Archetypal** critics might suggest that his earlier references to stars, moon, and sun were references that people from all cultures could understand and relate to. Now, however, he has moved from a broadly human perspective to one that is specifically Judeo-Christian. At the same time (**historical** critics might suggest), it is also possible to hear allusions in his words to the winged messengers of classical mythology. Thus, **dialogical** critics might note that both Romeo and Shakespeare are now in a kind of obvious dialogue with the Christian scriptures as well as in a kind of subtler dialogue with Greek and Roman writings. Meanwhile, **feminists** and **historicists** might find it interesting that the angel Shakespeare imagines is a male (2.2.31)—not, as often in popular culture today, a female.

**Longinus** might note that practically everything in this scene so far has been both literally and figuratively uplifting: Romeo literally looks up to Juliet's balcony and uses elevated language to express elevated, elevating ideas. A **traditional historical** critic might note that Elizabethan theaters were built so that Juliet would actually have an elevated platform on which to stand.

## Juliet Finally Speaks

When Juliet herself finally gets to say more than two words, she utters one of the most famous lines in English literature: "O Romeo, Romeo, wherefore art thou Romeo?" **Formalists** would note how the heavy use of repetition emphasizes just how important Romeo now is to her. **Thematic** critics would note how her line immediately reinforces the major theme of conflicting family identities. This same theme is reiterated in her next line: "Deny thy father and refuse thy name" (2.2.34). Some **feminists**, of course, might note how this line implies the patriarchal, patrilineal nature of society during the Renaissance. Meanwhile, Juliet's next two lines might interest **feminists** for another reason: "Or, if thou wilt not, be but sworn my love, / And I'll no longer be a Capulet" (2.2.36). Here and elsewhere, Juliet is an unusually assertive young woman, especially when we consider that she is only thirteen. She is determined to have her way, even if doing so means renouncing her own family. From a **historicist** point of view, she may both reflect and have helped contribute to the growing freedom and power of females that was increasingly developing during this period. Her determination to love as she wishes is one of the play's key **themes** and has also been a growing **historical pattern** for at least the last four hundred years, at least (**multiculturalists** might note) in European cultures.

Romeo's reaction to Juliet's lines—"Shall I hear more, or shall I speak at this?" (2.2.37)—is a richly "**metatheatrical**" moment—that is, a moment that calls attention to its own status as part of a theatrical production. Any such moment is also inevitably **dialogical**, and this one is doubly so: Romeo speaks to himself, but he also in a sense speaks to the audience. That, at least, is one way the moment could be played, perhaps for comic effect. Now, however, in a kind of balance that **formalists** would admire, it is Juliet who speaks at length and Romeo who stays relatively silent. Her ensuing speech contains several **dialogical** moments when she asks herself questions ("What's Montague?"; "What's in a name?") and then immediately answers them. She also reiterates one of the play's main **themes**—the distinction between individual selfhood and membership in a family. **Historicists** might note that family connections were especially important during Shakespeare's era; individualism was not as strong then as it tends to be in some democratic societies today. In fact, Shakespeare's play can be read as both a symptom of, and a contribution to, the slowly growing emphasis on individual rights that has become increasingly important in many cultures in the past four hundred years.

### Textual "Cruxes"

Is there a subtle hint of sensual desire in Juliet's language when she lists the various body parts that distinguish Romeo himself from his family name? **Psychoanalytic** and **Darwinian** critics might say so. "What's Montague?" Juliet asks. The name "Montague," she continues, "is nor hand, nor foot, / Nor arm, nor face" (2.2.4-41). **Formalists** would admire the emphatic listing here, including the way the iambic meter and monosyllabic words stress the key nouns, which are all accented. But at this point, the text becomes especially interesting from a **historical** point of view. In the 1599 first printing of the play (the so-called "first quarto"), Juliet's words continue as follows: "nor any other part. / What[']s in a name?" (See the facsimile in the Weis edition, 364). The first quarto, then, omits one and a half lines that most modern editions include: "nor any other part / Belonging to a man. O be some other name!" (2.2.42-43). These words come from later texts, and the reference to "any other *part / Belonging to a man*" (my italics) supports an erotic, **psychoanalytic** reading of Juliet's speech. Moments like these—moments where editors must choose from among various possible readings—are known as textual "cruxes," and they are especially interesting to **traditional historical** critics. These critics often try to establish "accurate," "reliable" texts of literary works—texts that reflect the author's probable final intentions. In contrast, **new historicist** critics are much more likely to assume that "establishing" "accurate," "reliable" texts is often difficult if not impossible, especially when dealing with Shakespeare's dramas. One key difference between **traditional historical** critics and **new historicists**, then, is that new historicists are much more open to ideas of uncertainty, multiple possibilities, and textual instability.

Another example of a textual "crux" appears a few lines later, when Juliet asks herself "What's in a name?" and then famously answers, "That which we call a rose / By any other word would smell as sweet." The 1599 first quarto prints "By any other *name*" rather than "By any other *word*" (my italics). Editors have often debated which term to choose and use. Most editors now choose "word" over "name," but here again the important point is that **historicist** critics of all kinds are the sorts of critics likely to be most interested in "establishing" (or refusing to establish) "correct," "final," "authoritative" texts. The choices they make are often crucial (a word derived from "crux") for all other kinds of critics, which is why **textual scholarship** or **textual criticism** seems so important to so many people.

However one chooses to settle such textual cruxes, it is clear that the rest of Juliet's speech here would interest **thematic** critics because it emphasizes one of the play's central "motifs"—the distinction between individual and family identities. The fact that this theme runs all throughout the play would also interest such theorists as **Aristotle** and modern-day **formalists**, who highly value a text's coherence and complex unity. Juliet ends this speech by offering to let Romeo (whose presence she doesn't yet realize) to "Take all myself." Romeo finally steps forward, makes his presence known, and speaks to her directly: "I'll take thee at thy word" (2.2.49). **Formalists** might be interested in the fact that he and Juliet actually (and symbolically) share a line (she speaks the first half; he speaks the second), just as they share so much else. Similarly, **formalists** would be interested in the way Romeo repeats and plays with her word "take." Shakespeare thereby again implies their connection: they even use the very same words. Some **feminists**, meanwhile, might find it interesting that Juliet explicitly offers herself (thereby implying that she is an independent agent) to be "take[n]" (thereby perhaps implying that she is still, in a sense, in a passive position in a male-dominated world).

## Critical Pluralism: A Final Overview

Romeo's final two lines at this point—"Call me but love, and I'll be new baptized. / Henceforth I never will be Romeo" (2.2.50-51)— are open to multiple responses from various critical perspectives. In fact, this might be a good point at which to survey the *many* different responses that might be offered to a mere two lines of Shakespeare's dramatic poetry. **Plato**, for instance, with his general skepticism about the value of literature, might question why this play is even worth reading or viewing. **Aristotle**, with his much more positive view of the importance and artistry of literature, might appreciate the ways these lines are consistent with Romeo's character throughout the drama. **Horace**, with his practical stress on the need to satisfy a diverse audience, might appreciate these lines for being simple, clear, and interesting to people of all sorts, especially both men and women. **Longinus**, concerned with lofty, elevating ideas and emotions, might enjoy Romeo's implication that loving Juliet symbolizes a new birth and transformation of his old identity. **Thematic** critics would certainly note that these lines contribute to two of the play's central motifs (romantic love and independent selfhood). And **traditional historical critics** would provide any necessary information about the actual processes and meanings of baptism in Shakespeare's culture.

Formalist critics might note the rich potential meanings of the single word "baptized," which can simultaneously imply being given one's name, achieving a new spiritual identity, being cleansed and transformed, and so on. **Psychoanalytic** critics might suggest that in these lines, Romeo brings the impulses of his id into line with the dictates of his ego and superego: rather than merely expressing basic erotic attraction, he sublimates (elevates) that attraction so that it is socially acceptable. **Archetypal** critics might argue that the romantic desire implied in Romeo's words is a key human trait; it is an impulse shared by almost all people of any era, place, or culture. **Marxist** critics might have little to say about these particular lines—a fact interesting in itself: not every theorist will have an insight to offer on every single detail of a work of art, and that fact alone helps suggest the nature of the detail. If pushed, a **Marxist** might allege that "baptism" is associated with a mystifying religion that ignores more important kinds of genuine transformation.

Some **feminist** critics might appreciate Juliet's power as a woman to effect such a profound change in Romeo: he even expresses a willingness to give up his own family name (as women in Shakespeare's culture were typically expected to do when they married). **Structuralist** critics, with their interest in the ways cultures use "binary opposites" to structure themselves, might note the various binaries implied in these two lines. Those binaries include male/female; Romeo/Juliet; Montague/Capulet; love/hate; old name/new name; past/future, etc. **Deconstructors**, interested in the ways binaries are unstable and bleed into one another, might note Romeo's willingness to give up his own identity to merge with Juliet. They might also note his willingness to submit himself to a woman's desires—thereby (paradoxically) achieving his own desires and thereby also (paradoxically) advancing her desires as well.

**Reader-response** critics, who emphasize the ways individual readers (or similar groups of readers) respond to texts based on their own personal experience and identities, might note that people who have faced family opposition to their romantic choices would especially be able to relate to Romeo's words. **Dialogical** critics, who stress the multitude of voices, tones, and allusions a text displays, might relate Romeo's language here to the influential tradition of Petrarchan love poetry. **New historicists**, who emphasize how every aspect of life is inherently political (involving issues of power) would note Romeo's desire to escape the power-structure that prevents him from enjoying an uncomplicated relationship with Juliet. **Multiculturalists**, who emphasize the multiplicity of subcultures that make up any larger culture, might note that even the simple, apparently neutral word "baptize" implies differences between

Christians and non-Christians and even between different kinds of Christians who define "baptism" in distinct ways. **Postmodernists**, who distrust grand systems and rigid rules, would surely sympathize with Romeo's desire for personal freedom. **Ecocritics**, like Marxists, might have little to say about these lines, partly because nature is not as prominently featured in this play as it is in some of Shakespeare's other works. Finally, **Darwinians** might see Romeo's efforts at actual courtship as literally bred deeply into the nature of most animals, including humans. For Darwinians, almost everything that happens in this play can easily be understood as the result of millions of years of evolution.

## Final Words

There are, of course, many other ways in which any lines (or even single words) of any author might be interpreted. The nearly twenty ways mentioned above are just a few of numerous possibilities. (I have not mentioned, for instance, various kinds of **"cognitive"** criticism nor the enormous variety of non-Freudian psychological approaches that could easily be employed.) Ultimately, the value of keeping many perspectives in mind when reading is simply the value of remembering that there *are* many different ways to interpret anything. Remembering that fact can enrich our response to any text, and doing so can also promote an interpretive humility and open-mindedness that are valuable in themselves.

## Note

1. For discussions of pluralism, and for fuller explanations of the various theories employed in this essay, see (for example) my book cited below and the many other books cited therein.

## Works Cited

Evans, Robert C. *Perspectives on Renaissance Poetry*. Bloomsbury, 2015.

Shakespeare, William. *Romeo and Juliet*, edited by René Weis, Bloomsbury, 2012. The Arden Shakespeare—Third Series.

# Comparisons and Contrasts: Some Filmed Versions of the "Balcony Scene" in Shakespeare's *Romeo and Juliet*

Eric J. Sterling

The so-called "balcony scene" in *Romeo and Juliet* is definitely one of the most famous episodes in Shakespearean drama. Even people who know little else about Shakespeare can quote lines from this scene—especially the line that opens the episode: "O Romeo, Romeo! Wherefore art thou Romeo!" (2.2.33). This moment, emphasizing the characterization of Juliet, is important in any staging of the play; it has probably never been cut from any production (unlike many other scenes and lines). Audiences wait for it to appear and are curious to see exactly how it will be performed. Stagings of Juliet's opening words on the balcony typically symbolize the choices made (by actors, directors, and scenic designers) for entire productions. Little wonder, then, that Juliet's first appearance on the balcony is a key moment in any filmed version of the drama. In this essay, I examine a number of different cinematic versions of Juliet's opening words. I thereby hope to suggest some of the ways in which this key moment, as well as the entire play itself, has been interpreted in different productions on film.

## The 1936 Cukor Production

One early filmed version of Juliet's initial speech appears in the 1936 version of the play directed by George Cukor. In this version, the British actor Leslie Howard starred as Romeo, while Canadian American actress Norma Shearer appeared as Juliet. Both leads were considerably older than the characters Shakespeare describes: Shearer was definitely not thirteen, and Howard had already begun to develop a receding hair line. Cukor's version was filmed in crisp black and white. When we first see Juliet, who looks middle-aged, she is wearing a billowing, finely crafted diaphanous gown as she leans with both hands propped against an ornately carved post.

Thick, white classical columns, with elaborately carved tops, can be seen behind her. She speaks her famous opening line slowly, sadly, and romantically as she stares off into the distance. Her mood changes when she utters her next line: "Deny thy father, and refuse thy name" (2.2.34). Now she pushes herself slightly away from the carved post and sounds determined and somewhat assertive.

The camera now quickly cuts below to Howard, costumed in a richly decorated, tight-fitting Renaissance-era outfit as he stands within a "V" created by the trunk of a mature tree and one of its thick lower limbs. He stares up at Shearer yearningly, his mouth slightly open and his expression excited, but he remains silent. In this one brief moment, then, we see many of the aspects that typified Cukor's entire production: authentic period costuming, rich sets, realistic staging, and acting that seems (at least by contemporary standards) a bit artificial and melodramatic. This is definitely a "romantic" moment (in all the many meanings of that adjective). It is staged in ways that suggest the lofty poetry and cultural prestige associated with Shakespeare in the first half of the twentieth century.

## The 1954 Castellani Production

The extravagant and ambitious 1954 Renato Castellani-directed Italian version of *Romeo and Juliet* stars Laurence Harvey as Romeo and Susan Shentall as Juliet. At the time of the film, Harvey was twenty-six, while Shentall was twenty. This movie, which is available in both English and Italian, sets the balcony scene in deep darkness. Adding to the foreboding nature of the darkness are the shadows, silence, and absence of music, especially since music often symbolizes harmony and order in other productions and is often used in big-budget films. In the Castellani movie, Romeo, hidden in shadows, is barely visible. Harvey wears a flowing cape and, before Juliet's entry, briskly walks up a flight of stone stairs towards her balcony. He is thus standing only a few feet to her right when she begins to speak. In many other productions, Romeo stands far below the balcony, but Castellani places the lovers almost at the same level. When Shentall does appear, she speaks a few words before we actually see her, from behind, leaning against a stone pillar. Her blonde hair (most filmed Juliets have been brunettes) is pulled back into a tight braided bun. She wears authentic period costuming, including a flowing and loose white gown. Shentall languishes as she leans on the pillar positioned behind the actual balcony itself. She speaks with emotion but without the excessive passion of a teenager. She does, however, cover her eyes and cries just after she speaks her famous line. She appears determined to be with Romeo and resolute in her affection, yet except for her weeping, she controls her passion, and when she removes her hands from her face she glances repeatedly toward the dark sky.

## The 1968 Zeffirelli Production

The Castellani production set an obvious precedent for the Franco Zeffirelli (1968) film. Both directors employed an elaborate and convincingly Renaissance Italian setting, clearly striving for period authenticity and verisimilitude. In the Zeffirelli balcony scene, dogs bark below as Juliet appears. Their barking portends trouble, in this case, the visit by a stranger who does not belong in the Montague garden. Romeo, played by the handsome, teenaged Leonard Whiting, with his thick brown hair cut in a style popular in the 60s, stands below in the night. He is hidden effectively behind rich Italian summer green vegetation in a garden beneath the balcony. Whiting wears a dark blue doublet and, underneath, a blue shirt with puffed shoulders and white stripes that extend from his shoulders to his hands. Just before Olivia Hussey (who plays Juliet) appears, light warmly illuminates the balcony as Romeo moves through the garden for a better view of Juliet. Soft music plays as he repositions himself, and the camera moves slowly before both Romeo and we—finally—catch a distant glimpse of Juliet, who seems far above, tiny in the distance. Romeo pushes thick foliage aside to get a better view of her and seems awestruck by her beauty.

When the camera finally cuts back to Hussey, she is leaning forward, one elbow on the stone wall of the balcony, and wearing a white dress with gold trim and elaborate gilt embroidery sewn into ornate patterns. Such costuming indicates, during a time of sumptuary laws, her family's wealth. Her authentic Renaissance dress, with a square, plunging neckline, exposes her ample breasts. In her flowing brown hair, she wears a crescent-shaped gold headpiece that contains red rubies and other jewels. A convincingly youthful and childlike Juliet, Hussey first stands and then lounges on the white sculptured stone balcony as she ruminates about her Romeo (although she cannot discern his appearance because he is hidden in the dark vegetation). The balcony is realistically imperfect: some stones are smooth while others are rough. These imperfections— those of an actual Renaissance Italian house—help remind us that we are not viewing an artificial movie set.

A misty fog shields Romeo in the night. At the time of filming, Whiting was seventeen and Hussey was fifteen—close to Juliet's actual age (thirteen) in Shakespeare's drama. The two actors look young and are fresh; they were at the beginning of their careers and were unknown to the public. In their youthfulness and innocence, Whiting and Hussey directly contrast with the significantly older Norma Shearer and Leslie Howard in Cukor's production. As Juliet prepares to speak, filmgoers hear the sound first of flutes and then of violins. Juliet then lounges on the edge of the balcony and looks to heaven as she speaks to Romeo as if he is not there. She pauses, then stretches both arms widely above her as she quietly exclaims "Ay, me." She then lifts herself onto the stone wall and stretches out before she sits, knee up, revealing most of her youthful gowned body before the camera moves in as she speaks her famous line. She accentuates the word "wherefore," making clearer than some actresses do that the question she asks is not about Romeo's physical location but about his name: *why* does he have to be named Romeo? In other words, why does he have to be a Montague (and thereby her family's enemy)?

## The 1976 Kemp-Welch Production

In contrast to the lavish but realistic film version directed by Zeffirelli, the 1976 version directed by Joan Kemp-Welch was a televised production featuring modest sets. It resembled more a televised stage version than a big-budget film. Romeo (Christopher Neame) and Juliet (Ann Hasson) both dress in period costumes. The broad-shouldered Neame, looking older than a teenager (he was roughly thirty when he played this part) wears a V-neck white shirt tied very loosely around his neck by a burgundy string. This shirt is beneath a burgundy and pink doublet, with puffed sleeves, made of crushed velvet that has a thick brown trim. It is tied in front of his chest with brown strings. Hasson wears a billowy white dress tied around her chest by a string. Both actors, then, wear V-neck white shirts that are tied in the front. The similarity in clothes suggests not only that they live in the same culture but also that despite the separation caused by the family rivalry, they are similar and belong together.

As Romeo abruptly dashes into the Capulet garden, he suddenly stops, awe-struck, as he sees Juliet already leaning on the balcony above him. He seems to smile as he speaks his own lines. Meanwhile, she looks almost angelic in her flowing white gown as she stares off into the distance and rests her arms on an aqua-colored wooden balcony while Romeo ruminates below. The balcony is painted to resemble old, distressed wood. Juliet is framed from behind by tall wooden arches that are yellow on top and black on the bottom. Just as Neame does not look like a teenager, neither does Hasson. Her long, flowing auburn hair is parted in the front and is combed back, showing lines on her forehead as she breaks into a broad, beautiful smile.

One distinctive element of this version is the contrast between the lead actors' styles of performance. Neame is extremely emotional and active: he lifts his eyes toward heaven and speaks with great intensity. Hasson is much more subdued and mature and far less emotional. She gazes into the distance just before she asks—slowly, still smiling, as if she cannot believe the irony of their situation— why Romeo bears the name that makes him a Montague. The contrast in intensity of emotions between the two lovers is disturbing; it may suggest either that she is more mature and less emotional or that he loves her more than she does him. The Kemp-Welch film shares with some other productions an unfortunate lack of chemistry between the lovers.

## The 1978 Rakoff Production

The same problem also handicaps the 1978 BBC film version, directed by Alvin Rakoff. It makes a strong and successful effort to be realistic in setting and costuming: much attention is given to period details. Patrick Ryecart, as Romeo, sports well-coiffed blonde hair and wears a white shirt and a crushed velvet brown Renaissance-era doublet. The doublet features light brown embroidery. True to the period, he also wears long stockings rather than pants. Rebecca Saire, who plays Juliet, wears a loose-fitting, simple white dress. Above this, she wears a more formal gown; it is light green and is decorated with pale white flower patterns and pink ribbons on the shoulders. Ryecart was twenty-five when he played Romeo, while Saire was merely fourteen; the age difference could explain their lack of chemistry, including in the balcony scene. Saire speaks her famous line softly and fairly quickly rather than languorously or erotically.

Most actresses who play Juliet in films are in their twenties (or older), even though they play a thirteen-year-old. Unlike some highly sexualized Juliets, Saire—in keeping with her real age—seems innocent and childlike, hardly ready for marriage and a sexual relationship. She speaks in a measured, unemotional manner, reciting her lines in a sad, contemplative, plaintive tone. She seems more curious than in love. The walls and door behind the balcony feature glass shaped into circular patterns; the significant amount of glass and the decorative patterns it features are noteworthy because in the Renaissance, glass was expensive, so only wealthy families used glass to decorate their homes. There is also an ornamental stone balustrade on which Saire leans. As in Zeffirelli's version, the garden is full of lush, green flowers and plants, although these are obviously indoor stage props rather than vegetation in a real outdoor garden. The balcony is made to look like stone, and Romeo moves rapidly toward it and stands directly beneath it when she speaks, so that he and Juliet are separated by roughly ten feet.

## The 1996 Luhrmann Production

In contrast to the quite literally stagey BBC televised production, the 1996 big-budget film, directed by Baz Luhrmann and innovatively titled *Romeo + Juliet*, made the most of its status as a full-screen movie. Influenced by the fast-paced music videos so popular at the time, it also drew on many other elements of pop culture to emphasize its many symbolic contrasts and juxtapositions. Set in the 1990s, the film is modern (even postmodern) in practically every respect. In the "balcony scene," Leonardo DiCaprio, looking much younger than his twenty-one years and wearing the grey chainmail shirt that had been part of his outfit in the preceding costume ball, stealthily enters a courtyard featuring a large, built-in swimming pool. After he reaches a certain point, security devices suddenly switch on bright lights that make the pool shimmer. Romeo comically scrambles for cover in an alcove, managing to knock over a metal plant stand in the process, and later, he suffers yet another comic misadventure when he approaches the wrong window by mistake.

When Juliet (played by seventeen-year-old Claire Danes) finally appears, Romeo is standing just to her right, on the other side of a white stone statue. He is literally only a yard or so distant from her and has to whisper his lines so she can't hear him. Danes wears a loose-fitting, sleeveless nightgown with two shoulder straps and a scoop neckline, exposing her entire neck and the top of her bosom. She also wears a small silver crucifix necklace. A thick white band wraps around her slim waist and is tied in a knot behind her. She looks straight ahead as she delivers the famous line, not realizing that DiCaprio is standing so close by.

Luhrmann's film is unique in that this balcony scene uses no actual balcony. In other films, Romeo stands far beneath Juliet. In those productions, a physical separation of twenty or thirty yards symbolizes that the two lovers have met only recently and know little about each other, that they have yet to consummate their love, and that their love is blocked by the family rivalry discussed by Juliet when she wishes that Romeo could change his name. The Luhrmann production differs by placing the lovers merely a few feet away from each other, suggesting the passion they feel. DiCaprio initially seems scared that she will discover him, yet once he hears Danes mention his character's name and knows she is in love with Romeo, he becomes emboldened. DiCaprio even follows Danes, as if stalking her.

Tension mounts when we see Juliet being followed by Romeo's shadow. Because she is still deep in her thoughts and words, she fails to notice. Her shock when she initially sees him implies terror, not pleasant surprise. Their genuine passion, however, is soon clear from their behavior (such as amorous, aggressive kissing) in the swimming pool in Juliet's courtyard. The lovers' behavior under water suggests their erotic desire, a feeling missing from other productions. In other films, Juliet is chaste and demure, demanding marriage before offering physical love. In the "balcony scene" in the Luhrmann production, she freely gives her body to Romeo. Another difference is also striking. In previous film productions, the camera focuses on Juliet as she quietly exclaims, "O Romeo, Romeo! Wherefore art thou Romeo!," accentuating the final word (2.2.33). Intriguingly, in Luhrmann's film, as Juliet utters this iconic line, the camera focuses solely on Romeo, as if to show how he reacts to finding out that she loves him. Finally, Luhrmann's version also seems unusual in employing so much humor in its non-balcony "balcony" scene.

## The 2010 Goold Production

The 2010 Royal Shakespeare Company production, directed by Rupert Goold at the Courtyard Theatre (whose empty seats are deliberately and plainly visible), is a videotaped staged version rather than an expensive Hollywood film. In the balcony scene, performed on a bare stage, Romeo (played by Sam Troughton) looks to be in his early thirties and is dressed in unelaborate modern street clothes, wearing a two-toned red shirt (light and dark red squares) that is not tucked in. Illuminated by a spotlight (another reminder that this is a *staged* play), he also wears a bluish gray jacket and faded gray jeans. His dark gray coat has a hood that he employs to cloak his identity from Juliet (played by Mariah Gale), who seems to be about thirty. When she abruptly appears, she stands silently, barefooted, on a platform at the back of the stage, her hand over her mouth. Unlike so many Juliets before her, she is dressed not in white but in a black, sleeveless knee-length dress.

After she loudly exclaims "Ay me," she suddenly sits down on her platform, her legs widely spread and her black dress tucked between them. When she finally speaks her famous line, Romeo comically collapses onto the stage with a loud thud. As she utters the words "Wherefore art *thou* Romeo!" (emphasis mine), the camera suddenly seems inches away from her face. We can now see that her dark brown hair, parted in the middle in a very simple style, is combed back except for a braid that extends around her head. We can also now see that she wears a modern, sleeveless, loose-fitting black dress with two shoulder straps and a scoop neckline, and her legs dangle over a simple black wrought-iron balcony. The balcony rests on what looks like a simple wrought iron fence. Few Renaissance women of Juliet's class would dangle their bare legs over the balcony as Gale does. She even spreads out her arms as she sits. The director seems to want (simultaneously) to portray and parody the famous balcony scene. Romeo appears not in a real garden with actual dirt, flowers, and trees, nor even in an obviously fake garden with artificial or potted plants. Instead, he stands on a wooden stage painted to resemble steel-gray concrete. It seems cold, somewhat like Juliet herself. Behind her is an alcove that is both solid black and dark yellowish black. The colors are uninviting and cold. The lovers may seem, to some viewers, to lack real chemistry. We are never allowed to forget that we are watching a play staged in an empty theater. This style of production may have been intended to remind audiences of Bertolt Brecht's so-called "alienation effect," also known as a distancing effect, in which a play self-consciously calls attention to itself *as a play*.

As Romeo, Troughton looks somewhat unkempt, and Gale, as Juliet, looks very tall and unconventionally plain. Troughton plays Romeo with great emotion, while Gale, in contrast, seems lethargic and unemotional. Gale delivers her famous lines deliberately, almost haltingly. She looks straight ahead yet fails to see Romeo, who is standing directly in front of her, unhidden but with his back to her and with his hood drawn over his head. He eventually reacts with loud, startling emotion to her slowly-delivered speech. This juxtaposition of an emotional and intense Romeo with a comparatively unemotional and subdued female Juliet resembles the similar contrast in the 1976 Kemp-Welch film. But whereas that film tried to look realistic, this balcony scene is about as stripped-down as possible.

## The 2013 Carlei Production

In contrast, the big-budget 2013 film directed by Carlo Carlei is strongly reminiscent of Zeffirelli's movie of the late 1960s. Carlei employs (1) an authentic Verona setting; (2) a dashingly handsome, youthful Douglas Booth as Romeo; and (3) a relatively plain (compared to Booth) but young and attractive Hailee Steinfeld as Juliet. The huge white Capulet stone mansion is so massive that Steinfeld seems dwarfed when she appears on the enormous balcony. The mansion's elegant splendor adds to the romance of the scene: the audience can see the wealth of the Capulet family that Juliet willingly sacrifices for love. The balcony contains three huge arches and above the windows rest stonecrafted drip moldings. The garden leading to the balcony contains much garden statuary. Steinfeld appears tiny while standing on the periphery of her family's huge home, just as Booth looks tiny as he hides within the massive hedges (which function as a kind of maze) in the large garden. The hedges are carefully manicured into severe rectangular shapes, looking rather artificial and contrasting with the lush, almost forested garden of the Zeffirelli film. Candelabra and torches illuminate the scene, again contributing to the authentic "period" look and contrasting greatly with the deep darkness of the Castellani film.

In that film's balcony scene, Laurence Harvey had been only barely visible. In Carlei's film, everything is done to make the good looks of the leading actors highly apparent. As Romeo, Booth (twenty-one and smoothly clean-shaven) wears a green robe with a green hood over his head to mask his identity (although viewers can easily see his well-lit face). His hood (ironically) makes him look almost like a young monk. As Juliet, Steinfeld also looks quite young (she was only fifteen when the film was made). When she steps onto the balcony, she is wearing a light pinkish blouse, with white decorative strings by her breast, beneath a white sweater. The white strings match the sweater and offer a nice contrast to the peach blouse. The outfit is plain, unlike the elaborate balcony, house, and garden. Her outfit now is much simpler than the beautiful necklace and elaborate green bodice she wore during the Capulet party hours before. Her simple costuming here makes her look like the girl she actually is. Steinfeld's lovely brown hair glows beautifully thanks to the lights from the candles behind her. She looks almost angelic. Two elaborate sets of candles stand behind her, one on each side. The candelabra, like the arches and the hedges, manifest the director's unmistakable desire for symmetry. (When Steinfeld appears, she of course stands underneath the middle arch.)

Reviewers of Carlei's film often complained about Steinfeld's performance. Although she was already an accomplished, Academy Award-nominated actress, she does sometimes struggle as she tries to play her role believably. She delivers her famous line in a wistful, unemotional manner, never indicating the excitement and feelings of young love Shakespeare seems to have intended. Before she says her lines, a quiet piano solo begins, presumably to help evoke a romantic mood. Steinfeld recites the line thoughtfully yet mechanically, without much sense of rhythm. Unlike other actresses who have played the part, she ignores the comma in "O Romeo, Romeo!," as if she is merely repeating his name but not actually thinking about him or their future together. Her colorless American accent also sounds oddly plain next to Booth's suave British delivery.

## The 2014 King Production

The Don Roy King version of *Romeo and Juliet* appeared on Broadway in 2013 and was made into a film (of the staged play) in 2014. This modern interpretation, which even features Romeo entering on a motorcycle, stars Orlando Bloom as Romeo and Condola Rashad as Juliet. The film is highly distinctive in that Romeo and all the Montagues are Caucasian while Juliet and all the Capulets are black. The contrast between the races symbolizes the separation and distrust between the two rival Italian families while also making a sociopolitical statement about race relations in the United States.

In the play's famous scene, Rashad dangles her legs over the balcony, as Mariah Gale does in the Royal Shakespeare Company version. Such an action would, of course, have been considered unfeminine and beneath the dignity of a Renaissance gentlewoman, but this version never tries (or wants) to be a "period piece." The lovers' clothes are also quite modern, with Bloom wearing a blue zip-up windbreaker jacket and modern-style blue jeans with fashionable holes. He also sports modern sunglasses that hang from his white shirt. As Juliet, Rashad wears a simple white slip and a gold hairpiece in her hair. The wooden balcony, like the entire set, is bare, sterile, and cold. For some viewers, chemistry between Bloom and Rashad may seem clearly lacking. Perhaps the age difference between the actors is part of the cause: Bloom was thirty-seven during the filming, while Rashad was twenty-eight. Bloom, in particular, seems too old to play an innocent teenage boy experiencing first love. Rashad speaks her famous lines without demonstrating much love or many emotions in her voice or actions, only frustration about the family rivalry. This production benefits, however, by being staged before a "live audience." Their laughter and other reactions show that the production was well received by many who viewed it in the theater. This audience "soundtrack" is another innovation in this particular filmed version of the play.

## Summary Comments

*Romeo and Juliet* has always been one of the most popular of Shakespeare's plays with audiences, actors, directors, and film producers. Within the play, the "balcony scene" has always been a favorite with all four groups. A quick search of YouTube will show how often—and how variously—this particular scene has been recreated by numerous groups, both professionals and many amateurs. High school and college students seem to love staging (and often parodying) the scene, but the balcony episode also creates a real challenge for professional performers. Precisely because the scene *is* so well known, performances of it often serve as a kind of litmus test of entire productions. The balcony scene perfectly illustrates how variously all of Shakespeare's plays can be imagined and presented, whether on stage or (increasingly) on video or film.

## Works Cited

*Romeo and Juliet*. Directed by Carlo Carlei, Relativity Media, 2013.

*Romeo and Juliet*. Directed by Renato Castellani, United Artists, 1954.

*Romeo and Juliet*. Directed by George Cukor, Metro-Goldwyn-Mayer, 1936.

*Romeo and Juliet*. Directed by Rupert Goold, Royal Shakespeare Company, 2010.

*Romeo and Juliet*. Directed by Joan Kemp-Welch, Thames Television, 1976.

*Romeo and Juliet*. Directed by Don Roy King, Inception Media Group, 2014.

*Romeo + Juliet*. Directed by Baz Luhrmann, 20th Century Fox, 1996.

*Romeo and Juliet*. Directed by Alvin Rakoff, BBC Television, 1978.

*Romeo and Juliet*. Directed by Franco Zeffirelli, Paramount Pictures, 1968.

# CRITICAL READINGS

# Imagining *Romeo and Juliet*_____

Maurice Hunt

This essay's title has several applications. It refers at times to Shakespeare's imagining his characters and their speeches; at other times, it refers to Romeo's and Juliet's imagining their love, its fulfillment, and its consequences. These imaginings usually find expression in speeches informed by metaphors, that is, by poetic imagery of varying degrees between basic similes and ingenious complex metaphors made up of several parts. Shakespeare and his fellow dramatists called these complex metaphors "conceits." Shakespeare of course does what I have just described in all his plays, but he does so especially in *Romeo and Juliet*. Everyone admires the sheer beauty of Romeo's and Juliet's imaginative poetry expressing their love.

Worth noting, however, are the times when a lover's metaphors for the beloved are conventional or when they seem artificial, at least according to the love poetry of Shakespeare's age. Sometimes Romeo's and Juliet's poetic imaginings appear dangerous because they are excessive or morbid, catapulting them into perilous behavior. Shakespeare himself seems to be unable to resist coining memorable imaginative metaphors that we value even though they do not conform to later ages' ideas of decorum, of what is fitting to their speakers' social class, age, and amount of education (if any). This suggests that Shakespeare enjoyed the sheer pleasure of exercising his luxuriant imagination. And yet he appears to grasp the fact that the imagination, given loose reins, could overwhelm one's reason and judgment, for he shows that happening to Romeo and Juliet at crucial moments.

Shakespeare's contemporaries eyed the faculty of imagination warily. When *Romeo and Juliet* appeared in 1595, "terms like 'phantasy,' 'fantsie,' even 'fancy,' are used interchangeably with "'imagination,'" often in a negative sense (Rossky, esp. 49). Skeptical Mercutio refers to dreams as "the children of an idle brain,

/ Begot of nothing but vain fantasy, / Which is as thin of substance as the air" (1.4.97-99).[1] "Fancy" could refer to the impressionable, untrustworthy imagining gathered from the senses, especially that of sight. In this respect, the word "fancy" was interchangeable with "infatuation," never moving deeper than eye-liking. Portia, in *The Merchant of Venice*, has her musicians sing to Bassanio, in the lottery for her hand in marriage, to warn him against choosing the gold or silver casket as the receptacle of her portrait:

> Tell me where is fancy bred:
> Or in the heart or in the head;
> How begot, how nourished?
> . . . . . . . . . . . . . . . . . . . .
> It is engend'red in the eye,
> With gazing fed: and fancy dies
> In the cradle where it lies. (3.2.63-65, 67-69)

Fancy, the song implies, is temporary, fleeting. Romeo is taken by Rosaline's and Juliet's beauty. One might think, therefore, that Romeo's love for both women depends upon his fancy. But his love for Rosaline quickly dies when he sees Juliet. In Portia's terms, his love for Rosaline never evolves beyond an eye-love, a fancy, but his love for Juliet, while it may start in his eye, is fundamentally bred in his heart. But no adversity is so great that it can lessen the love he feels for Juliet.

## Language and Love

Shakespeare shows that Romeo's love for Rosaline is conventional, not heart-felt, so to say, by making his imaginative expression of it filled with what had become poetic clichés. They involve what are called Petrarchan conceits. Francis Petrarch was a great Italian writer of sonnets in the Middle Ages. Petrarch sometimes describes his feelings for Laura at war within himself by yoking together contrary sensations. "I burn in winter, and freeze in summer" he wrote in Rima—Sonnet—132. These combinations of incongruous antitheses were called oxymora (oxymoron in the plural). Petrarch often condenses an oxymoron in a single phrase, such as "sweet bitter life," "O living death," and "My sweet pain." (Rime 129, 132, 164). When Benvolio in Act 1 attempts to get Romeo to name the woman he dotes upon, Romeo, noting the recent fray of Capulets and Montagues, exclaims,

> Why, then, O brawling love, O loving hate,
> Of anything of nothing first create,
> O heavy lightness, serious vanity,
> Misshapen chaos of well-seeming forms,
> Feather of lead, bright smoke, cold fire, sick health,
> Still-waking sleep that is not what it is.
> This love feel I that feel no love in this.
> Dost thou not laugh? (1.1.178-81)

"Cold fire," "sick health"—these simultaneous contrary feelings, original to Petrarch, seemed artificial, even trite, because of overuse by uninspired poets in Shakespeare's time. Mercutio says, "Now is [Romeo] for the numbers that Petrarch flowed in. Laura to his lady was a kitchen wench" (2.4.38-40). René Weis believes that "Romeo is keeping Benvolio at bay with a parody of lovers' artificial discourse, to forestall his question about the identity of his beloved" (136). But Romeo's claim, "This love feel I that feel no love in this," is not necessary for parody; in fact, it seems to work against parody by appearing heart-felt. Romeo's oxymora may be parody, but they seem to be expressive of a real emotion. They do seem artificial (as other poets had made them appear), and so they suggest the emotion involving Rosaline is somewhat artificial. Later Juliet's language recalls Petrarch when she cries, "My only love sprung from my only hate" (1.5.137), but her words here reflect the tragedy inherent in loving a man her clansmen hate (but one whom she does not, nor never could).[2]

When Romeo sees Juliet, his imagination explodes in a striking metaphor, whereby she "hangs upon the cheek of night / As a rich jewel in an Ethiop's ear." Hers is a "Beauty too rich for use, for earth too dear" (1.5.44-46)—heavenly, star-like. Eclipsed is his fancy for Rosaline. Nevertheless, Shakespeare is never a dramatist of the easy development of true love. Romeo's subsequent wooing is courtly, clever. Romeo's and Juliet's talk creates a rhyming poem, a sonnet, infused by an elaborate pilgrim/pilgrimage metaphor for their lips and hands.

| ROMEO | If I profane with my unworthiest hand |
| | This holy shrine, the gentle sin is this: |
| | My lips, two blushing pilgrims, ready stand |
| | To smooth that rough touch with a tender kiss. |
| JULIET | Good pilgrim, you wrong your hand too much |
| | Which mannerly devotion shows in this, |
| | For saints have hands that pilgrims' hands do touch, |
| | And palm to palm is holy palmer's kiss.[3] |
| ROMEO | Have not saints lips and holy palmers too? |
| JULIET | Ay, pilgrim, lips that they must use in prayer. |
| ROMEO | O then, dear saint, let not lips do what hands do— |
| | They pray; grant thou, lest faith turn to despair. |
| JULIET | Saints do not move, though grant for prayers' sake. |
| ROMEO | Then move not while my prayer's effect I take. |
| | (1.5.92-105) |

Dancing, Romeo has taken Juliet's hand and then, as they move together, their clasped hands become two pressed palms, as he finally begs a kiss. The first eight verses of this dialogue form the initial two quatrains of a Shakespeare sonnet, rhyming abab, cdcd. The third quatrain of the sonnet rhymes efef, before the concluding shared couplet, rhyming gg. This form and rhyme appear in lines 95 to 105 of Romeo and Juliet's dialogue. The total metaphor is ingeniously articulated (developed), including at least one pun on "palm" ("inside of the hand"/ "leaf frond of a pilgrim") at the end of the second quatrain. A certain intellectual artificiality attaches to this wooing dialogue. Romeo and Juliet are not yet profoundly in love. Auditors have to be listening for the sounds of words as much as or more so for their content to cooperatively create the precise rhyme of a sonnet. Likewise, they must concentrate on the similar sounds of words to make the wordplay appearing here.

---

After Romeo takes his kiss, they fashion one more rhyming quatrain:

ROMEO      Thus from my lips by thine my sin is purged.
JULIET     Then have my lips the sin that they have took.
ROMEO      Sin from my lips? O trespass sweetly urged!
           [*Kisses her.*]
JULIET     You kiss by th' book. (1.5.106-9)

Juliet's phrase "by th' book" is interpreted as meaning "according to the rules." But in this context, it could also convey a certain bookish—academic—quality.

Romeo refigures the bright jewel-like beauty of Juliet when he imagines her as the sun (2.2.3). And yet he almost immediately loses this burst through further imagining that runs away into a conceit so excessive it becomes an astronomical absurdity:

Two of the fairest stars in all the heaven,
Having some business, do entreat her eyes
To twinkle in the spheres till they return.
What if her eyes were there, they in her head?
The brightness of her cheek would shame those stars
As daylight doth a lamp. Her eyes in heaven
Would through the airy region stream so bright
That birds would sing and think it were not night.
See how she leans her cheek upon her hand.
O, that I were a glove upon that hand,
That I might touch that cheek! (2.2.15-25)

Romeo displaces the effect this conceit makes by reimagining Juliet coherently as a "bright angel," who is:

As glorious to this night . . . . . . . . . .
As is a winged messenger of heaven
Upon the white-upturned wondering eyes
Of mortals that fall back to gaze on him
When he bestrides the lazy-puffing clouds
And sails upon the bosom of the air. (2.2.26-32)

## Shakespeare as Renaissance Writer

Shakespeare lived during the period labeled the Renaissance, which involved learning how to read Ancient Greek so as to value freshly classical Greek and Roman writers. This period also valued the expansion, the dilation, of human capacities. It is no accident that Michelangelo's statue of David is about fourteen feet tall. Poets amplified, enlarged, and spun out their imagery into the length of the conceits we see in *Romeo and Juliet*. Sometimes they seem to be a bit out of control. Sometimes Shakespeare purposely shows uncontrolled conceits usually to characterize a speaker by their effect. Every so often, he seems to lose control himself, perhaps through a fondness for what he is writing. The effects of the conceits we have analyzed so far seem to be intended. Still, it is hard often to guess at a writer's intentions. But the repeated experience of watching and reading Shakespeare's plays puts us on firmer ground for our speculations.

A good example of Shakespeare's lack of realistic decorum, of what the eighteenth century would especially require of poets and dramatists—and which they faulted Shakespeare for lacking—is an early speech of Juliet's mother, Lady Capulet. Early in the play, Lady Capulet comes to tell her daughter that Lord Paris seeks her for a wife.

> What say you, can you love the gentleman?
> This night you shall behold him at our feast.
> Read o'er the volume of young Paris' face,
> And find delight writ there with beauty's pen;
> Examine every married lineament,
> And see how one another lends content;
> And what obscured in this fair volume lies
> Find written in the margent of his eyes.
> This precious book of love, this unbound lover,
> To beautify him only lacks a cover.
> The fish lives in the sea, and 'tis much pride
> For fair without the fair within to hide.
> That book to many's eyes doth share the glory
> That in gold clasps locks in the golden story

So that you share all that he doth possess,
By having him, making yourself no less. (1.3.80-95)

The Nurse comically undercuts Lady's Capulet's conclusion by exclaiming "No less? Nay, bigger—women grow [become pregnant] by men" (1.3.96). Lady Capulet's extended metaphor, her conceit, is likely the longest, the most imaginatively articulated poetic construction in the play. Its beginning depends upon one of the oldest poetic comparisons, that of the human face to a page of a manuscript or a book.[4] What suggested this metaphor was probably the fact that both faces and books have "lines" which can be "read" for meaning. So the basic comparison is not original to Shakespeare. What is original—creative—about this conceit is the fineness of the fabric spun, so to speak.

Lady Capulet personifies Beauty and gives her a pen, to write the lines on the "volume" of Paris's face. She then puns on "lines" / "lineaments," the latter meaning not just his features but the limbs of his body, which complement one another in a harmonious (handsome) whole. A second pun occurs with the word "content." Paris's lineaments not only give a viewer "content" (satisfaction, pleasure); they also give Paris "content," in the sense of "substance." In Shakespeare's lifetime, explanations of ideas in a page of text were often printed next to them in the margin. They were called "marginalia." Juliet's mother draws on this idea when she says that any obscurities in Paris are clarified by "the margent of his eyes," that is to say, a feature of his handsome face. She then imagines him as a book of unbound pages, which only lacks a beautiful cover. This would be lovely Juliet. Paris, in another pun, is "unbound" because he is not yet bound by wedding vows. She concludes by saying that Juliet's "golden clasps" (her clamp-like binding, i.e., her embracing of Paris) shall share in the glory of his rich, inner content (substance)—here, his "story."

The image of Juliet as Paris's cover demeans her in two ways. It suggests that she herself lacks substance or depth of meaning, that is, she is all outside show. Moreover, it has a sexual overtone, of lying with this man. The latter is surprising—indecorous—for a mother to apply to her daughter, who is not yet fourteen. Lady Capulet never shows much empathy for her daughter as Old Capulet orders her to marry this lord. Nor would it be surprising if Shakespeare's playgoers supposed she had much formal education. Even well-born women often lacked it. Moreover, Lady Capulet's other speeches in the play give no evidence of the rich imagination that her book conceit requires. In other words, Shakespeare doesn't fit her conceit to her character. (It is not decorous). But then, we don't expect him to. The conceit is his, spun because he wants to weave it. The imagining in this case seems more his own (not his character's) than many of the other conceited imaginings in *Romeo and Juliet*.[5]

Whatever the case, many of the metaphors in *Romeo and Juliet* cause a playgoer to appreciate better the unforgettable originality and succinct quality of Romeo's and Juliet's poetic imagining of their love. "Come, gentle night, come, loving black browed night," Juliet murmurs,

> Give me my Romeo, and when I shall die
> Take him and cut him out in little stars,
> And he will make the face of heaven so fine
> That all the world will be in love with night
> And pay no worship to the garish sun.
> O, I have bought the mansion of a love
> But not possessed it, and though I am sold,
> Not yet enjoyed. So tedious is this day
> As is the night before some festival
> To an impatient child that hath new robes
> And may not wear them. (3.2.20-31)

When Juliet does express her mysteriously self-renewing love, she uses a simple simile tenderly to express it:

> My bounty is as boundless as the sea,
> My love as deep; the more I give to thee,
> The more I have, for both are infinite (2.2.133-35)

"Conceit more rich in matter than in words," Juliet says at one point, "Brags of his substance, not of ornament" (2.6.30-31). In one sense, metaphor, and poetic imagery in general, can be thought of as ornamenting thoughts and their expression. Surprisingly, in this play loaded with conceits, when Romeo and Juliet pledge their love, they do so in speech devoid of metaphor, made up of many one- or two-syllable words. Juliet says,

> Fain would I dwell on form, fain, fain deny
> What I have spoke; but farewell, compliment.
> Dost thou love me? I know thou wilt say "Ay,"
> And I will take thy word; yet, if thou swear'st,
> Thou mayst prove false. At lovers' perjuries,
> They say, Jove laughs. O gentle Romeo,
> If thou dost love, pronounce it faithfully,
> Or if thou think'st I am too quickly won,
> I'll frown and be perverse and say thee nay,
> So thou wilt woo, but else not for the world.
> In truth, fair Montague, I am too fond,
> And therefore thou mayst think my haviour light.
> But trust me, gentleman, I'll prove more true
> Than those that have more cunning to be strange. (2.2.88-101)

When Romeo responds by wanting to swear by some outside authority: "Lady, by yonder blessed moon I vow, / That tips with silver all these fruit-tree tops" (2.2.107-8), she interrupts him:

> O swear not by the moon, th'inconstant moon.
> That monthly changes in her circled orb,
> Lest that thy love prove likewise variable. (2.2.109-11)

"What shall I swear by," Romeo asks. "Do not swear at all," Juliet concludes:

> Or if thou wilt, swear by thy gracious self,
> Which is the god of my idolatry,
> And I'll believe thee. (2.2.112-15)

---

Juliet's professing her love rings true because the simple, unadorned language by which she voices it seems immediate, honest, without the gathering of calculated thought necessary to refigure it in metaphors. She soon does that though through the wonderful metaphor of the sea and its boundless breadth and depth. But that comes a little bit later. At the moment, she utters her love, her unornamented language seems the only medium for projecting it. Romeo disturbs that impression by wanting to swear by the goddess of the moon, Diana. Juliet says that he is the god of her idolatry. Making an idol of someone, whether a god or not, would have been suspect for Shakespeare's Christian playgoers, whether Protestant or Catholic. That was what Christ warned his believers to refrain from doing and what the Old Testament God punished the Hebrews for doing. Shakespeare creates a trail of allusions, for the most part conventional, to a god perhaps ruling Romeo and Juliet, an enslaving god according to conceits about him, who becomes remarkably original in his embodiment—one who turns a somewhat trite personification into a unique presence.

## Gods and Goddesses of Love

This god, of course, is Cupid, the little son of Venus, the goddess of earthly love. At the time, Shakespeare wrote there were two Venuses and two Cupids, the Venus and Cupid of Earthly Love, the sensual love between men and women that everyone is aware of, and the Venus and Cupid of Heavenly Love, the spiritual love that, for Christians at least, involved self-sacrifice (agape). This is the love of another unmerited by the beloved. In visual art, one could tell the difference between the pairs by whether Cupid wore a blindfold. Cupid blindfold symbolized erotic love, blind love—love without regard to reason or calculation. Cupid carried a little bow and arrows; these he shot at either his mother's direction or at will on his own, without regard to his victims' appearance or choice. When the invisible arrow pierced the heart, the result was love at first sight. If the arrow had a golden head, the man or woman beheld at the instant of impact returned the love; if the head was leaden, the other did not. This is Romeo's situation at the beginning of the play, for he blindly loves Rosaline, but she will have nothing to do with him.

Poetic accounts of Cupid and his shooting of arrows, of piercing lovers, of a cold beloved and of his tyranny, appeared in the literature of the Middle Ages, and they abounded in the love poetry and literature of the Renaissance, Shakespeare's age. Like the oxymora of Petrarch, they had become worn and expected, ho-hum even. Of Rosaline, Romeo tells Benvolio,

> . . . . . . . . . . . . . . . . . . She'll not be hit
> With Cupid's arrow. She hath Dian's wit,
> And in strong proof of chastity well armed
> From love's weak childish bow she lives uncharmed. (1.1.206-9)

When Benvolio wonders what apology they shall make for crashing Capulet's ball, Romeo says,

> We'll have no Cupid hoodwinked with a scarf,
> Bearing a Tartar's painted bow of lath [wood]
> Scaring the ladies like a crow-keeper. (1.4.4-6)

Romeo confirms certain playgoers' opinion that the conceit of blindfold Cupid and his bow is a bit shopworn, mainly by his remarking that Cupid is currently played by lovers with cheap props for those of the love-boy. Mercutio jokes with Romeo nevertheless: "You are a lover; borrow Cupid's wings, / And soar with them above a common ground" (1.4.17-18).

Romeo's reply seems to indicate that he subscribes to the reality of what Cupid represents:

> I am too sore empierced with his shaft
> To soar with his light feathers, and so bound
> I cannot bound a pitch above dull woe;
> Under love's heavy burden I sink. (1.4.19-22)

Romeo appears unaware of who he will become when he commands, "Give me a torch, I am not for this ambling, / Being but heavy I will bear the light" (1.4.11-12). Torches were called links in Shakespeare's age, and people carried them at night along dark, narrow streets unlit by any meaningful lighting. Despite this common practice, a few playgoers, probably the more learned ones, might have thought him Cupid personified at the moment he takes his torch; for Cupid was sometimes depicted as holding aloft a burning torch, to signify the burning passion he prompted. This image seems anything but hackneyed.

Later, when Romeo has leapt the Capulet orchard wall and his friends cannot find him, Mercutio wittily asks him to discover himself by uttering "[o]ne nickname for [Venus's] purblind son and heir, / Young Abraham Cupid, he that shot so trim / When King Cophetua loved the beggar maid" (2.1.12-14). Mercutio implies that King Cophetua lived a long time ago. Abraham was an Old Testament patriarch. By the phrase "Abraham Cupid," Mercutio sarcastically suggests that the love-god is an "old boy."[6] Paradoxically, Cupid was born in the Ancient world, and yet he through the centuries has never gotten older. Here, the motif of Cupid merges with Petrarch, for Mercutio has coined an oxymoron.

At this point, Shakespeare has breathed new life into stereotyped Cupid, for he becomes Romeo—or rather, Romeo becomes Cupid. Before he was Cupid, the little love god was Eros, the Greek god of love—not just that between a man and woman—but love as the force driving all things together to mate and breed—indeed the force driving the four elements together to shape the material world. Eros as this god was a handsome, full-sized man, who soon was given beautiful rainbow-colored wings. He appears as such in one of the most famous myths of the Ancient world, that of Cupid and Psyche. Eros/Cupid becomes beautiful Psyche's secret lover, wedding her and visiting her nightly. Fearful of his mother, he orders this mortal woman, after their lovemaking in the dark, to never try to see his face. When, curious, she suddenly shines a light on him, she sees the handsome winged god, who flees. This moment was a favorite subject of Renaissance painters such as Titian and Rubens. When Juliet tells Romeo to cast off his Montague name and take all herself, he says, "I take thee at thy word. / Call me but love and I'll be new baptized" (2.2.49-50). And when she asks how he got over the "high and hard to climb" orchard walls, he clearly identifies himself as Eros by saying "[w]ith love's light wings did I o'erperch these walls" (2.2.66). Imaginatively, Shakespeare capitalizes on the full-size figure of Eros. So this is the god of Juliet's idolatry, one so beautiful that she wants to become one with him through love.

Shakespeare thus shows Cupid—Eros—casting off his clichéd appearance and becoming imaginatively alive. Still, such moments compete with occasions when Romeo's and Juliet's imaginations become excessive, overwrought. Romeo's strange conceit, wherein, distraught over his exile, imagines insects—flies—doing what he cannot: court Juliet. "They may seize":

On the white wonder of dear Juliet's hand
And steal immortal blessing from her lips,
Who even in pure and vestal modesty
Still blush, as thinking their own kisses sin. (3.3.35-39)

This expanded comparison vaguely resembles a poem of John Donne, Shakespeare's contemporary, titled "The Flea." Donne imagines the flea he sees drawing blood from him and then from his mistress, as enjoying in their mingled blood within it what she refuses: as marrying them so as to rationalize his marrying her blood and his through the act of lovemaking. Shakespeare's comparison is almost as imaginatively ingenious as Donne's. Romeo imagines Juliet's lips red from her blushes that the fly should steal a kiss from them. Not only does the fly simply crawl on her; he imagines it crawling across her lips. The grotesqueness of the image registers the morbid disturbance of Romeo's imagination brought about by his despair over his exile.

Given the Friar's scheme involving Juliet's drinking a life-suspending potion and being placed in the Capulet tomb so as to awaken at the moment Romeo arrives, she gradually becomes so fearful of what she will see and smell once inside the tomb that she hallucinates. Seeing Tybalt's ghost terrorizes her into impulsively drinking the potion. Her imaginings have become so real that they smother all other faculties of her mind:

. . . . . . . . . . [I]s it not very like
The horrible conceit of death and night
. . . . . . . . . . . . . . . . . . . . . . . . . . . . .
Where bloody Tybalt, yet but green in earth,
Lies festering in his shroud . . . . . . .
. . . . . . . . . . . . . . . . . is it not like that I,
So early waking, what with the loathsome smells,
And shrieks like mandrakes torn out of the earth,
That living mortals, hearing them, run mad—
Or, if I wake, shall I not be distraught,
Environed with all these hideous fears,
And madly play with my forefathers' joints,
And pluck the mangled Tybalt from his shroud
And, in a rage, with some great kinsman's bone,
As with a club, dash out my desperate brains? (4.3.36-37, 42-43, 45-54)

Shakespeare here follows his source, Arthur Brooke's *The Tragicall Historye of Romeus and Juliet* (1562; 1587; see 284-363, esp. 347). In this poem, "The force of her ymagining, anon dyd waxe so strong" that she sees the specter of Tybalt. In both Brooke and Shakespeare, this force triggers Juliet's drinking the elixir, most likely to escape her awful imaginings.

### Reason and Friar Laurence

Friar Laurence's emphasis upon reason sets off Romeo's and Juliet's imaginings, both the lovely lyrics as well as the uncontrolled flights. He repeatedly counsels them to moderate their feelings, and he does so mainly by urging them to use reason to deal with their predicaments. Concerning Romeo's calling his exile death, the Friar says,

O deadly sin, O rude unthankfulness!
Thy fault our law calls death, but the kind Prince,
Taking thy part, hath rushed aside the law,
And turned that black word "death" to banishment.
This is dear mercy, and thou seest it not. (3.3.24-28)

When Romeo insists that "banishment" also means "death," the rational Friar replies, "I'll give thee armour to keep off that word, / Adversity's sweet milk, philosophy, / To comfort thee though thou art banished" (3.3.54-56). Playgoers generally side with Romeo; the Friar seems to be playing with words, and his philosophy is barren. "Yet banished! Hang up philosophy!" Romeo exclaims,

> Unless philosophy can make a Juliet,
> Displant a town, reverse a prince's doom,
> It helps not, it prevails not. Talk no more. (3.3.57-60)

While Romeo's and Juliet's imaginings cannot do these things, they have a fertility absent in the Friar's reasonable thinking. Friar Laurence's rationalizations about how fate-cursed Romeo is "happy" work neither for him nor for the audience (3.3.134-44). Finally, playgoers judge the Friar's rationalizations as downright callous, insensitive to the Capulets' grief over Juliet's sudden "death." The Friar begins with his typical playing with the meanings of words; if the Capulet's sought Juliet's "promotion," they should be glad she is "advanced" to "heaven" (4.5.71-74). "She's not well married that lives married long," the man who has never known marriage pronounces:

> But she's best married that dies married young.
> Dry up your tears, and stick your rosemary
> On this fair corse, and, as the custom is,
> And in her best array, bear her to church;
> For though fond nature bids us all lament,
> Yet nature's tears are reason's merriment. (4.5.77-83)

The grotesque lack of empathy for the distraught parents in saying that reason bids them to be merry turns auditors away from reason back to the attraction of Romeo's and Juliet's memorable imaginings. True to Shakespeare's portraying his characters as woven of mingled yarn—possessing paradoxical traits—the Friar has the capacity to imagine. But his one act of imagining—the scheme involving the potion, Juliet's "death" and burial, and the letter to Romeo to come rescue her from a tomb—is so wildly improbable, depending as it does on no accidental interference and on incredible timing, that it serves to remind us that Friar Laurence is unused to imagining.

In conclusion, this remarkably imaginative play with set speeches rich in detail, such as Romeo's portrait of the Apothecary, with his "tattered weeds" "overwhelming brows," and his "needy shop," containing among its many details "a tortoise," an "alligator stuffed," and "other skins / Of ill-shaped fishes" (5.1.37-54). Mercutio's aria, a bravura set piece, about the monarch of dreams, the fairy Queen Mab, is internationally famous (1.4.53-94). For denseness of exotic detail, such as her chariot, "an empty hazelnut" with "wagon-spokes made of long spinners' legs, / The cover of the wings of grasshoppers" (1.4.60, 62-63), Mercutio's imagining has no rival among Shakespeare's dramas. Not surprisingly, the skeptic Mercutio says that dreams "are children of an idle brain, / Begot of nothing but vain fantasy" (1.4.98-99). Here, Mercutio seems to be using the word "fantasy" as a negative term for imaginings ("fancies"), in accord with the negative definition of the faculty of mind current in Shakespeare's time, which was set forth at the beginning of this essay. "So full of shapes is fancy, / That it alone is high fantastical," Duke Orsino says at the beginning of Shakespeare's comedy *Twelfth Night* (1.1.14-15). The various imaginings of *Romeo and Juliet* appear fantastical at times, and yet at others—the distinct majority—they possess the clear ring of truth.

## Notes

1. All quotations of *Romeo and Juliet* come from Weis's edition. Those of texts from other Shakespeare plays are taken from Greenblatt et al.

2. Admittedly, Juliet uses a string of oxymora for Romeo the moment after the Nurse tells her Romeo has killed her kinsman Tybalt: "Beautiful tyrant," "fiend angelical," "Dove-feathered raven" . . . "damned saint," "honorable villain" (3.2.75-76, 79). But in a matter of seconds, she reprimands herself for her outburst: "Upon his brow shame is ashamed to sit / For 'tis a throne where honour may be crowned / Sole monarch of the universal earth. / O, what a beast was I to chide at him!" (3.3.92-95).

3.  Pilgrims to Jerusalem were sometimes called "palmers" because they often brought back palm branches as tokens of their visit (Weis 174).

4.  Curtius (316, 318, 332, 335-38). Curtius in fact cites Lady Capulet's speech among his many examples of the metaphor (335), some of which come from Shakespeare's plays.

5.  Readers recollect Lady Capulet's conceit when Juliet, momentarily vilifying Romeo for Tybalt's death, says, "Was ever book containing such vile matter / So fairly bound?" (3.2.83-84). This kind of residue periodically emerges in Shakespeare's writing, perhaps surfacing semi-consciously, from a previous metaphor.

6.  In *Love's Labor's Lost*, Shakespeare likewise calls Cupid "Signor Junior" (3.1.175).

7.  For more evidence of the compulsive power of the imagination, see Montaigne, "Of the power of the imagination."

## Works Cited

Brooke, Arthur. *The Tragicall Historye of Romeus and Juliet, Narrative and Dramatic Sources of Shakespeare, Volume I: Early Comedies, Poems, Romeo and Juliet*, edited by Geoffrey Bullough, Routledge and Kegan Paul, 1957. 8 vols.

Curtius, Ernst Robert. *European Literature and the Latin Middle Ages*. Translated by Willard R. Trask. 1953. Harper & Row, 1963.

Montaigne, Michel de. "Of the power of the imagination," *The Complete Essays of Montaigne*. Translated by Donald M. Frame. 1957. Stanford UP, 1965, pp. 68-76.

Petrarch. *Petrarch: Selected Poems*. Translated by Anthony Mortimer, U of Alabama P, 1977.

Rossky, William. "Imagination in the English Renaissance: Psychology and Poetic." *Studies in the Renaissance*, vol. 5, 1958, pp. 49-73.

Shakespeare, William. *The Norton Shakespeare*, edited by Stephen Greenblatt et al., Norton, 2016.

_____. *Romeo and Juliet*, edited by René Weis, Bloomsbury, 2012. The Arden Shakespeare—Series Three.

# The Artificiality of *Romeo and Juliet*

Frances Teague

Some teachers inform their students that *Romeo and Juliet* reflects the universal experience of first love. One editor even declares:

> *Romeo and Juliet* is a play of young love. No other conveys so well the impetuous, idealistic passion of youth. [. . .] The universal longing for a perfect romantic love, for the union of physical desire with selfless self-surrender, finds full expression in this play [. . . ]. (Hankins 14)

In fact, googling the terms "Romeo and Juliet" *and* "universal" produces almost half a million results. Many admirers of this play think that the play reflects the world of young love in a transcendent way and argue that this reflection of reality is what makes the play great.

But I am a contrarian about *Romeo and Juliet*. The idea that *Romeo and Juliet* is great art because it is so universally reflective of life seems to me to be accurate only if you have a taste for melodrama. While two young people falling in love and behaving recklessly is common enough, rarely does adolescent passion result in six deaths (Mercutio, Tybalt, Paris, Romeo, Juliet, and Lady Montague). Surely the spate of homicide, suicide, and grieving oneself to death does not reflect some universal situation.

What I like about this play is its artificiality. Specifically, I admire the way that the speeches play with heightened language, while the plot plays with heightened action. In the plot, Romeo and his friends brawl in the streets, fence with one another, dance, leap walls, and climb balconies. Because most of Juliet's scenes are domestic, her action is limited, although she too dances, makes love with Romeo, and drinks the potion that stills her, and the Nurse promenades the streets of Verona seeking Romeo. Accompanying this action is exuberant language. What attracts my attention, however, is the wonderful rhetoric, the speech-making in which images and paradoxes and metaphors pour out in aria-like verse. When I say as much in class, my students recoil slightly. In part, they resist the idea that listening to long stretches of poetry can be enjoyable (although the success of *Hamilton* may change that misconception) and, in part, because they often believe that great plays will "hold. . . the mirror up to nature," as Hamlet tells the players. Artificiality is bad in their minds. Instead they measure art by how well it reflects their own lives, by how "relatable" they judge it to be.[1]

Yet art can also be artifice, something that delights and moves us because it is emphatically not true to life. For example, Fabergé eggs could never be mistaken for actual eggs. Peter Carl Fabergé created gifts for the Tsars of Russia to present to family members at Easter. Fashioned of precious metals, decorated with enameling and jewels, and containing diminutive objects like a miniature carriage, a ship, portraits, and a tiny hen, Fabergé eggs are art precisely because they are not eggs. Instead they are extraordinarily complex and personal jewels in an egg-shaped case, which make a meaning specific to the Russian royal family.

Fig 2 Peter Carl Fabergé, *Memory of Azov Egg* (Moscow, 1891).
Kremlin Armoury Museum.
Photograph Stan Shebs (own work), via Wikimedia Commons. Web.

In this photograph, for example, we see the Fabergé egg that was an Easter gift from Tsar Alexander III to his wife in 1891. The egg itself is jasper, decorated with gold and diamonds. Inside the egg in a nest of green velvet is a miniature ship, a replica of an actual cruiser called *Memory of Azov* on which two of the Russian princes had sailed the previous year. While beautiful, no one would serve this egg for breakfast.

Like the egg, *Romeo and Juliet* is artifice, not a replication of people talking and acting in a naturalistic way, but rather a presentation of characters who speak lyric poetry and act with reckless passion within the culture of the sixteenth-century. The way that the play uses artificial language to create lyricism and paradox is what engages me. I shall go further: the way that the language of the play swings between lyrical beauty and paradox allows me to read and view the play over and over without becoming jaded. I especially admire a particular paradoxical image, suitable to a horror movie, which recurs throughout the play and then abruptly stops.

## Paradox and Lyricism

Paradox is defined by E. H. Behler in *The Princeton Encyclopedia of Poetry and Poetics* as follows:

> A daring statement that unites seemingly contradictory words but that on closer examination proves to have unexpected meaning and truth ("The longest way round is the shortest way home"; "Life is death and death is life"). (996)[2]

Paradox is at the heart of the play, both at its most lyrical and its most horrific. The play begins with the Prologue's paradoxical declaration that its subject is "Two households, both alike in dignity / In fair Verona" "Where civil blood makes civil hands unclean" (Prol. 1-2, 4). The paradox of the lines underscored by the repetition of "civil," for what could be less civil than one civilized family trying to kill another civilized family that is "alike in dignity"? The verbal paradox that opens the play is sometimes undercut today by the way that production after production shows the Montagues and the Capulets as households that differ in important ways, despite being "alike in dignity." From contrasting costumes (the Montagues in blue, for instance, while the Capulets wear red), to contrasting ethnicities (of race or ethnic origin), to opposed political positions (the opposite sides of a civil war), such productions ignore the bitter paradox that the play's text offers us of feuding characters willing to kill and die, although they are very like their enemies.

Moreover, the play underscores that paradox. In his first appearance, Romeo comments on his family's feud with the Capulets, telling his cousin Benvolio:

> Here's much to do with hate, but more with love.
> Why then, O brawling love, O loving hate,
> O anything, of nothing first create!

O heavy lightness, serious vanity,
Misshapen chaos of well-seeming forms!
Feather of lead, bright smoke, cold fire, sick health,
Still-waking sleep that is not what it is!
This love feel I that feel no love in this.
Dost thou not laugh? (1.1.173-181)

Simply counting what Behler calls "contradictory words" becomes complicated by the way that terms are combined and echoed, as when "hate" and "love" become "brawling love and loving hate." Romeo recognizes that the feud has no basis in difference, but rather is created of nothing (although another of Shakespeare's plays tells, "Nothing can come of nothing"). Next, Romeo spirals into a list of oxymorons, a paradoxical figure of speech, and asks his cousin if that list does not provoke laughter. His brittle use of paradox and oxymorons continues throughout the play's opening scenes until he finally begins to dance with Juliet at the Capulet ball.

Then his language shifts into the lyrical: he moves into the opening of a sonnet in which he declares himself a pilgrim who seeks to worship at the shrine of Juliet's beauty. Juliet, whose previous speech has been anything but eloquent, answers him with the second quatrain of the sonnet he has started, telling him he may hold her hand in the dance, but should not kiss her. Both of them play with the image of a religious pilgrim adoring a shrine, joining hands to pray and leaning in to kiss a sacred relic. The two conclude the sonnet together, exchanging line for line as Romeo steals his kiss. The scene is charming, lyrical, and completely (wonderfully) artificial. The dancers' sonnet also enacts a paradox: their desire as they rhyme with one another is anything but holy if one believes that religion imposes chastity on the young and unmarried. When the dance concludes, and the Nurse identifies Romeo, Juliet laments in paradox:

My only love sprung from my only hate.
Too early seen unknown, and known too late.
Prodigious birth of love it is to me,
That I must love a loathed enemy. (1.5.137-40)

Like Romeo, who adds "brawling" and "loving" to love and hate, Juliet combines the terms "love" and "hate" in this passage and then complicates them with the next line when she links "early" and "late" with "known" and "unknown." Well aware of the paradoxical relationship that she and Romeo must have, Juliet yearns to join with her love, yet is separated from him by her family's feud. She struggles to reconcile herself to her position, for although she has no doubt of her love for an enemy, a fundamental tenet of her religion, she is unsure of what will come of that love, since an equally fundamental tenet of her family identity tells her to hate him.

In the balcony scene that follows, Romeo acknowledges their difficulties:

> My name, dear saint, is hateful to myself
> Because it is an enemy to thee.
> Had I it written, I would tear the word. (2.2.55-7)

He is willing to surrender his identity and his family because the Montagues are enemies to her family. When she protests, fearing her kinsmen will find and kill him as he talks with her, he is indifferent to his danger:

> I have night's cloak to hide me from their eyes,
> And but thou love me, let them find me here.
> My life were better ended by their hate,
> Than death prorogued, wanting of thy love. (2.2.75-8)

His response is to embrace hate's destruction so that he may enjoy his love, a vow that hints at what is to come. In both passages, Romeo's love leads him to speak of self-destruction, an ominous foreshadowing. The bulk of the balcony scene is lyrical, but the tension created by the feud depends on paradox, as the love that they feel is threatened by the hate with which they must live.

The beauty of the language in the balcony scene is a mainstay of the play's reputation. Juliet is Romeo's sun, his bright angel, and when she "leans her cheek upon her hand," he wishes, "O, that I were a glove upon that hand, / That I might touch that cheek" (2.2.24-25).

She muses on how foolish it is to regret his name is Montague, for "What's in a name? That which we call a rose / By any other name would smell as sweet" (2.2.43-44). While the scene has the two speaking to themselves initially, each attains even greater lyricism as they come together and begin to converse, demonstrating the truth of Romeo's observation, "How silver sweet are lovers' tongues by night, / Like softest music to attending ears" (2.2.165-66). The imagery of the stars and moon in the night sky, of birds and flowers, crowds the scene as the two declare their love. Just as their first meeting allowed them to compose a sonnet as they danced, they now share rhyming couplets at the end of the scene:

> Juliet: Good night, good night! Parting is such sweet sorrow,
> That I shall say good night till it be morrow.
> Romeo: Sleep dwell upon thine eyes, peace in thy breast.
> Would I were sleep and peace so sweet to rest! (2.2.184-87)

Anyone who enjoys rich poetry enjoys this scene, at least in part because no one talks this way in the ordinary world. The wonderful language is fabricated by an artist who crafts those images, who makes the iambic pentameter dance, who creates beauty with the spoken word.

## Death, the Bridegroom

While the play's lyrical language is lovely, it is accompanied throughout the play by a recurring paradox that we may find disturbing, the repeated reference to personified Death as a lover. Images of death wooing a maiden are often found in medieval and Renaissance Europe, enough so that the image of "Death and the Maiden" becomes a commonplace. Two such sixteenth-century images, one a painting by Hans Baldung and the other a boxwood carving by Hans Schwarz, illustrate the motif.

Hans Baldung, *Der Tod und das Mädchen* (Strasbourg, 1517).

Hans Schwarz, *Death and the Maiden* (Augsburg, 1520)

In both of these works, Death is personified and portrayed as a particularly repellent skeleton, with scraps of flesh and hair still clinging to his bones; in both, the maiden is very much alive and revolted by her skeleton-lover, but each version emphasizes her living flesh. The linkage between death and sex, between a decaying corpse and a fertile body, is one that Shakespeare's culture would recognize at once. As the friar reminds Romeo in 2.3, "the earth that's nature mother is her tomb: / What is her burying grave, that is her womb" (2.3.5-6). The idea lingers from the *memento mori* tradition of the medieval period that one must always keep one's mortality in mind. This particular form of *memento mori*, by imagining Death as a lover, becomes profoundly disturbing because it violates multiple taboos about handling dead bodies, especially the taboo against necrophilia. The imagery of Death and the Maiden is intended to shock and fascinate.

Repeatedly, the play suggests that Romeo's chief rival is not Tybalt or Paris, but Death. In 1.5.133-4 as Juliet asks about Romeo's identity, she says she fears he might be married: "If he be married, / My grave is like to be my wedding bed." Death, in this comparison, becomes her husband, for only Death can meet her in her wedding bed if it is to be her grave. The idea of the bride going to her grave as if she were joining her lover and husband is extreme, but not unusual in the sixteenth century, when the trope of "Death and the Maiden" was active.

In 3.2, when Juliet contemplates her wedding night, she is eager for a human lover, however, anticipating the "amorous rites" and happy to "lose a winning match / Play'd for a pair of stainless maidenheads" (3.2.8, 12-13):

Come night, come Romeo, come thou day in night,
For though wilt lie upon the wings of night
Whiter than new snow upon a raven's back.
Come gentle night, come loving black-brow'd night,
Give me my Romeo. . . . (3.2.17-21)

At this point, Juliet's bridegroom is Romeo, and the two shall experience sexual union for the first time together. Yet when the Nurse brings word of Romeo's exile, Juliet despairs and then says, "I'll to my wedding bed, / And death, not Romeo take my maidenhead" (3.2.136-37). Romeo has been pushed aside by his rival Death for the moment, until Friar Laurence makes his plan to save the lovers.

The unexpected complication that Juliet must face—her parents' determination to have her marry Paris on short order—first makes Juliet resist her parents' will. Not knowing why her usually obedient daughter is so stubborn, Lady Capulet says, "I would the fool were married to her grave" (3.5.140). When Juliet resists her father's wishes, Lord Capulet tells her that he will marry her to

Paris, and if she refuses, "hang! Beg! Starve! Die in the streets!" (3.5.192). Unwittingly, the father and the mother echo one another: their daughter will take death as her bridegroom and the grave as her wedding bed. In her misery, Juliet begs for a delay: "or if you do not, make the bridal bed / In that dim monument where Tybalt lies" (3.5.200-201). Telling Friar Laurence about this wedding, Juliet vows to kill herself rather than violate her marriage vows with Romeo. Indeed, she swears:

> O, bid me leap, rather than marry Paris,
> From off the battlements of any tower,
> Or walk in thievish ways, or bid me lurk
> Where serpents are. Chain me with roaring bears,
> Or shut me nightly in a charnel-house,
> O'ercover'd quite with dead men's rattling bones,
> With reeky shanks and yellow chapless skulls.
> Or bid me go into a new-made grave,
> And hide me with a dead man in his shroud—
> Things that, to hear them told, have made me tremble—
> And I will do it without fear or doubt,
> To live an unstain'd wife to my sweet love. (4.1.77-88)

The final image in this list of horrors, that she would crawl into a shroud and share it with a dead man, inverts the erotic image of two lovers wrapped in a sheet.

Juliet's revulsion, the thing that would make her tremble, as she says, is a normal response. She fears death and the grave. Indeed as she prepares to take the potion that Friar Laurence has prepared, she begins to doubt the plan because she is so terrified of waking too early and finding herself in the family tomb with the corpse of Tybalt and the bones of her ancestors.

> How if, when I am laid into the tomb,I wake before the time that
> RomeoCome to redeem me? There's a fearful point! Shall I not then
> be stifled in the vault, To whose foul mouth no healthsome air breathes
> in, And there die strangled ere my Romeo comes? Or, if I live, is it
> not very like, The horrible conceit of death and night, Together with
> the terror of the place, As in a vault, an ancient receptacle, Where,

for these many hundred years the bones Of all my buried ancestors are pack'd: Where bloody Tybalt yet but green in earth Lies festering in his shroud; where, as they say, At some hours in the night spirits resort;— Alack, alack! Is it not like that I So early waking, what with loathsome smells, And shrieks like mandrakes torn out of the earth, That living mortals, hearing them, run mad— O, if I wake, shall I not be distraught, Environed with all these hideous fears, And madly play with my forefather's joints, And pluck the mangled Tybalt from his shroud, And, in this rage, with some great kinsman's bone As with a club, dash out my desperate brains? O, look, methinks I see my cousin's ghost Seeking out Romeo that did spit his body Upon a rapier's point! Stay, Tybalt, stay! Romeo, Romeo, Romeo, here's drink! I drink to thee! (4.3.30-58)

This speech is superb, as the character moves closer and closer to hysteria and desperation. Note, for example, the single sentence from line 36-54: despite the dashes that allow the performer to breathe, it demands that Juliet speak more and more disjointedly as it proceeds.[3] The speech in the unreliable first quarto is far briefer and less effective, but in both the authorized texts of the second quarto and first folio, the punctuation is clear: the speech shows Juliet's fear of the grave, and it is written in such a way that the person who performs Juliet has to show that fear as well (for the various texts, see the Sadlack edition).

The play's reiteration of the love-death linkage moves with each instance closer to making Death the bridegroom to Juliet. When her family discovers her catatonic body the next morning, her father seems to complete the metaphor, telling Paris:

O son, the night before thy wedding-day
Hath Death lain with thy wife. There she lies,
Flower as she was, deflowered by him.
Death is my son-in-law, Death is my heir.
My daughter he hath wedded. I will die,
And leave him all: life, living, all is Death's. (4.5.35-40)

A few scenes later, Paris comes like a pilgrim to the tomb of the Capulets to say farewell to Juliet. Seeing Romeo enter, Paris says he fears the intruder "is come to do some villainous shame / To the dead bodies" (5.3.52-53). In this line, one can hear a hint at the many taboos against handling corpses. Finally, when Romeo, having killed Paris, sees Juliet's body laid out, he acknowledges that he has lost his wife to a rival lover, Death.

> Death that hath suck'd the honey of thy breath
> Hath had no power yet upon thy beauty.
> Thou art not conquer'd.
>                    [. . .] Ah, dear Juliet,
> Why art thou yet so fair? Shall I believe
> That unsubstantial Death is amorous,
> And that the lean abhorred monster keeps
> Thee here in dark to be his paramour? (5.3.92-4, 101-105)

Death has seemingly become the lover who steals Juliet from Romeo, although the dramatic irony of the scene allows the audience to know that Juliet is actually alive because the strength of her love has not allowed her to betray her husband with death. While Romeo kills himself to join his love, she awakes just moments too late.

I want to conclude by arguing that when Juliet awakes, the richly artificial language that has sustained the play comes to an abrupt stop. The paradox, the repeated imagery, the elaborate speeches all end. Juliet regains consciousness as Friar Laurence enters the tomb. He tells her that both Paris and Romeo, her parents' choice and her own choice, have died, so she must leave "that nest / Of death, contagion, and unnatural sleep" (5.1.151-52). She refuses and seeing that Romeo is dead, quickly kisses him in hope that some poison remains on his lips. Her fear and revulsion at death, her wrestling with the paradox of love and hate, her fanciful imagery about her lover all give way. In four words, Shakespeare halts the play's rich rhetoric and by choosing a literal statement achieves what may be the most powerful moment of the entire play. Juliet simply says:[4]

> Thy lips are warm. (5.3.166)

---

The play's incessant, near-obsessive use of figurative language—paradox, metaphors, imagery—stops. Juliet kisses a corpse and observes that his lips are still warm. The flat declarative statement emphasizes how recently the character has lived, but the flatness also works. After the richness of the play's language, the contrasting plainness lends that simple statement poignancy. Romeo, the ever-active, ever-speechifying hero of the play is dead and cannot come again, although his death is so recent that his lips are still warm.

Juliet's suicide is hurried, and I find the lines that follow unsatisfying in every way. The adult characters come into the scene, trying to determine who is to blame or retelling and lamenting events. Their poetry is generally ineffective compared to that of the lovers, yet the play continues for almost 150 lines after Juliet's death. The contrast underscores what makes the play succeed for me—the wonderful language that Romeo and Juliet use, juxtaposed with the horrific *memento mori* images—and once they are silent in death, the talk that persists is irritating. The world of the play has lost its magically artificial language as Death unites both bridegroom and bride.

## Notes

1.  "Relatable" poses problems in any serious critique; see Rebecca Onion, "The Awful Emptiness of 'Relatable.'"

2.  On paradox in *Romeo and Juliet*, see Chang.

3.  Try reading the speech aloud. Neither I nor my students can resist speeding up and increasing our volume as we read, and I have taught this play for decades.

4.  I break here with the Arden edition, which ends the line with an exclamation point. Both the second quarto and the first folio end with a period since printers rarely used exclamation points in the English Renaissance.

## Works Cited

Baldung, Hans. *Der Tod und das Mädchen* (Kunsthistorisches Museum). Strasbourg, 1517. *The Yorck Project: 10.000 Meisterwerke der*

*Malerei.* DVD-ROM, 2002. DIRECTMEDIA Publishing GmbH. *Wikimedia Commons.* Accessed 12 Sept. 2016.

Behler, E. H. "Paradox." *The Princeton Encyclopedia of Poetry and Poetics*, edited by Roland Greene et al., Princeton UP, 2004, pp. 996-97.

Chang, Joseph S. "The Language of Paradox in *Romeo and Juliet.*" *Shakespeare Studies*, vol. 3, 1967, pp 22-42.

Fabergé, Carl. *Memory of Azov Egg*, (Kremlin Armoury Museum). Moscow, 1891. Photograph Stan Shebs (own work).*Wikimedia Commons.* Accessed 12 Sept. 2016.

Hankins, John. "Introduction." *The Pelican "Romeo and Juliet,"* edited by John Hankins, Penguin, 1978, pp.14-23.

Onion, Rebecca. "The Awful Emptiness of 'Relatable.'" *Slate.* The Slate Group Inc., 11 Apr. 2014, slate.com/blogs/lexicon_valley/2014/04/11/relatable_the_adjective_is_everywhere_in_high_scchool_and_college_discussions.html/. Accessed 9 Sept. 2017.

"Showcase 20. Panagias of the 18th-19th Centuries. Production of the Fabergé Firm." *Kremlin Armoury Chamber/Moscow Kremlin State Historical and Cultural Museum and Heritage Site*, 2017, armoury-chamber.kreml.ru/en-Us/exposure/view/vitrina-20-panagii-xviii_____xix-vekov-yuvelirnye-izdeliya-firmy-faberzhe/. Accessed 12 Sept. 2016.

Schwartz, Hans. *Death and the Maiden* (Bode-Museum). Augsburg, 1520. Photograph Till Niermann (own work). *Wikimedia Commons.* Accessed 12 Sept. 2016.

Shakespeare, William. *The Arden "King Lear,"* edited by R. A. Foakes, 3rd ed., Bloomsbury, 1997.

_____. *The Arden "Romeo and Juliet,"* edited by Brian Gibbons, Methuen, 1980.

_____. *Romeo and Juliet*, edited by Erin Sadlack, Internet Shakespeare Editions/University of Victoria, 19 Apr. 2013. Accessed 12 Sept. 2016.

# *Romeo and Juliet* on Film

Christopher Baker

My graduate school Shakespeare professor once related an experience he witnessed while returning home aboard a troopship after World War II. Weather permitting, films were shown on a screen at the ship's stern to entertain the soldiers during the long voyage. One evening, it was announced that the 1936 film of *Romeo and Juliet* would be shown. The GIs groaned with disapproval, but as the film went on, the crowd grew increasingly quiet and attentive. Finally, the film ended, the screen went dark, and for a moment, the audience was silent. Then from the back of the crowd came a voice: "Shakespeare, you son of a bitch!"[1] Just as he had done centuries earlier on the London stage, on that ship Shakespeare was able to reach out to an audience of persons from all walks of life, emotionally drawing them into an intense human tragedy. That most of the shipboard soldiers were themselves not much older than the characters they were watching must certainly have sharpened their reactions. It is fair to say that probably every author of a popular tragic love story since the play's first appearance has had at least a knowledge of, if not some direct debt to, this famed drama and its impact on audiences.[2]

Moviemakers since the turn of the twentieth century have also been quick to recognize that this play is both good drama and good box office; it is the most-filmed of all of Shakespeare's plays (Brodie 42). Beginning with the silent film era, this chapter offers an overview of the most critically significant films of the play (as distinct from films of staged theatrical productions). Just as Shakespeare himself adapted his drama from an earlier source (Arthur Brooke's 1562 poem *The Tragical History of Romeus and Juliet*, itself based on Pierre Boaistuau's 1559 French version of Matteo Bandello's 1554 Italian novella), each director melds the genres of stage and screen to produce a unique cinematic experience. Director Franco Zeffirelli sees the task of adaptation this way: "The only revolutionary claim any director can make is to have seen what no one has bothered to see since the author compiled the work" (qtd. Cartmell 216). Thus, as critic Harry Keyishian writes, "We need to ask of any 'Shakespeare film', what kind of *movie* is this?" (72). Each version is, as Kenneth Rothwell defined Zeffirelli's *Taming of the Shrew* (1967), "an imaginative filmic reconstruction of the play's essential concerns" (130). The versions of four directors in particular—George Cukor (1899–1983), Renato Castellani (1913–1985), Franco Zeffirelli (born 1923) and Baz Luhrmann (born 1962)—have gained the greatest popular and critical attention, but several other more recent productions will be noted later as well.

It has been said that playing *King Lear* is difficult because when an actor is old enough to fully grasp the part, he may not have the stamina to perform it, especially when he must carry Cordelia's dead body across the stage. A comparable director's task in *Romeo in Juliet* is to motivate young actors—especially one playing a Juliet not yet fourteen—to convey the onrush of adolescent passion and then rather quickly launch into the emotional depths of an inescapable tragedy. This challenge is increased by the screen's ability to magnify emotional intensity (or its absence) in extreme close-ups or intimate dialogues. If Barry O'Neill's 1911 film produced by the Thanhouser studio typifies the several silent versions of the play that appeared between 1908 and 1924, it is clear that the actors were twice the age of their characters. Julia M. Taylor with long, dark hair plays Juliet, and a paunchy George A. Lessey is Romeo; both were in their early thirties. This film is notable as one of the first two-reel films of a Shakespeare play; "it marked a new departure in advertising, foreshadowed a different system of distribution, and paved the way to a new tendency in production" (Ball 70). Only the second of the film's two reels survives (it is available on Youtube), running less than fourteen minutes and condensing the tragic portion of the play to its most action-packed and romantic scenes—the death of Tybalt, Juliet's rejection of Paris (Dave Andrada), Romeo's murder of Paris, and the lovers' final death scene, all rendered in the typically exaggerated gestures of the silent screen. Moviemakers could not assume that audiences would already know the story, and intertitles could only offer snippets of dialogue or summary. A reviewer in 1911 noted that "The Thanhouser adaptation is a work of skill and conscientious effort and makes the story very plain to every grade of intelligence, a merit which cannot be estimated too highly" (*Moving Picture World*). A bit of stage history lies in its casting of Mrs. George Walters as the Nurse, outfitted with a lace cap, fan, and cane, and walking with a stooped limp. Walters, born in 1835, had played opposite Sir Henry Irving on the English stage; she made a specialty of playing old ladies in silent films and died four years after this film was finished.

## George Cukor's 1936 Version

The challenge of casting older actors to play youthful parts is more apparent in George Cukor's 1936 version produced by Irving Thalberg for Metro-Goldwyn-Mayer. Thalberg's goal was to "make the production what Shakespeare would have wanted had he possessed the facilities of cinema" (qtd. Brodie 44). It offers the lavish spectacle of a would-be Hollywood blockbuster, presenting Shakespeare as middlebrow culture for the masses. The studio hired Professor William Strunk Jr. (who, in 1959, joined E. B. White to produce the popular writing handbook *The Elements of Style*) to ensure that the film would preserve a fidelity to Shakespeare's text. The play is presented with imagery connoting a classic aura: the opening credits unroll on a scroll, and the Chorus reads the Prologue from a scroll against a panoramic background styled as a Renaissance painting that is given a canvas-like texture. Of thirteen principal actors—"a veritable waxworks of British upper-class snobbery" (Rothwell 39)—only three were born in the twentieth century; the oldest, C. Aubrey Smith (Capulet) was seventy-six. Leslie Howard (Romeo) was forty-three, and Norma Shearer (Juliet) thirty-four. Thus, though the staging, costumes (requiring 38,000 yards of cloth [Rothwell 40]), and music are memorable, the film itself emerges as a bardic artifact from the past, a period piece arousing respect and reverence more than popular enthusiasm. As contemporary reviewer Otis Ferguson noted, "'Romeo and Juliet' must be accepted (and will be widely) as the framing of an old picture rather than the execution of a new one" (qtd. Willson 67). Thalberg (Shearer's husband at the time) evidently hoped that Depression-era audiences would want to escape into the Renaissance for "the two hours' traffic of our stage" (Prologue 12) as they had with Warner Brothers' popular version of *A Midsummer Night's Dream* the previous year, but his $2 million film lost nearly half of its production cost (Willson 65).

Howard and Shearer carry a "star quality" into their roles. Most, though not all, of Romeo's lines are delivered with an expressive authority stemming from Howard's stage experience. As Juliet warms to her new love, Shearer is often shot in extreme close-ups, gazing wistfully into the middle distance, her hair constantly backlit. Her light-colored, rhinestoned dancing gown and gauzy balcony peignoir are cleverly lit so as to virtually glow from within; in the opening scenes "with a beatific smile on her face, her portrait-like image throughout, she emerges as an icon representing a cross between Snow White and the goddess Diana" (Willson 60).[3] More disconcerting are the stylized movements of her hands (often raised, palms out, to express surprise or delight) that seem a holdover from her silent films (by 1928, Shearer had filmed forty-six silents). In the latter half of the film, her costumes become darker to match her tragic fate; her soliloquy at the end of act four, scene three, in an extreme close-up of her terrified face, is a passionate meditation on the *memento mori* theme.

Other cast members have a Dickensian individuality but remain largely one-dimensional. Basil Rathbone (Tybalt) bears a supercilious grudge against practically everyone, while Edna Mae Oliver as the zanily squinting, cackling Nurse anticipates Margaret Hamilton's Wicked Witch of the West from *The Wizard of Oz* three years later. As Mercutio, John Barrymore is a belching, low-comic raconteur whom the other characters seem to endure as much as enjoy. But his Queen Mab speech bubbles with energy, and his single earring mimics the famed Chandos portrait of Shakespeare.[4] When he offers a jug of wine up to a balcony of simpering, portly prostitutes, we are treated to a bawdy burlesque of the lovers' own balcony scene. The dueling scenes of Romeo, Tybalt, Mercutio, and Paris are suitably swashbuckling, but the opening clash between the Montagues and Capulets—dozens of young men wearing improbably ornate, immaculate costumes—resembles a brawl among angry bellboys. Cukor's production was energetic, expensive, and sincerely respectful of the play as a monument of the theatre, but the film remains very much of its own era.[5]

## Renato Castellani's 1954 Version

In 1954, Renato Castellani directed Laurence Harvey, a familiar English movie star, and the nineteen-year-old Susan Shentall, an untrained actress who never appeared in another film, in a version proclaiming that, despite its English author, this was assuredly an *Italian* story. Though produced in cooperation with the English Pinewood Studios, the film was shot in ten different Italian cities, including Verona, Siena, Florence, and Venice using period buildings and Renaissance streets to create a realistic *mise-en-scène*. Castellani cut over 60 percent of Shakespeare's text (such as the apothecary's part and Mercutio's Queen Mab speech) and added new details "to portray Renaissance Verona, its rigid class system, Roman Catholicism, and feuding families" (Tatspaugh 138-39). Rothwell credits Castellani's version with having "inaugurated the vogue for 'authentic' Renaissance settings in Shakespeare movies and teleplays" (125). This film's strong evocation of Italian culture would later influence Zeffirelli, but Castellani's decision to replace much of Shakespeare's text with vivid images of buildings and costumes (shot in the heavily-saturated hues of Technicolor, especially a deep, Titian red for the Capulet's ball) means that the film's *visual* text challenges its *poetic* text in importance, as it later would much more strongly in Baz Luhrmann's media-rich version.[6] In the balcony scene, Castellani (who had studied architecture) frames Juliet within huge Moorish arches suggesting Capulet power and makes liberal use of contemporary paintings to fashion his shots, combining the stylistic features of Vermeer, Filippo Lippi, Pisanello, and Lorenzo Monaco (Brodie 49). The boy choir at the dance resembles a group of angelic *putti*, and indoor scenes are recognizably painterly. Shentall—whom Castellini chose for her lustrous skin and blonde hair—often seems to be posing within a frame rather than acting; as she prepares to drink the sedative (4.3), she is even filmed from the back so that her intricate, golden braids take our attention instead of her face.

Although Laurence Harvey's acting rises above Shentall's indifferent performance, he speaks affectedly in what Maurice Hindle calls a "fruity diction" (35), confirming Romeo's complaint that Juliet's beauty "hath made me effeminate" (3.1.114).[7] His fighting scenes are brief rather than athletic; he kills Tybalt with a single stab and later brains Paris with a large candlestick, then uses it to pry open Juliet's tomb. In the supporting cast, Sebastian Cabot is an imposing Capulet. His scene-chewing condemnation of Juliet in 3.5 recalls Lear's rage at Cordelia but from someone of Falstaffian girth. Flora Robson's garrulous Nurse rejects Edna Mae Oliver's slapstick, becoming a comforting confidante of Juliet, still enjoying ribald innuendo but more of an intimate Emilia to Juliet's Desdemona. Mervyn Johns plays Friar Laurence as a cartoonish, slow-minded gardener, pottering among his plants and distractedly puzzled that his plan has gone awry.

At one point, however, Castellini uses the Friar to inject yet more Italian culture into Shakespeare's text. When another monk warns him against speaking to Juliet, Laurence gently chides him saying, "*Omnia munda mundis*"—"to the pure, all things are pure." This biblical statement (Titus 1.15) appears in a similar context in Alessandro Manzoni's 1827 *I Promessi Sposi* (*The Betrothed*), the most popular Italian historical novel, which, like the play, also includes a young couple that desires to marry against the wishes of powerful opponents. Castellani's allusion echoes his membership in the early 1940s in a group of Italian directors, the "calligraphers," who scorned fascistic propagandistic themes by instead basing their films on nineteenth-century literary works.[8] Pierre Leprohon comments that "All his later films were in fact concerned with very young heroes still imbued with all the ingenuousness and sincerity—sometimes the selfishness and cruelty—of childhood," and Andre Bazin notes that his film "*Two Pennyworth of Hope* is *Romeo and Juliet* on the dole" (qtd. Leprohon 124).

## Franco Zeffirelli's 1968 Version

Fourteen years after Castellani's production, Franco Zeffirelli completed what can still be regarded as the best traditionally Shakespearean film of the play to date. Zeffirelli avoids Cukor's error of casting too-old actors by choosing relative unknowns Leonard Whiting and Olivia Hussey (seventeen and sixteen, respectively) for the leads. Following Castellani, he uses Italian locations and rich costuming but in far more natural color. Nino Rota's musical score adds the title theme "What is a Youth?," a cloying ballad that became a popular song in its own right. Laurence Olivier (who had originally been offered the role of Romeo in Cukor's version) spoke the Prologue offscreen as well as various other crowd voices. Zeffirelli had produced this play on the London stage, so audiences eagerly awaited its film version; with a modest original studio budget of $800,000, the movie would eventually reap $48 million in profits. Zeffirelli also pares down the text as Castellani had (speeches are shortened, the apothecary scene and Paris' death are cut) but his quicker pacing and visual symbols combined with a more realistic acting style create a brisker cinematic experience. The film benefits from the "use of gesture, of looking, of touching, and of using music and the choreography of bodily movement" (Hindle 173).

Zeffirelli was fortunate in his two leading actors. Whiting is attractive, agile, and emotive in his role, without falling back on the stiffly theatrical postures of previous Romeos. Hussey is even better, in the first half conveying moods of the romantic young girl as well as the coy mistress with a natural beauty that sidesteps the contrived glamour of a Hollywood matinee idol. The film aroused comment by showing Romeo's bare buttocks in Juliet's bedroom after their night of love. Although Brooke in his 1563 poem had written of the "unfortunate lovers . . . attempting all adventures of peril for the attaining of their wished lust" (qtd. Wells 149), Zeffirelli's inclusion of nakedness here manages to be erotic without being prurient.[9] The most impressive supporting roles belong to Peter McEnery (Mercutio), Pat Heywood (the Nurse) and Milo O'Shea (Friar Laurence). McEnery is engaging as an actor playing an actor without falling into self-parody like Barrymore. He has fun with his lines, even when speaking them while neck-deep in a fountain. His role is complicated with a darker, more introspective side, creating a "powerful manic depressive" (Rothwell 137). Heywood believably steers a middle course between Edna Mae Oliver's caricature and Flora Robson's amiable compatriot. With a genuine affection for Juliet, she almost seems to believe she could become a Capulet herself but for her crooked teeth, Cockney accent, and shameless guzzling of wine. Unlike Mervyn Leroy's befuddled friar, Milo O'Shea plays a quick-witted and resourceful cleric, but his air of confident control dissolves when he discovers Romeo's body; at the sound of the approaching watchman, he abandons Juliet and flees into the night, screaming "I dare no longer stay" (5.3.159). Zeffirelli's sixties film was "particularly intended to attract the counter-culture youth, a generation of young people, like Romeo and Juliet, estranged from their parents, torn by the conflict between their youthful cult of passion and the military traditions of their elders" (Sarah Munson Deats qtd. in Tatspaugh 140). For its sense of color, movement, music, and sheer vitality, it will continue to interest audiences.[10]

## Baz Luhrmann's 1996 Version

Despite their various differences, each of the previous three productions strove to *look* and *sound* Shakespearean in costuming, props, set design, and music. Well-read audiences and scholars would have little problem situating each film within a literary and historical context based on the influence of such cultural pillars as Dante, Petrarch, the Bible, the sonnet tradition, and early modern treatises on providence and fate. This would change in 1996 when Australian director Baz Luhrmann released *William Shakespeare's Romeo + Juliet*, "far and away the most profitable and popular Shakespeare film produced in the last 30 years" (Cartelli and Rowe 10). Luhrmann shifted the play's imaginative framework from historic texts to contemporary cultural images, from the Good Book to the comic book. Often termed a "postmodern" production, this is more precisely a post-textual production in which the visual images of the movie overtake the verbal text of the play itself. The film is relocated from a pre-Enlightenment locale to a hip, technological metropolis: televised news, gaudy Hawaiian shirts, skimpy bikinis, chrome pistols, outlandish cross-dressing costumes, hovering police helicopters, and glitzy customized cars all compete for our attention in a directorial style of rapidly shifting camera shots. Although the location in "Sycamore Grove" recalls Romeo's languishing in a "sycamore [sick-*amour*] grove" (1.1.121), the crumbling theatre proscenium on the beach suggests that our ideas of a historic theatre have been supplanted by the electronic screen; the film's references and allusions are no longer anchored in the Elizabethan page and stage but rather in the wired world of pop culture. Audiences of Cukor's film were taken into the past to reverentially experience the power of great literature, while Zeffirelli's and Castellani's viewers were transported to a sensuous Italian milieu. For Luhrmann's spectators, however, there is almost no cultural gap to be crossed apart from the play's language.

Leonardo DiCaprio (Romeo) and Claire Danes (Juliet) are near-teens themselves playing the perennial lovers, creating what Ariane Balizet calls a "Shakespeare teenpic" (124). The opening fight between the Montagues (an Anglo family) and the Capulets (Latinos) is worthy of Quentin Tarentino at his violent best, and the soundtrack mingles church choirs, police sirens, hard rock, beeping pagers, and squealing tires. In the view of critic Janet Maslin, this was "a classic play thrown in the path of a subway train." For Luhrmann, Shakespeare was a dramatist who was remarkably like the director himself:

> He was a rambunctious, sexy, violent, entertaining storyteller. We're trying to make this movie rambunctious, sexy, violent and entertaining the way Shakespeare might have if he had been a filmmaker. . . . Everything that's in the movie is drawn from Shakespeare's play. Violence, murder, lust, love, poison, drugs that mimic death, it's all there. (Luhrmann qtd. in Modenessi 67-68)

Though Romeo and Juliet live *in* this world, they are not *of* it; seen at the ball, Juliet's costume wings mark her as an angel on earth, while Romeo's chivalric armor suggests him as the knight in pursuit of an ideal courtly lady. Frequent shots of them in, near, or through water (such as Juliet's courtyard pool or her aquarium) imply their liminal position between the earthly corruption around them and the spirituality of their love. Luhrman's MTV-like camera work bombards the audience with rapid cuts, pans, slam zooms, and visual juxtapositions, all in eye-poppingly vivid colors. Critics have noted how saturated this film is with religious imagery, especially crosses, as if the seamy, raucous culture of Los Angeles or Miami Beach has reduced traditional values to mere signs without meaning. Yet their persistent presence implies, even in this materialistic society, a divine dimension to which—unlike those around them—Romeo and Juliet alone finally gain access through their love and death.

In casting two young heart-throbs in the leading roles, Luhrmann is relying on the allure of star-power to express his idiosyncratic conception. Danes (fifteen at the time) is calf-eyed and enraptured with Romeo, while DiCaprio (twenty-four but looking younger) is both Shakespeare's hero and a James Dean-like angry young man. Luhrmann impishly slips in cinematic allusions; when, on the barren plain of Mantua, Romeo agonizingly screams "Juliet! Juliet!" we recall Marlon Brando shouting "Stella! Stella!" in the 1951 film of Tennessee Williams' *A Streetcar Named Desire*. Other characters seemed modeled on film stereotypes: Paul Sorvino's Capulet is a boorish Mafia don; Mercutio (Harold Perrineau) is a black, gyrating transvestite; and Paris (Paul Rudd) a feckless preppy. Shakespeare's language is not always delivered with the precision it deserves, but Pete Postlethwaite, playing Friar Laurence like an aging biker with a large cross tattooed on his back, speaks with clarity and vigor. John Leguizamo's tightly-wound, paranoid Tybalt is eager to empty his pistol into the first Montague he sees. Most of the cast speak with little sense of poetic pacing, instead allowing the energetic camerawork to become its own visual language. But if we resist the urge to compare Luhrmann's film too closely with Shakespeare's play and instead see it as a work that is of, by, and for the cinema, it gains a provocative identity that leads us, in an ironically postmodern way, to appreciate anew the meaning of a Shakespearean "adaptation."[11]

## Other Versions

Other, less influential, productions have appeared since the 1960s. Joan Kemp-Welsh directed the play in a 1976 Thames television production starring Ann Hasson and Christopher Neame. Hasson, in her mid-twenties, manages well the transition from a girlish ingénue to a terrified woman facing the prospect of death, her soliloquy in 4.3 delivered almost as a single, long shriek. Neame's Romeo is at first a dreamy, too-precious lover, but after Tybalt's death he soon conveys a deeper tragic awareness. When he screams at Friar Laurence, "Thou canst not speak of what thou dost not feel" (3.3.64), we feel real rage destroying his former Petrarchan prettiness. Patsy Byrne is a satisfyingly rambunctious, blowsy nurse, and Robin Nedwell's Mercutio is a quick-witted yet physically agile and combative sidekick to Romeo. His duels with Tybalt (David Robb) gain dramatic intensity from the direction of William Hobbs, who forty years later would choreograph the fight scenes in *Game of Thrones*. Clive Swift as Friar Laurence shows a genuine, meditative concern for the young lovers and guilty frustration when his plans go tragically wrong. Despite its lack of immediately recognizable stars, this unpretentious production still effectively delivers the play's emotional range.

As part of the BBC series of Shakespeare's plays, Alvin Rakoff directed *Romeo and Juliet* two years later in what has been generally judged to be one of its least effective presentations. The problem of age versus skill again plagued the casting of the principal roles. Rebecca Saire, only fifteen at the time, captured Juliet's youthful innocence but her waif-like temperament carries on for too long into the tragic second half, where she seems to be merely speaking her lines instead of acting them.[12] More convincing is older Patrick Ryecart's Romeo, who is emotionally dynamic even in his briefest speeches. Anthony Andrews presents Mercutio as a wise-cracking showoff full of frantic posturing that recalls Barrymore, and, in his first screen role, Alan Rickman displays in Tybalt the trademark sneer that would mark his part as Severus Snape in the Harry Potter films twenty-five years later.

Carlo Carlei directed Hailee Steinfeld and Douglas Booth in his production on location in Verona in 2013. Shot in high-definition digital format, the film looks even more sumptuous than Zeffirelli's; interior scenes are painstakingly filled with opulent furniture, paintings, and period props. Carlei follows Cukor and Zeffirelli in seeking to bring Shakespeare to a popular audience through a rich visual tapestry; he exploits Italian locales as did Castellani and Zeffirelli; and like Zeffirelli and Luhrmann he uses young actors and visual symbolism: the row of glowing blue crosses in Juliet's tomb at the close of *Romeo + Juliet* he reimagines as a double row of flaming torches within the blue-frescoed grotto where the dead lovers lie.

Unfortunately, the performances of the two young actors fail to match the grandeur of their surroundings. Though under twenty, neither has the skills to command Shakespeare's diction, and the balcony scene is uncomfortably chatty rather than soaringly poetic, owing as well to the maladroit screenplay by Julian Fellowes (of *Downton Abbey* fame). It is standard practice to shorten the play text for films, but Fellowes not only cuts but rewrites and even adds his own faux-Shakespearean lines to this adaptation. In an interview included with the film's DVD version, he explains that the play "needed to be accessed for a new generation and made simpler in a way but also more straightforward" so that audiences are "never puzzled." The result is a script sprinkled with creaking lines typical of a pulp romance. Friar Laurence, hoping that the lovers have not slept together before marriage, tells Romeo, "I pray you were not playing Satan's game!" and Capulet barks at his wife, "Do you want legal offspring from our loins?" As Juliet kisses Romeo for the last time, her original line—"Thy lips are warm" (5.3.167)—is flattened into "Your mouth is warm." When Fellowes has Romeo ask Benvolio, "Is something here amiss?" we know the answer.

Hailee Steinfeld is eagerly romantic but lacks the emotional variety and verve of Olivia Hussey. Douglas Booth, reprising Leonardo DiCaprio as a teen idol, has the tousled hair and chiseled face of a male model (critic Susan Wloszczyna says of him, "Romeo should never be prettier than Juliet"), and he is inexplicably portrayed as an artist, first seen carving a block of stone, later sketching in a studio. The more experienced actors shine by comparison. Damian Lewis (Capulet) outdoes Sebastian Cabot in his rage at Juliet, hurling her to her bed with his face as red as his hair. Leslie Manville plays the Nurse as a flustered, worried nanny but with few of the role's comic elements. Paul Giammatti is effective as a gruff, irascible Friar Laurence, eager to dispense advice to the lovers and performing an extended Latin marriage for them but finally reduced to tears on seeing their dead bodies.

Luhrmann's extravagantly visual and intercultural version of the play, as well as various interracial theatre productions, are evidence that future film adaptations will be limited only by the creativity of new directors.[13] Of course, not all reconceptions are created equal; neither the fantasy cartoon *Gnomeo and Juliet* (2001) nor the gratuitously sexual, cult mash-up *Tromeo and Juliet* (1997) qualifies as a legitimate attempt to capture the spirit of the original text. But even these testify to the play's stature as a classic, a work that, as Italo Calvino has defined it, "has never exhausted all it has to say to its readers" (5). Ben Jonson famously wrote in his dedicatory poem to the First Folio edition of Shakespeare's plays (1623) that the dramatist was "not of an age, but for all time" (43), and we should expect fresh film adaptations to offer new opportunities for this classic tragedy to continue to speak to future audiences.

## Notes

1.  The professor was the late Peter G. Phialas of the University of North Carolina at Chapel Hill.

2.  For example, when Zora Neale Hurston near the end of her novel *Their Eyes Were Watching God* (1937) asks, "Who was it didn't know about the love between Tea Cake and Janie?" (185), we hear a not-too-distant echo of the play's final couplet: "Never was a story of more woe / Than this of Juliet and her Romeo" (5.3.309-10).

3.  Our first glimpse of Juliet is of her feeding a tame deer in a wooded grove. The deer wears a jeweled necklace, prompting us to wonder if Cukor (or Strunk) is reaching back to Sir Thomas Wyatt's Henrician poem "Whoso list to hunt" for an image of forbidden love.

4.  See the Chandos portrait at the National Portrait Gallery website: www.npg.org.uk/collections/search/portrait/mw11574/William-Shakespeare/.

5.  Gary Cary's judgement is more severe: "Hollywood has rarely seen such an elaborate production—done without any imagination or taste" (58).

6.  Stephen Buhler notes that Castellani "suggests that the film might bring audiences closer to Shakespeare than even his words can" (77).

7.  Terrence Pettigrew wrote that Harvey "mouths his words like a carpet salesman" (82).

8.  Castellani's first film, *Un colpo di pistol* (*A Pistol Shot*) was based on the Pushkin story, "A Shot." On Castellani and the "calligraphers" see Armes (38-40) and Leprohon (76-78 and 120-24).

9.  For more on sexuality in the play and later adaptations, see Wells, chapter 6; Kidnie; and Burt.

10. On Zeffirelli's production, see also Hapgood; chapter 5 of Jorgens; and Pilkington.

11. Luhrmann's cinematic style is discussed by Anderegg, Loehlin, and chapter 8 of Crowl.

12. Willson notes that "the actress used her press interviews to attack the director's treatment of her and his interpretation of Juliet's role as too childlike and asexual" (16).

13. Two recent interracial theatrical productions, both available on DVD, are David Leveaux's version with a white Romeo (Orlando Bloom) and a black Juliet (Condola Rashad), and Dominic Dromgoole's production with a black Romeo (Adetomiwa Edun) and a white Juliet (Ellie Kendrick).

## Works Cited

Anderegg, Michael. "James Dean Meets the Pirate's Daughter: Passion and Parody in *William Shakespeare's Romeo + Juliet* and *Shakespeare in Love*." *Shakespeare, The Movie, II: Popularizing the Plays on Film, TV, Video, and DVD*, edited by Richard Burt and Lynda E. Boose, Routledge, 2003, pp. 56-72.

Armes, Roy. *Patterns of Realism*. Barnes and Company, 1971.

Balizet, Ariane M. "Teen Scenes: Recognizing Shakespeare in Teen Film." *Almost Shakespeare: Reinventing His Works for Cinema and Television*, edited by James R. Keller and Leslie Stratyner, McFarland, 2004, pp. 122-36.

Ball, Robert Hamilton. *Shakespeare on Silent Film*. Theatre Arts Books, 1968.

Boose, Lynda E., and Richard Burt. *Shakespeare, the Movie: Popularizing the Plays on Film, TV, and Video*. Routledge, 1997.

Brodie, Douglas. *Shakespeare in the Movies*. Oxford UP, 2000.

Buhler, Stephen M. *Shakespeare in the Cinema: Ocular Proof*. State U of New York P, 2002.

Burnett, Mark Thornton, and Ramona Wray, editors. *Shakespeare, Film, Fin de Siècle*. Macmillan, 2000.

Burt, Richard. "The Love That Dare Not Speak Shakespeare's Name: New Shakesqueer Cinema." Boose and Burt, pp. 240-68.

Calvino, Italo. *Why Read the Classics?* Vintage, 2001.

Cartelli, Thomas, and Katherine Rowe. *New Wave Shakespeare on Screen*. Polity Press, 2007.

Cartmell, Deborah. "Franco Zeffirelli and Shakespeare." *The Cambridge Companion to Shakespeare on Film*, edited by Russell Jackson, Cambridge UP, 2000, pp. 212-21.

Cary, Gary. *Cukor & Co.: The Films of George Cukor and His Collaborators*. The Museum of Modern Art, 1971.

Crowl, Samuel. *Shakespeare at the Cineplex*. Ohio UP, 2003.

Hapgood, Robert. "Popularizing Shakespeare: The Artistry of Franco Zeffirelli." in Boose and Burt, pp. 80-94

Hindle, Maurice. *Studying Shakespeare on Film*. Palgrave Macmillan, 2007.

Jorgens, Jack. *Shakespeare on Film*. Indiana UP, 1977.

Keyishian, Harry. "Shakespeare and the Movie Genre: The Case of *Hamlet*." *The Cambridge Companion to Shakespeare on Film*, edited by Russell Jackson, Cambridge UP, 2000, pp. 72-84.

Kidnie, Margaret Jane. "'The Way the World is Now': Love in the Troma Zone." Burnett and Wray, pp. 102-20.

Leprohon, Pierre. *The Italian Cinema*. Secker & Warburg, 1972.

Loehlin, James N. "'These Violent Delights Have Violent Ends': Baz Luhrmann's Millenial Shakespeare." Burnett and Wray, pp. 121-36.

Maslin, Janet. "Soft! What Light? It's Flash, Romeo." *New York Times*, November 1, 1996, p. B1.

Modenessi, Alfredo Michel. "(Un)Doing the Book 'without Verona walls': A View from the Receiving End of Baz Luhrmann's *William Shakespeare's Romeo + Juliet." Spectacular Shakespeare: Critical Theory and Popular Cinema*, edited by Courtney Lehmann and Lisa S. Starks, Fairleigh Dickinson UP, 2002, pp. 62-85.

*The Motion Picture World*, August 19, 1911, p. 446.

Pettigrew, Terrence. *British Film Character Actors: Great Names and Memorable Moments*. Barnes and Noble, 1982.

Pilkington, Ace G. "Zeffirelli's Shakespeare." *Shakespeare and the Moving Image: The Plays on Film and Television*, edited by Anthony Davis and Stanley Wells, Cambridge UP, 1994, pp. 163-79.

Rothwell, Kenneth. *A History of Shakespeare on Screen: A Century of Film and Television*. Cambridge UP, 1999.

Shakespeare, William. *Romeo and Juliet. The Riverside Shakespeare*, edited by G. Blakemore Evans, 2nd ed., Houghton Mifflin, 1997.

Tatspaugh, Patricia. "The Tragedies of Love on Film." *The Cambridge Companion to Shakespeare on Film*, edited by Russell Jackson, Cambridge UP, 2000, pp. 135-59.

Wells, Stanley. *Shakespeare, Sex & Love*. Oxford UP, 2010.

Willson, Robert F., Jr., *Shakespeare in Hollywood, 1929–1956*. Fairleigh Dickinson UP, 2000.

Wloszczyna, Susan. "Romeo and Juliet." *RogerEbert.com*, 11 Oct. 2013. www.rogerebert.com/reviews/romeo-and-juliet-2013/. Accessed 22 Feb. 2017.

# Soliloquies in *Romeo and Juliet*: An Empirical Approach

James Hirsh

## Introduction

In analyzing soliloquies in *Romeo and Juliet*, I have made use of evidence I uncovered in the course of my long-term investigation into the history of soliloquies in Western drama. At the outset of the project, I decided to conduct a systematic, empirical survey and analysis of passages in plays from throughout Western theatrical history that share the following specific characteristic:

> *that the character portrayed by the actor who speaks the passage does not direct the passage at the hearing of any other character.*

I selected this type of passage to investigate in order to leave the following questions to be answered by a systematic survey of *evidence* rather than by an a-priori fiat:

> One, does a given soliloquy represent an interior monologue, that is, unspoken thoughts passing through the mind of the character, or does it represent the spoken words of the character?
>
> Two, if a given soliloquy represents the spoken words of the character, does it represent a self-addressed speech, or does it represent a speech knowingly addressed by the character to playgoers?

In the course of my investigation, I found plentiful, varied, conspicuous, unambiguous, and overwhelmingly one-sided evidence that provides surprisingly clear-cut answers to each of those questions and that led to other, sometimes surprising, results.[1] Among the many findings of my investigation are the following:

1. that conventions governing soliloquies are not trans-historical or universal (they have varied significantly from age to age; conventions governing soliloquies have a history);

2. that, over the course of Western theatrical history, there have been three kinds of soliloquies (audience-addressed speeches, self-addressed speeches, and interior monologues);

3. that from ancient times until the middle of the seventeenth century, soliloquies represented speeches by characters, not their unspoken thoughts;

4. that in England, conventions governing soliloquies underwent a profound change in the late 1580s and early 1590s, and the new conventions remained in place until the closing of the London theaters in 1642;

5. that during this period, soliloquies by characters engaged in the action represented self-addressed speeches as a matter of convention;

6. that the dramatists most responsible for the establishment of this new convention in no uncertain terms were Thomas Kyd, Christopher Marlowe, and Shakespeare;

7. that the convention of self-addressed speech was employed ubiquitously in plays of all genres and is one of the most distinctive hallmarks of late Renaissance drama;

8. that a large set of surprisingly precise subsidiary conventions arose that governed soliloquies in eavesdropping situations;

9. that these subsidiary conventions were actively maintained (they were employed pervasively and conspicuously in plays of all genres);

10. that these conventions were rarely if ever overridden by major dramatists of the period;

11. that, rather than adhering to the complex conventions in a reluctant or perfunctory fashion, major dramatists actively competed with one another to employ the conventions in novel, complex, and subtle ways;

12. that the hands-down winner of this competition was Shakespeare;

13. that these conventions were not revived after the eighteen-year hiatus in London theatrical activity from 1642 to 1660;

14. that since the late seventeenth century, a collection of demonstrably false notions about soliloquies in Shakespeare's plays arose and became deeply embedded in theatrical and scholarly traditions.

In late Renaissance drama, conventions governing soliloquies intersected with those governing asides. In the course of my investigation, I also located passages with the following key characteristic:

> *that the character guards the speech from the hearing of at least one other character.*

Some asides are directed at the hearing of one or more other characters onstage; they are shared asides. But some asides are *not directed at the hearing of any other character*. These asides thus possess the characteristic of a soliloquy specified above. The two kinds of passages were overlapping rather than mutually exclusive categories; characters frequently guard soliloquies in asides from the hearing of all the other characters of whose presence they are aware. Like any other skill, guarding a soliloquy required active attention. If a character became so preoccupied by what she was saying to herself that she became oblivious of the presence of others, those characters would begin to hear the speech or bits of it. According to another nuance of the convention, a character could *not* guard a soliloquy from the hearing of another character *unless* the speaker was specifically aware of the presence of the other character.

*Romeo and Juliet* marked a major watershed in Shakespeare's employment of the late Renaissance dramatic convention of self-addressed speech. Plentiful evidence demonstrates that, in the process of writing *Romeo and Juliet*, Shakespeare, like the two main characters, fell madly in love. In his case, what he fell in love with were the exciting dramatic possibilities created by the convention governing soliloquies that he himself had helped to establish.

## Soliloquies as the Representation of the Spoken Words of Characters

The most conspicuous kind of evidence demonstrating that soliloquies represented the spoken words of characters as a matter of convention rather than their unspoken thoughts is that, whenever an eavesdropper is present, he overhears the soliloquy of a character who is unaware of the presence of the eavesdropper. This occurs with astonishing frequency in Shakespeare's plays of all genres from early in his career to the end (see Hirsh, *History* chapter 5). *Romeo and Juliet* contains a remarkable total of ten instances in which a soliloquy is overheard or partially overheard by one or more other characters—more instances of this type than in any earlier play by Shakespeare—and it contains *the* example that immediately springs to mind when the topic of overheard soliloquies is raised.

The scene in which Romeo and Juliet fall in love contains three partially overheard soliloquies. (1) When Romeo first sees Juliet at the Capulet feast, he describes her beauty in a speech that he does not direct at the hearing of any other character (1.5.44-53) and that therefore possesses the key characteristic of a soliloquy. Romeo initially guards the speech in an aside from the hearing of other characters. But at some point, he becomes so intensely focused on Juliet's beauty that he becomes oblivious of the presence of others and ceases to guard his soliloquy adequately. Tybalt overhears enough of what Romeo says to recognize his voice: "This, by his voice, should be a Montague" (54). (2) Except for a command to a servant, Tybalt's own response, like Romeo's preceding speech, is not directed at the hearing of any other character and so constitutes a soliloquy. Like Romeo, Tybalt is so overwhelmed by emotion—in his case, rage at the presence of a Montague—that he, too, fails to guard his own speech adequately. As a result, Tybalt's soliloquy, like Romeo's, is partially overheard by another character, in this case by Lord Capulet who questions him: "Why, how now, kinsman, wherefore storm you so?" (60). (3) Still later in the same scene, the Nurse partially overhears Juliet's soliloquy, which Juliet fails to guard adequately because she is stunned by the news that the man with whom she has just fallen in love is a Montague.

Nurse:  His name is Romeo, and a Montague,
        The only son of your great enemy.
Juliet: My only love sprung from my only hate!
        Too early seen unknown, and known too late!
        Prodigious birth of love it is to me
        That I must love a loathed enemy.

| Nurse: | What's tis? what's tis? |
|---|---|
| Juliet: | A rhyme I learnt even now |
| | Of one I danced withal. (136-43) |

After unintentionally allowing the Nurse to overhear a fragment of her soliloquy, Juliet tries to explain it away.

In the balcony episode, once Juliet finds out that Romeo has overheard her soliloquies, she cannot play hard-to-get, as she explains in some detail. For example,

I should have been more strange, I must confess,
But that thou overheardst, ere I was ware,
My true love passion. (2.2.102-04)

As a direct result of the contingency that Romeo overheard Juliet's soliloquies, the relationship between them becomes one of mutuality and equality. The episode dramatized a compelling alternative to the conventional, hierarchical model of courtship in which a woman was expected to play hard-to-get and the man posed as her servant. This milestone in the history of love was brought about by an overheard soliloquy.

The next scene (2.3) begins with the entrance of Friar Laurence, who proceeds to speak at length. In the most substantial quarto of the play (Q2) and in the 1623 Folio, a stage direction "*Enter Romeo*" occurs in the middle of the speech. Most entrances and exits in surviving play-texts of the period are located between speeches. It is unlikely that a compositor would have inserted this entrance into the middle of a speech unless the copy-text located the entrance at that point. Romeo listens to eight lines of the Friar's speech before making his presence known. Romeo does not explicitly comment on the Friar's speech in a soliloquy of his own guarded from the Friar's hearing. But alert late Renaissance playgoers would have been in no doubt that Romeo overhears the part of the Friar's soliloquy spoken after Romeo's entrance. This episode immediately follows the scene in which Romeo conspicuously and memorably overheard soliloquies by Juliet. That Romeo overhears part of the Friar's soliloquy sets up a dramatic irony. In the passage spoken after the entrance of Romeo, the Friar speaks about "Poison" (24), and later in the play, Romeo, implicitly influenced by the overheard soliloquy of his spiritual adviser, chooses poison to end his life. It is also noteworthy that within the course of two consecutive scenes, Romeo violates the privacy of two loved ones. By depicting Romeo as a serial eavesdropper, Shakespeare dramatizes that even an otherwise admirable person might succumb to the temptation to listen in on another person's self-addressed speech, a violation of privacy analogous to voyeurism. Regular late Renaissance playgoers themselves were serial eavesdroppers on a grand scale. They eavesdropped on the self-addressed speeches of countless characters.

The final scene of the play (5.3) contains a series of overheard soliloquies. The scene opens with the entrance of Paris and his page. Paris commands his page to "stand aloof" (line 1) to serve as a lookout. The page must remain onstage because he speaks and exits at line 71. At line 17, the page whistles to alert Paris that others are approaching. In a soliloquy guarded in an aside from his servant and the entering characters, Paris decides to take up a position in order to eavesdrop: "Muffle me, night, a while" (21). The entering characters are Romeo and his servant Balthasar. Romeo gives Balthasar instructions and sends him away. Believing he is alone, Romeo speaks to himself. Trained by memorable episodes in earlier plays and by memorable episodes earlier in *this* play to understand the conventions that governed soliloquies, asides, and eavesdropping, regular playgoers would have understood that anything said by the two entering characters, including their soliloquies, would be overheard as a matter of course by the eavesdropping characters. Ignorant of the fact that Romeo is the beloved husband of Juliet, Paris tragically fails to understand Romeo's soliloquy and presumes that this Montague plans to desecrate the Capulet tomb. The episode dramatizes a profound epistemological issue: even if one had the opportunity to eavesdrop on another person's self-addressed speech, one might not understand the significance of what one was hearing if one lacked crucial contextual information.

Paris and his page are not the only characters to overhear Romeo's soliloquy, nor is Romeo the only character whose soliloquy is overheard. Balthasar disobeyed his master's command to leave. In the course of a soliloquy guarded in an aside from his master, Balthasar gave voice to his decision to take up a hiding place from which to eavesdrop on his master:

> For all this same, I'll hide me hereabout,
> His looks I fear, and his intents I doubt. (43-44)

There are now three eavesdroppers onstage in three separate locations. According to the same familiar convention by which Paris and his page overhear Romeo's soliloquy, Balthasar implicitly overhears it as well. Romeo's soliloquy confirms Balthasar's worst fear. Romeo gives voice to his resolve to commit suicide.[2] Balthasar does not intervene, however, presumably because Romeo had threatened him with death if he did so: "I will tear thee joint by joint" (35). The episode contains concentric circles of eavesdroppers: Balthasar eavesdrops on Romeo; Paris and Paris's page eavesdrop on both Romeo and Balthasar.[3]

After Paris challenges Romeo and they begin to fight, the page exits the stage to get help. After Romeo kills Paris, he speaks to himself at length, still unaware of the continuing presence of Balthasar. When questioned by Friar Laurence later in the scene, Balthasar says,

> As I did sleep under this yew tree here,
> I dreamt my master and another fought,
> And that my master slew him. (137-39)

Balthasar is obviously lying about having fallen asleep. He took up a hiding place in order to eavesdrop on his beloved master because he was worried that his master intended to commit suicide. Immediately following the soliloquy guarded in an aside from Romeo in which Balthasar expresses that fear, he overhears Romeo formulate just such an intention. Immediately after that shocking speech, Paris steps forward and threatens the life of Balthasar's master; the two men fight; Romeo mortally wounds Paris; Romeo speaks at length about his intention to kill himself, drinks poison, and dies. It is not credible that Balthasar dozed off at any point in this sequence. The obvious reason that he lies to Friar Laurence is that he is ashamed that he did not intervene to prevent his beloved master from killing himself. He is ashamed even though the reason he did not intervene was that his master threatened his life if he did so. The poignancy of the death of Romeo is compounded by the poignancy of Balthasar's helplessness and shame.

In *Romeo and Juliet*, Shakespeare also carried to a new level the device by which a character guards a soliloquy from the hearing of at least one other character in an aside. Seven different characters—Romeo (1.5), Tybalt (1.5), Juliet (1.5, 3.2, 3.5), the Friar (4.1), Paris's page (5.3), Paris (5.3), and Balthasar (5.3)— guard, at least initially, a total of seventeen soliloquies, several of which have already been discussed.

The convention whereby soliloquies represented the spoken words rather than the unspoken thoughts of characters is not a trivial, purely technical matter. One of the fundamental features of the human condition is that no person has direct access to the mind of a fellow human being. We make inferences about the mental states of others by observing their outward appearance and behavior, including their speeches, and by obtaining secondhand reports by other observers. The ability to read minds directly is one of the traits whereby the divinity of Jesus was established in the Christian New Testament. By dramatizing in no uncertain terms that soliloquies represented the *spoken* words of characters, their *outward* behavior, rather than their unspoken thoughts, late Renaissance dramatists refrained from conferring on playgoers the fantasy experience of having the godlike power to read minds. Instead, the evidence demonstrates that late Renaissance playgoers had to draw inferences about a character's hypothetical motives based on the character's outward behavior, including the character's soliloquies. There is often an explicit or implicit gap between the words spoken by a character in a soliloquy and the implied hypothetical state of the character's mind. After articulating an intention to repent in a long soliloquy, Claudius acknowledges in a follow-up soliloquy just such a gap between his spoken words and his mental state:

> My words fly up, my thoughts remain below:
> Words without thoughts never to heaven go. (3.3.97-98)

The notion that soliloquies in Shakespeare's plays were meant to represent a character's unmediated "innermost thoughts," a notion that first became a critical commonplace during the Romantic period,[4] is untenable in light of the vast, conspicuous, wholly one-sided evidence that those passages were meant to represent the spoken words of characters.

## Soliloquies as Self-Addressed Speeches

Another profound feature of soliloquies in late Renaissance drama is that they represented *self*-addressed speeches, not audience-addressed speeches, as a matter of convention. Plentiful, varied, conspicuous, unambiguous, and overwhelmingly one-sided evidence demonstrates that this was the convention operative from around 1590 until the closing of the theaters in 1642. Of the many kinds of evidence, three often occur separately and often together: (1) self-address by name, title, epithet, or feature of the character's consciousness; (2) self-address by a second-person pronoun; and, (3) commands directed at the speaker himself, not playgoers. Each instance of one of these kinds of evidence constitutes a verbal marker of self-address.

A single poetic line in the soliloquy in which Romeo gives voice to his decision to enter the Capulet garden contains four unambiguous markers of self-address (each word or phrase is in boldface):

> **Turn back**, **dull earth**, and **find thy** centre out. (2.1.2)

Romeo addresses himself by an epithet ("dull earth") and a second-person pronoun ("thy") and gives himself two commands ("turn

---

back" and "find"). In the final scene, Romeo gives himself another momentous command:

> **Thou** desperate **pilot**, now at once **run on**
> The dashing rocks **thy** sea-sick weary bark! (5.3.117-18)

Romeo repeatedly gives commands to his eyesight:

> Did my heart love till now? **Forswear** it, **sight!** (1.5.52)
> **Eyes, look your** last! (5.3.112)

The most common verbal markers of self-address in soliloquies are apostrophes in the sense of *passages addressed by speakers to imaginary listeners*. Apostrophes are understandably very rare in speeches directed by a character to the hearing of other characters because it is incongruous to address an *imaginary* audience if one is knowingly directing one's speech at an *actual* audience other than oneself. In sharp contrast, apostrophes occur with conspicuous frequency in soliloquies. The obvious explanation for this huge differential is that soliloquies represented self-address rather than audience address.

Soliloquies in *Romeo and Juliet* are pervaded by apostrophes. Juliet repeatedly and famously addresses Romeo in the balcony episode and apostrophizes him in soliloquies in three other scenes (3.2, 4.3, 5.3). She also addresses an array of other imaginary audiences, including: horses pulling the chariot of the sun god (3.2), personifications of night (3.2) and fortune (3.5), her Nurse (3.5), her mother (4.3), the vial containing the sleeping potion (4.3), a knife (4.3), and Tybalt (4.3). In the final scene, she addresses not only Romeo but Romeo's dagger (5.3). Romeo also addresses a wide variety of imaginary listeners in his soliloquies. He addresses Juliet in soliloquies in four scenes (2.2, 3.1, 5.1, 5.3). In 5.1, he addresses the personification of mischief and the poison. In the final scene, he addresses the Capulet tomb, the corpse of Paris, the personification of death, the corpse of Tybalt, his own arms and lips, and the Apothecary. In the final scene, Paris addresses Juliet and the personification of night. Apostrophes in soliloquies occur on a vastly greater scale in *Romeo and Juliet* than in any earlier play by Shakespeare.

In addition to verbal markers, there are many other kinds of evidence of self-address in soliloquies in Shakespeare's plays. Overheard soliloquies constitute evidence not only that soliloquies represented speech but that they represented *self*-addressed speech. In the balcony episode, Romeo eavesdrops on a self-addressed speech by Juliet. He does not witness Juliet in the act of announcing her feelings to thousands of strangers. Whenever a character in a play by Shakespeare speaks a soliloquy, playgoers do what Romeo does in the balcony episode. They eavesdrop on the character's self-addressed speech. During the balcony episode, they eavesdrop not only on Juliet's self-addressed speeches but also on the self-addressed speeches that Romeo guards from the hearing of Juliet.

If a sympathetic character had been depicted as addressing a non-rhetorical question to playgoers, it would have been appropriate for playgoers to have shouted out answers, guesses, or preferences. During the balcony episode, Romeo asks in a soliloquy guarded from Juliet's hearing,

Shall I hear more, or shall I speak at this? (2.2.37)

Romeo is depicted as engaged in the process of making up his *own* mind. Playgoers understood that he was not seeking guidance from themselves.

In many soliloquies, sympathetic characters arrive at fateful decisions on the basis of assumptions that playgoers know to be erroneous. If playgoers had thought that these speeches were addressed to themselves, it would have been appropriate for them to have shouted out corrections. If, instead of *privately* grieving for the death of Juliet in self-addressed speeches (in 5.1 and 5.3), Romeo had openly *shared* his grief and his intention to commit suicide with thousands of playgoers, it would have been appropriate for them to have shouted out that Juliet is not in fact dead.

Shakespeare's plays contain a number of passages in which a character mentions either that he engaged in self-addressed speech offstage or that he overheard another character's offstage self-addressed speech. Romeo recalls his own behavior in response to observing the poverty of the Apothecary:

"Noting this penury, *to myself I said,* . . . ." (5.1.49, italics added)

And what follows is a verbatim quotation of his self-addressed speech. In *All's Well That Ends Well* the Steward gives the Countess a report on Helen's offstage behavior:

[She] did communicate to herself her own words to her own ears; she thought, I dare vow for her, they touch'd not any stranger sense. (1.3.107-10)

In regard to an *onstage* soliloquy, playgoers are in a situation analogous to that of the Steward in his account of an *offstage* situation. Playgoers *eavesdrop* on the self-addressed speeches of characters.

Soliloquies in *Romeo and Juliet* contain a total of 160 distinct verbal markers of self-address. Romeo's dying soliloquy (5.3.74-120) contains forty-five such markers. That soliloquy depicts a character overwhelmed with grief for the death of his wife and fixated on his intention to commit suicide. It does not depict a character who, supposedly on the verge of committing suicide, engages in a public-spirited effort to keep thousands of strangers up to speed about his state of mind. As indicated above, in addition to verbal markers, there are numerous other kinds of evidence of self-address in the play.

It was necessary to survey in some detail the huge body of evidence demonstrating that soliloquies represented self-addressed speeches as a matter of convention in order to refute the currently dominant scholarly consensus that soliloquies typically represented audience address. Many prominent and influential scholars are proponents of that theory, including Janet Adelman, John Barton, Stephen Greenblatt, Brian Vickers, Harold Bloom, David Bevington, Marjorie Garber, Margreta de Grazia, Jonathan Bate, and Robert Weimann.[5]

*Romeo and Juliet* does contain two unambiguously audience-addressed speeches, but those are spoken by the Chorus, who does not interact with characters engaged in the fictional action. At no point in *Romeo and Juliet* does any character engaged in the action acknowledge the presence of playgoers. One major function of the choral monologues is to set up a direct contrast between the overtly audience-addressed speeches by the Chorus and the emphatically self-addressed soliloquies of characters engaged in the action. This contrast is most conspicuous when the second choral monologue is immediately followed by a brief soliloquy by Romeo that contains four unambiguous markers of self-address ("Turn back, dull earth, and find thy centre out").

The evidence presented here demonstrates that Shakespeare was willing to challenge playgoers to follow complex operations of the convention of self-addressed speech. He had the confidence of a great artist that he could make the operations of the convention so interesting that he could induce playgoers to make the intellectual effort to understand them. It is certain that most playgoers of the time not only understood the complex convention but enjoyed episodes in which it was employed. Throughout his career and in plays of all genres, Shakespeare created many episodes that entail complicated, subtle, fast-moving, and sometimes novel operations of the convention. He would not have continued to do so if such episodes had not met with the enthusiastic approval of playgoers.

That soliloquies represented self-address rather than audience address has profound artistic and philosophical implications. If a soliloquy in a late Renaissance public theater had been knowingly addressed to playgoers by the speaking character, it would have represented the *most public* form of speech possible in the period. The character's implied, hypothetical motive in speaking would have been to inform, to entertain, to provoke, to manipulate, or otherwise to have an effect on a large assembly of strangers. In fact, the overwhelming evidence shows that soliloquies in late Renaissance drama represented self-addressed speeches, the *most private* form of speech possible. Soliloquies in Shakespeare's plays dramatize how a character interacts *with herself*. Soliloquies depict characters engaged in a huge variety of *self*-directed actions: self-congratulation, self-justification, self-reassurance, self-control, self-determination, self-denigration, self-manipulation, self-deception, and so on. Formulating or reviewing a plan in private is a different activity than announcing a plan to a multitude. In many soliloquies, a character is depicted as attempting to talk himself into a belief.[6] That is a very different psychological, rhetorical, and dramatic situation from one in which a character seeks to convince a large group of strangers to share a belief.

In addition to radically altering the implied hypothetical psychology of characters, the widespread post-Renaissance assumption that soliloquies in Shakespeare's plays were meant to represent speeches knowingly addressed to playgoers creates thematic muddles. For example, one of the most conspicuous themes in *Romeo and Juliet* is the potential conflict between an individual and a social group. By demonstrably speaking only to herself, whether alone or in an aside in the presence of other characters, each speaker of a soliloquy in *Romeo and Juliet* ipso facto sets herself apart from others at least momentarily and thereby engages in an act of individuation.[7] Post-Renaissance commentators who incorrectly assume that those speeches were public addresses and therefore communal acts radically alter a major theme meticulously constructed by Shakespeare.

Any convention can be overridden in a particular instance by a conspicuous, unambiguous signal. In the case of a pervasively reinforced convention, such as the late Renaissance convention of self-addressed speech, the signal would have to have been conspicuous and unambiguous because the benefit of any doubt would have gone to the convention. Having witnessed countless instances in which characters engage in unambiguously self-addressed speech, intelligent regular playgoers would have assumed that that convention was in operation unless unambiguously and conspicuously violated. A small number of conspicuous, unambiguous violations would not seriously undermine a well-established convention, and the convention of self-addressed speech was as well-established as a convention gets. The plays of Shakespeare alone contain literally hundreds of unambiguous markers of self-addressed speech as well as many other kinds of evidence of self-address. Evidence of self-addressed speech is also pervasive in plays of other major dramatists of the period. Shakespeare and other major dramatists rarely if ever overrode the convention. The obvious explanation for this extraordinary restraint is that the convention was too artistically important and productive to weaken even a little with violations. The convention was a magnificent tool to depict how a character interacts with himself. The nuances of the convention governing eavesdropping situations produced countless memorable episodes in late Renaissance drama, the greatest age of eavesdropping episodes in Western drama. Playgoers of the period evidently took a voyeuristic kind of pleasure in eavesdropping on the most private speeches of characters and were not interested in what a character might say to themselves if the character knew that she was merely a character in a play.

## Conclusion

Shakespeare's employment of the convention of self-addressed speech in *Romeo and Juliet* is also impressive in other respects. The play contains thirty-three self-addressed speeches by eleven characters. Self-addressed speeches occupy 410 lines, 14 percent of the total number of lines in the play (2964). That percentage is double the percentage in *Hamlet*. All major characters have self-addressed speeches except Mercutio and the Prince. Romeo's sixteen self-addressed speeches occupy a total of 159 lines, which amount to 27 percent of the total lines he speaks in the play (591). Juliet's dozen self-addressed speeches occupy 156 lines, which amount to 31 percent of the lines she speaks (509). Those are astonishing statistics considering the fact that Hamlet's self-addressed speeches occupy only 13 percent of the total number of lines *he* speaks. The balcony episode contains a remarkable sequence of six consecutive soliloquies, occupying forty-nine lines without any intervening dialogue between characters. Shakespeare's love of the convention of self-addressed speech is also demonstrated by his brilliant exploitation of a possibility raised by two nuances of the convention in combination: that soliloquies could be overheard and that in soliloquies characters frequently addressed imaginary listeners. In the balcony episode, not only does Romeo overhear Juliet's soliloquies, he overhears her address *himself* in apostrophes. It is a charming dramatic irony that, unbeknownst to Juliet, her imaginary listener is an actual listener. *Romeo and Juliet* is quite demonstrably the work of an author who imaginatively, exuberantly, daringly, and pervasively exploited the very precise features of a complex convention to create many fascinating and profound dramatic situations that would not have been possible without strict adherence to the convention.

## Notes

1. Instead of conducting an empirical investigation, some scholars adopt the easy, shortcut method of defining *soliloquy* according to its etymology (*loqui*, "to speak" in Latin; *solus*, "alone"). This procedure for describing stage practices without going to the trouble of actually examining stage practices is patently wrong-headed. No sane dramatist would tailor a dramatic situation so that it would conform to the etymology of a word, and the evidence shows that Shakespeare did not do so.

2. In an apostrophe to the Capulet tomb, Romeo says, "I'll cram thee with more food" (5.3.48).

3. Amazingly, this is neither the first nor the last episode devised by Shakespeare that involves concentric circles of onstage eavesdroppers. Memorable examples occur in *Love's Labor's Lost* 4.3 and *Troilus and Cressida* 5.2. See Hirsh, *History* 128, 139-40, 148, 150-51.

4. Charles Lamb, for example, described Hamlet's soliloquies as "the silent meditations with which his bosom is bursting, reduced to *words* for the sake of the reader" (29). Coleridge asserted that Hamlet's soliloquies represented the character's "inward brooding" (165). Later in the century, Algernon Charles Swinburne described Hamlet's "How all occasions" soliloquy (4.4.32-66) as the "effusion of all inmost thought" (xxx).

5. A few scholars, including Bernard Beckerman, Anne Righter Barton, and Stephen Mullaney, recognized that soliloquies were not audience addresses but did not provide evidence to support their intuition. Gary

M. McCown correctly describes Juliet's "Gallop apace" soliloquy at the beginning of 3.2 as a "debate with herself" (164), "spoken in solitude" (166), rather than as a public address explaining her mental state to thousands of strangers. For surveys of scholarly commentary on the issue of the direction of address of soliloquies, see Hirsh, *History*, especially chapter 9, and Hirsh, "Late Renaissance."

6.  Self-persuasion is an overt theme in the main source of the play, Arthur Brooke's *The Tragicall Historye of Romeus and Juliet*:

    Oh how we can persuade, our self to what we like,
    And how we can dissuade our mind, if aught our mind mislike.

    (429-30)

7.  Silvia Bigliazzi has persuasively differentiated the kind of selfhood exhibited by Juliet in her soliloquies in Q1 from the kind of selfhood exhibited in her soliloquies in Q2. Juliet's soliloquies in Q1 tend to exhibit her sense of oneness with Romeo, whereas her soliloquies in Q2 tend to express her sense of solitary selfhood. Bigliazzi's research is in accord with the evidence catalogued in the present essay demonstrating that soliloquies represented self-address rather than audience address. Each of the kinds of selves delineated by Bigliazzi is a *private* self, constructed by Juliet for herself alone, rather than a *public* self-constructed by Juliet for the edification of thousands of strangers in the theater audience. The argument presented here about the psychological and thematic implications of Shakespeare use of self-addressed speeches complements Paul A. Kottman's philosophically astute exploration of the theme of "self-realization" in the play (3).

## Works Cited

Bigliazzi, Silvia. "Female Desire and Self-Knowledge: Juliet's Soliloquies in *Romeo and Juliet*." *Rivista di Letterature moderne e comparate*, vol. 68, new series, 2015, pp. 243-65.

Brooke, Arthur. *The Tragicall Historye of Romeus and Juliet. Narrative and Dramatic Sources of Shakespeare*, edited by Geoffrey Bullough, vol. 1, Routledge, 1957–75, pp. 269-363.

Coleridge, Samuel Taylor. *Coleridge's Writing on Shakespeare*, edited by Terence Hawkes. Capricorn, 1959.

Hirsh, James. *Shakespeare and the History of Soliloquies.* Fairleigh Dickinson UP, 2003.

_____. "Late Renaissance Self-Address Fashioning: Scholarly Orthodoxy versus Evidence." *Medieval and Renaissance Drama in England,* vol. 27, 2014, pp. 132-60.

Kottman, Paul A. "Defying the Stars: Tragic Love as the Struggle for Freedom in *Romeo and Juliet." Shakespeare Quarterly,* vol. 63, 2012, pp. 1-38.

Lamb, Charles. "On the Tragedies of Shakespeare." 1811. *Charles Lamb on Shakespeare,* edited by Joan Coldwell. Colin Smythe, 1978.

McCown, Gary M. "'Runnawayes Eyes' and Juliet's Epithalamium." *Shakespeare Quarterly,* vol. 27, 1976, pp. 150-70.

Shakespeare, William. *The Riverside Shakespeare,* edited by G. Blakemore Evans. 2nd ed., Houghton Mifflin, 1997.

Swinburne, Algernon Charles. *A Study of Shakespeare.* 1880. W. Heinemann, 1918.

# Trauma in *Romeo and Juliet*

Robert C. Evans

Trauma—for good reason—has been the subject of much recent
literary and cultural commentary. The Holocaust, the aftermath of
various wars, the rise of terrorism, and the prevalence of "mass
shootings" (to mention just a few examples) have all helped make
trauma a much-discussed topic, especially in literary criticism.[1] Thus
it's surprising that very little discussion seems to exist of trauma
in Shakespeare in general or in *Romeo and Juliet* in particular.[2]
I therefore hope to offer a comprehensive overview of traumatic
moments in this play, focusing especially on the scenes involving
the deaths of Mercutio and Tybalt as well as the later scenes leading
up to and involving Juliet's apparent death in her parents' home. As
I hope to show, Shakespeare's play illustrates many points made
by recent theorists of trauma, and trauma is central to much of this
drama's enduring power.[3]

## Recent Trauma Theory

One especially fine contribution to thinking about trauma is
*Shattered Assumptions: Towards a New Psychology of Trauma* by
Ronnie Janoff-Bulman. Janoff-Bulman (hereafter abbreviated as
"JB") argues that trauma occurs when a person's most fundamental,
most reassuring assumptions about the world are shattered by some
catastrophe. People often believe, for instance, that the world is good,
that life makes sense, that their own lives are worthy, that the world
is just, and that we have some control over what happens to us (JB
5-12). These assumptions are often unconscious, taken for granted,
and rooted in early life, especially in our relations with parents and
others (JB 13-19). Until truly bad things happen, we tend to assume
that we are invulnerable, and we tend to downplay the possibilities
of personal suffering (JB 19). Our positive assumptions tend to
persist even in the face of minor contradictory evidence; we tend to
see threatening persons or developments as anomalies (JB 28-40).

We resist abandoning our stereotypes; only truly severe crises cause such change, and this is one reason trauma both causes and results from "shattered assumptions" (JB 40-53).

Of course, bad things almost inevitably happen to good people, but not all bad events cause trauma. Standard losses, extended sickness, financial setbacks, tension in relationships—such developments are not necessarily traumatic (JB 54). Traumatic events usually involve some powerful threat of death, either literally or figuratively (JB 56-60). Suddenly, assumptions that had seemed relatively stable are threatened with "massive disintegration" (JB 60). The world abruptly appears terrifying, malevolent, and meaningless (JB 61-63). Physically and psychologically, traumatized persons become hyper-aroused and hypersensitive, sometimes permanently (JB 65-72). If their sufferings seem accidental or "acts of God," trauma is likely; if their sufferings seem the result of their own failings or others' evil, trauma often results (JB 76-78). Trauma often leads the traumatized to judge themselves and/or others harshly (JB 77-78). They are likely to feel victimized, vulnerable, and/or even guilty (JB 79-80). Persons who previously saw the world most positively are likely to be most easily and deeply traumatized, but they also have an easier time recovering (JB 88-90). Persons who are already cynical, hardened, or damaged are less subject to traumatic reactions (JB 90).

## Trauma in *Romeo and Juliet*: The Opening Scene

Prospects of trauma in *Romeo and Juliet* occur even before the play begins. The Prologue already mentions the likelihood that "civil blood" will make "civil hands unclean" (Pr. 4), just as it also mentions death, pity, fear, and rage—all usual causes of trauma (a word etymologically suggesting deep psychic "wounds"). The prologue also implies "civil" trauma affecting society at large rather than one or two persons in particular. Individual trauma is bad enough; a traumatized culture is even worse. Shakespeare reiterates this theme of social trauma throughout the play, especially in scenes where the prince appears.

---

Critical Insights

When the play itself begins, potential trauma is already implied by prominently mentioned—and prominently visible—"swords and bucklers" of the Capulet servants named Samson and Gregory (1.0.sd). Potential woundings and deaths are already suggested by these very blatant details of costuming, and wounding insults are already implied by the very first line (1.1.1). Sampson epitomizes potential hostility and conflict, while Gregory symbolizes potential good humor and play. Two basic tones are thus immediately implied. Samson repeatedly promises violence (1.1.1, 3, 5, 7, 10-11, 15-17, 20-22), but the appearance of two Montague servants prompts both Capulet servants to draw their swords (1.1.31 sd, 32-33). Eventually, in a pattern repeated later, potential violence results in real violence (1.1.6-63). Multiple swords are drawn, but the playwright already clearly distinguishes Benvolio (who draws his sword to suppress fighting [1.1.64-65, 66]) from Tybalt (who draws his sword in genuine hatred [1.1.65, 68-69]). Ironically, unnamed but armed "Citizens" soon arrive (1.1.71) and try to suppress violence *through* violence. Even greater violence—between Capulet and Montague themselves, not merely their servants and allies—seems in the offing (1.1.73-78).

Only the abrupt appearance of Prince Escalus and his armed followers (1.1.79 sd) prevents further bloodshed. He calls the combatants "beasts" (1.1.81) and threatens them with "pain of torture" (1.1.84). He implies that the current fight has been literally bloody (1.1.83-84) and that it follows two previous brawls (1.1.87, 89), and he threatens Montague, Capulet, and their followers with death if further disturbance occurs (1.1.95, 101). Although no actual deaths apparently result from this initial conflict, real wounds are suffered, and Shakespeare raises the possibility of traumatic deaths while still (at this point) postponing their actual appearance. In none of his other tragedies is the prospect of massive social trauma raised so immediately and at such length: fighting is quickly reported in *Macbeth*, but it occurs off-stage and involves military combat. The other tragedies begin in relative peace. It is as if Shakespeare wanted to underline, in *Romeo and Juliet*, the possibility and reality of trauma right from the start. Potentially violent chaos always lurks just beneath the play's surface and then bursts out into actual, devastating bloodshed. Disputes between the Montagues and Capulets repeatedly unleash widespread social trauma. Their fighting threatens to shatter the city's peace (1.1.89-95).

After the Prince departs, Benvolio explains the details of the recent turmoil, describing it in ways that imply real trauma, even if things could have been far, far worse (1.1.102-13). Attention soon shifts, however, to Romeo. He, as it turns out, seems traumatized in his own way, but his wounds are romantic and seem trivial in light of the just-concluded violence. He has been shedding "tears," exhaling "deep sighs," and turning himself into an "artificial night" (1.1.130-31, 138). "Black and portentous must this humour prove," his father predicts (1.1.139)—not realizing, of course, how true his prediction will be. Romeo's early pains are nothing compared to his later suffering. The play's early acts allude to, and even almost present, different *possible* traumas, but only later do true traumas appear in great abundance.

Romeo's early sadness can actually sound almost comic and overblown (1.1.159, 174-180). Perhaps Benvolio even finds Romeo's exaggerated rhetoric laughable, although Benvolio (good man that he is) instead claims to weep at his cousin's words (1.1.181). In any case, Romeo soon returns to lamenting "Griefs" lying "heavy" in his "breast," and then he even claims to grieve at Benvolio's answering sadness (1.1.184-87). He feels like "groan[ing]" over his painful infatuation with Rosaline (1.1.198), compares himself to a sad, sick man facing death (1.1.200), laments Rosaline's chastity (1.1.208)—even when he tries to bribe her financially (1.1.212)—and suggests that her refusals make him "despair" (1.1.220). Her chastity makes him feel "dead" (1.1.222). In short, he feels traumatized in ways that almost seem comic.

Romeo's exaggerated romanticism seems foolish. Perhaps we laugh gently because we have all thought, felt, and behaved with similar foolishness. Even if we find Romeo completely sympathetic and admire his melancholy, his trauma here will eventually seem quite minor. Repeatedly, this play uses trivial trauma to highlight, by contrast, the real thing. Shakespeare uses Romeo's opening imagined trauma to emphasize the true traumas that appear later. The play's second half repeatedly echoes (in design, language, and characterization) its first, but always in ways that emphasize real tragedies and traumas no one can even begin to anticipate in the opening scene.

## Late Traumatic Moments

One example of this ironic foreshadowing is a passing comment by Capulet about Juliet. In a line not included in the first quarto, Capulet says "Earth hath swallowed all [his] hopes" except his daughter (1.1.14n). Even without that line, Capulet's larger, surrounding speech shows just how much he truly loves his girl. Later, of course—in an especially traumatic episode—he will violently berate her, profess to hate her, and wish she had never been born (3.5.141-204). The whole drama brims with such touches: hints of trauma, or allusions to past traumas, seem mild compared to later, deeper traumas. The play's first half often alludes to traumas that never seem quite real or very serious. Thus, Benvolio speaks of Romeo's romantic "pain," "anguish," and "desperate grief" (1.2.45, 47), and he lightly alludes to poison and death in ways that will eventually seem utterly ironic (1.1.49). Romeo, meanwhile (still smitten with Rosaline), claims to be "Shut up in prison, kept without my food, / Whipped and tormented," and full of "misery" (1.2.54-57). Perhaps he is partly joking, but even early jokes about pain seem ironic in light of the work's later genuine traumas.

There are, however, some early hints of real, undeniable pain. Often these are quite touching, especially when the Nurse remembers the deaths of her daughter and husband. Her daughter, Susan, was Juliet's contemporary, but Susan has died, and the Nurse simply but poignantly remarks, "Well, Susan is with God; / She was too good for me" (1.3.20-21). Later, mentioning her husband's death, she remembers him fondly and says simply, "God be with his soul, / 'A was a merry man" (1.3.40-41). The Nurse's pain (and her mature responses to it) seems far more moving than Romeo's early, overblown romantic suffering. Even her suffering, however, will later seem mild; she, in fact, will later be traumatized in especially memorable ways. Meanwhile, Romeo laments his romantic heaviness (1.4.12), although it is hard to know just how seriously he takes himself when he declares (for instance), "I have a soul of lead / So stakes me to the ground I cannot move" (1.4.15-16). His language is often so inflated that we can never be quite sure that even *he* is very serious about it (1.4.19-22, 25-26). Thus he says,

> I am too sore enpierced with [Cupid's] shaft
> To soar with his light feathers, and so bound
> I cannot bound a pitch above dull woe.
> Under love's heavy burden do I sink. (1.4.19-22)

Ironically, the more seriously he takes himself and his romantic pain, the less easy it may be to sympathize. The more traumatized he claims to feel, the less convincingly traumatized he truly seems. There are, however, moments when his words do ominously foreshadow the genuine trauma he and others will later experience, as when he worries that

> Some consequence, yet hanging in the stars,
> Shall bitterly begin his fearful date
> With this night's revels, and expire the term
> Of a despised life closed in my breast
> By some vile forfeit of untimely death. (1.4.107-111)

Here he adumbrates more truly than he could ever imagine the undeniable traumas to come.

Hints of those traumas occur even at Capulet's festive party. There, Tybalt recognizes Romeo and hopes to "strike him dead" (1.5.58). Of course (ironically), it will be Romeo who eventually and traumatically kills Tybalt, but for the moment, any conflict is prevented (again, ironically) by old Capulet. Capulet refuses to let Tybalt start a disruptive quarrel. His forceful rebuke of Tybalt (1.5.75-87) ironically foreshadows his later, traumatic dressing-down of Juliet (already mentioned). Shakespeare lets us see just how ferocious Capulet can be when crossed. Tybalt probably feels a bit traumatized by his uncle's harsh words, but it is Juliet who

---

will *truly* suffer trauma from his anger; Tybalt, by contrast, gets off relatively easy.

In the meantime, many early references to death and suffering prove double-edged. Thus, when Romeo and Juliet independently realize that they are in love with a nominal enemy, each immediately thinks of death (1.5.117, 134). In both cases, their words are more ominously accurate than they can know. As Act 2 opens, the play continues to abound in ironies obvious to anyone who knows the tragedy's eventual outcomes. Thus Romeo says of Mercutio (soon to be slain by Tybalt) that "He jests at scars that never felt a wound" (2.2.1). He hopes Juliet, his metaphorical sun, will "kill the envious moon" (2.2.4), although the only killing she commits involves her own eventual suicide. References to hatefulness, enemies, death, murder, swords, enmity, and grief permeate the famous balcony scene (2.2.55-56, 64, 70, 72-73, 77-78, 152), but for the time being, the play is dominated by feelings and words of romantic love. Romeo, now obsessed with Juliet, easily forgets his early excessive trauma over rejection by Rosaline (2.3.42). Describing his new infatuation with Juliet, he uses his typical Petrarchan metaphors ("one hath wounded me / That's by me wounded" [2.3.46-47]). Such language typifies how the play's phrasing at first lightly foreshadows grim traumas that appear later in full force. Friar Laurence, stunned by Romeo's easy abandonment of Rosaline aside, recalls his earlier trauma:

> Jesu Maria, what a deal of brine
> Hath washed thy sallow cheeks for Rosaline! . . .
> The sun not yet thy sighs from heaven clears,
> Thy old groans yet ringing in mine ancient ears.
> Lo, here upon thy cheek the stain doth sit
> Of an old tear that is not washed off yet.
> If e're thou wast thyself and these woes thine,
> Thou and these woes were all for Rosaline. (2.3.65-74)

As so often in the play's first half, these lines highlight later, genuine traumas by implicitly contrasting them with the earlier, shallow traumas. Romeo, Juliet, and practically everyone who knows and cares about them will feel truly traumatized before the play ends.

---

## True Traumas Break into the Play

Not until Act 3, however, do true traumas really appear, this time in an encounter replicating the opening scene. The true trauma is preceded, in typical Shakespearean fashion, by much ominous joking by Mercutio at the expense of Benvolio (3.1.1-33). Practically one third of these lines contain some reference to possible death. Soon, the hot-headed Tybalt and his men come upon Benvolio and the equally hot-headed Mercutio. A quarrel erupts—verbal sparring that rapidly leads to actual killings. As Romeo tries to break up the fight, Tybalt fatally stabs Mercutio (3.1.34-90). Now the play plunges into one quick trauma after another: Mercutio, although initially trying to minimize his wound, is genuinely traumatized when he realizes he will die (3.1.91-110). Romeo is traumatized by Mercutio's death—a death he ironically caused by trying to prevent it (3.1.111-13). Romeo feels traumatized by Tybalt's insults, Mercutio's death, and Juliet's softening impact on his character (3.1.113-17). Benvolio is traumatized first by Mercutio's quick demise (3.1.118-20) and then by witnessing Romeo kill Tybalt, especially since Romeo may himself now die (3.1.134-37). Romeo, traumatized by all these sudden developments, soon flees (3.1.138). The tragic events soon traumatize the citizens, the Capulets, the Montagues, and the Prince (3.1.139-88). And Romeo's friends and family are surely traumatized by the Prince's decision to banish Romeo (3.1.188-99). Into less than two hundred lines, Shakespeare has crammed more traumas—and more *kinds* of trauma—than perhaps in any similar section of his other works. Friends are traumatized; families are traumatized; citizens are traumatized; Romeo is traumatized; even the Prince (related by blood to Tybalt) is traumatized. And, of course, readers and audiences feel traumatized, too. In fact, Act 3, Scene 1 traumatizes *us* for several reasons: the traumas come rapidly; they are embedded in carefully staged chaos; and they seem so completely irreversible. And Shakespeare quite literally doubles the traumas by having them first enacted and then thoroughly described by Benvolio (3.1.154-77). First we *witness* the traumatic events, and then we read or hear about them all over again. We can easily imagine the traumatizing impact these events will have on the couple's relationship. But we can never quite imagine just exactly *how* traumatizing—in particular ways—the wounds they suffer will turn out to be. Eventually, practically everyone's assumptions will be shattered, and intense pain will be felt by almost all the work's characters.

## Traumatic Aftermaths of the First Killings

Act 3, Scene 2, like much of the rest of the play, is full both of ironic foreshadowings of trauma and of genuinely traumatized reactions. Thus, although Juliet does not yet know that Mercutio and Tybalt are dead and Romeo banished, her opening speech contains numerous unintended ironies. She embraces darkness, mentions "runaways," praises blackness, alludes to bloodshed, and uses "night" no less than eleven times in thirty-five lines (3.2.4-6, 10-11, 13-14, 15, 17, 18-24, 29-35). When the Nurse finally appears and reveals the deaths and banishment, both her own response and Juliet's reactions are so traumatic that there is no point in quoting all the examples. Both women overflow with traumatic emotions (3.2.37-143), so that sometimes their rhetoric can seem almost *too* rhetorical, too contrived. And, of course, there is the added (sometimes almost perversely comic) complexity that the Nurse at first laments for Tybalt, while Juliet laments for Romeo. Once again, even during this genuinely traumatic moment, Shakespeare is postponing even deeper traumas. He drags us ever deeper into ever more disturbing traumatic episodes. Although Juliet and the Nurse are sincerely traumatized, their language here is sometimes so elaborately artificial that we notice the language almost more than the underlying emotions. The trauma both characters feel can hardly be denied, but even harsher traumas are yet to come.

Elaborately artificial language appears again when Romeo visits Friar Laurence (3.3). He insistently laments his "banishment" (3.3.12-23), even (bizarrely) envying "carrion flies" (35) that can land on the lips he can no longer kiss (!). Many readers and listeners will sometimes wonder just how seriously to take the lovers, and surely this is one such moment. Certainly Laurence finds it hard to listen to Romeo's odd self-pity (3.3.54-63), especially when Romeo

---

literally falls to the ground in grief (3.3.69-70). Eventually the Nurse, who now arrives, joins Laurence in rebuking Romeo, even as she reports Juliet's similar behavior: "Even so lies she, / Blubbering and weeping, weeping and blubbering" (3.3.86-87). Clearly both youths are truly traumatized (their physical reactions are more convincing than their mere words), and both older characters face real difficulties in trying to deal with these adolescent traumas.

As therapists readily acknowledge (see, for instance, Bicknell-Hentges and Lynch, hereafter abbreviated as "BH&L"), responding appropriately to any traumatized person is difficult enough. Responding to traumatized adolescents is even harder. Youths are especially likely to engage in "avoidance, denial, rationalization, and distraction" (BH&L), and young males are particularly likely to resist direct assistance (BH&L). Traumatized adolescents are particularly likely to succumb to "rage, depression or despair, anxiety or terror" (BH&L), and traumatized people in general can easily be "retraumatized" if the counselors trying to help them are insufficiently careful (BH&L). This is especially true when the traumatized persons are suffering from "Level Three" trauma (the most serious kind), in which the traumatized person "is extremely stimulated" and displays emotions close in intensity "to the original [traumatic] response . . . . It is as if s/he is actually reliving the trauma," even "crying uncontrollably, gasping for breath, or displaying . . . regressed behaviors such as rocking and thumb sucking" (BH&L). Severely traumatized persons are likely to be "self-destructive" and feel "overwhelmed" (BH&L). Certainly Romeo's actions (far more than his actual words) in 3.3 indicate severe trauma: he falls on the ground (3.3.69), weeps uncontrollably (3.3.83), and even attempts to kill himself (3.3.107). These behaviors tell us far more about his actual mental state than all his elaborate language. Shakespeare convincingly depicted genuine trauma long before the term "trauma" was ever used by modern psychologists.

Shakespeare also realistically depicts trauma long before psychologists and psychiatrists invented the various methods now often used to try to alleviate traumatic suffering. Often those methods, today, involve at least in part some treatment with drugs, but the only drugs used in Shakespeare's play lead (ironically) not to healing but to death. Instead, the play's characters who try to help traumatized persons must rely mostly on so-called "talking cures." These involve "talking about the traumatic event" so as to "retrieve traumatic memories and review them" (BH&L). But such methods can further traumatize the traumatized patient (BH&L). Therapists today therefore often resort (in addition to drugs) to such other methods as "relaxation training, stress reduction exercises, [and] cognitive modulation of affect through self-talk" as well as "problem-solving, behavior change and emotional regulation" (BH&L). When dealing with Level Three traumas, counselors are advised to use such methods as

> asking content questions not specifically related to trauma (e.g., "How old were you at that time?"); using a hypnotic voice tone to calm; asking the client to stop talking about the trauma and anchor them to the present; repeating and rephrasing what the client has just said; getting the client to open eyes and describe the current setting; using relaxation and breathing techniques in session; and asking the client to talk about neutral events in the present not related to the trauma. (BH&L)

No one, in *Romeo and Juliet*, uses such methods, partly because they had not yet been formally invented and partly because the various potential "therapists" (especially Benvolio, Juliet's parents, the Nurse, and Friar Laurence) are too immediately caught up in a rush of unexpected, chaotic, and ever-complicating events to have the time, patience, and foresight to use them. In dealing with Romeo's trauma, Laurence's own words are initially emotional and condemning (3.3.107-33): he displays the very passion he rebukes. Only when he comes close to using something resembling modern "cognitive therapy" (by trying to reason with Romeo [3.3.107-53]) does his own tone become calmer and more logical. Finally, his words begin to have some positive effect. Like a good modern cognitive therapist (or a good Renaissance stoic), he tries to change Romeo's thinking in order to change Romeo's emotions. (As various critics of Laurence have noted, he resorts to philosophy rather than to Christian counsel, which might have worked even better.) By encouraging Romeo to be rational, he at least helps Romeo deal with his trauma. The fact that the Nurse commends Laurence's words (3.3.158-59) is no automatic or necessary reason to question his counsel. It does, after all, calm Romeo so that he is no longer weeping, throwing himself to the ground, or threatening suicide. We will never know if a more explicitly religious approach might ultimately have been more effective.

## The Most Traumatic Scenes of All?

In the play's next major scene of trauma—perhaps the most genuinely traumatic, traumatizing episode of all—Juliet's parents also at first try various strategies to assist their grieving daughter. Capulet's wife initially mixes reason and rebuke (3.5.69-76), then moves to seeking vengeance on Romeo (3.5.78-92), then tries to cheer Juliet by revealing plans for the girl's impending marriage to Paris (3.5.112-15). Juliet (already secretly married to Romeo) resists all these efforts, and things fare no better when her father tries to counsel her. He, too, at first tries various tactics, including tenderness and humor (3.5.129-37), but when he learns of her refusal to marry Paris, he at first seems stunned (3.5.141-45) and then explodes (3.5.149-68, 176-96), using extraordinarily ferocious language. His phrasing, which grows fiercer and fiercer the longer he talks, seems more truly hateful than just about anything said so far. Eventually, it stuns not only Juliet, the Nurse, and Juliet's mother, but even Shakespeare's readers and listeners. Paradoxically, Capulet's words here are both foreshadowed and contradicted by his much earlier (much briefer) anger at Tybalt when Tybalt wanted to confront Romeo at Capulet's party (1.5.59-91). Capulet had then used his own anger to defuse Tybalt's. But nothing really prepares us (or anyone) for his sheer violent anger at his own daughter. Even his wife seems stunned ("Fie, fie, what, are you mad?" [3.5.157]). And, perhaps more surprisingly, even the Nurse rebukes him and repeatedly defends her right to do so (3.5.169, 172, 173). Intriguingly, René Weis, the play's latest Arden editor, notes that much "of the detail of Capulet's harangue is Shakespeare's invention" (3.5.157n). It is as if the playwright wanted to underline the trauma here and stun literally everyone who experiences or witnesses Capulet's attack.

Even more trauma, however, is yet to come when Juliet's supposedly dead body is discovered the next morning. Now it is *Capulet's* turn to suffer, along with his wife, the Nurse, Paris, and presumably other members of the household. Their trauma seems profound, and, ironically, the less articulate it is, the more profound it seems. Thus, when the Nurse first assumes that Juliet is dead, she exclaims "Lady, lady, lady!" (4.5.13). Later she exclaims "Alas, alas, help, help! My lady's dead!" (4.5.14). Similarly simple exclamations from the Nurse punctuate the entire scene, but even the other characters use such language, as when Capulet's wife exclaims, "O me, O me, my, child! My only life!" and then bursts out, "Help, help, call help!" (4.5.19, 20). Capulet himself is eventually the most articulate, polished speaker in responding to the tragedy and trauma, but even he admits that death "Ties up my tongue and will not let me speak" (4.5.32). Perhaps the most interesting extended reaction, however, comes from the Nurse:

> O woe, O woeful, woeful, woeful day!
> Most lamentable day, most woeful day
> That ever, ever I did yet behold!
> O day, O day, O day, O hateful day!
> Never was seen so black a day as this.
> O woeful day, O woeful day! (4.549-54)

These are not, obviously, great lines of poetry, but perhaps that is the point: the Nurse's grief and trauma are *so* deep that she cannot wax eloquent. She cannot (as the other characters eventually do to some extent) launch into artificially contrived speeches. A talented actress could make these lines seem truly gut-wrenching even while also, perhaps, suggesting how they reflect the Nurse's taste for melodrama. In any case, all the characters now resort, in varying degrees, to mere lists of exclaimed words (as when Capulet exclaims "Despised, distressed, hated, martyred, killed!" [4.5.59]). This kind of chaotic language can have a power all its own, especially on stage when spoken by gifted actors. This is exactly the kind of unpolished language that truly traumatized people typically use. The play's phrasing, in this scene, is often as shattered as the characters' assumptions and emotions. Perhaps nowhere else do we see so many characters so profoundly traumatized all together and all at once. Even the scenes of widespread public brawling can seem tame in comparison.

Paradoxically, however, readers and spectators are perhaps less traumatized here than by the earlier scene in which Capulet viciously attacked his own daughter. That scene caught everyone, including us (and perhaps even Capulet) completely by surprise. In the present scene, the characters' trauma is enormous, but readers and spectators are much less traumatized because *we* know (or at least strongly suspect) that Juliet is not really dead. Once again, then, Shakespeare gives us yet another variation of the sheer *possibilities* of different *kinds* of trauma. Sometimes the trauma the play depicts is widely social; sometimes it is deeply personal. Sometimes it seems foolish; sometimes it seems profound. Sometimes it affects some characters and not others; sometimes it affects many characters at once. Sometimes readers and spectators are themselves traumatized (as in Capulet's attack on Juliet); sometimes the audience's perspective is more distanced and informed (as in the discovery of Juliet apparently dead).

## Trauma in Act 5

Of course, traumatic moments and scenes appear regularly in Act 5. Romeo is stunned by Juliet's supposed death (5.1.24-30), but now his response is far more subdued and, in some ways, more mature than when he faced earlier traumas. Now, when he contemplates suicide, his behavior and speech are far less frantic (and in that sense somewhat more ominous) than when he had earlier tried to kill himself (5.1.34-36, 85-86). Instead of speechifying, he responds with grim resolution. Paris, too, seems full of grief—so much so that he visits the cemetery where Juliet is entombed and plans to do so "Nightly" (5.3.15-17). When Romeo himself arrives at the churchyard, he announces that his "intents are savage-wild" (5.3.36-37). Paris, still assuming that a traumatized Juliet died from grief over Tybalt's death (5.3.49-51), is soon himself quite literally traumatized—stabbed and killed by Romeo (5.3.72-73). Romeo then feels distraught over this killing (5.3.81-83). Surprisingly, he is less traumatized by seeing Juliet's apparent corpse than we might have expected. Partly this is because she still looks beautiful (after all, she is not really dead).

But Romeo, in general, simply appears more mature than he had earlier seemed. All the traumas he has so far suffered have, in a sense, inoculated him against this moment. He is, perhaps, now so thoroughly traumatized, so inured to tragedy, that he no longer feels any need (or possesses any ability) to further rant and rave. All the traumas he has endured have stripped him of much of the overblown emotions he had earlier expressed. At this point, he himself seems less overtly traumatized than many readers and spectators are likely to feel when he does, in fact, drink the poison that quickly kills him (5.3.120). Now, ironically, it is Laurence—who had earlier seemed to offer a certain sort of wise, rational counsel—who appears traumatized when discovering that Romeo has killed Paris (5.3.139-47) and who quickly flees (leaving Juliet alone in the tomb) as others approach (5.3.159). Paradoxically, Juliet seems far from traumatized by the sight of Romeo's dead body, and, after speaking less than ten lines, she abruptly kills herself (5.3.161-70).

Shakespeare could easily have made all the deaths in this scene more elaborate, both in language and in action. He could easily have given all the eventually dead characters long, eloquent speeches. But he seems to have realized that less was more. Readers and spectators, rather than the characters, seem most fully traumatized by the deaths enacted here. But even readers and spectators have perhaps concluded, by this point, that the deaths are inevitable, impossible to avoid, and therefore less traumatizing than some earlier events. Certainly characters and citizens *within* the play are described as being traumatized (5.3.174-76, 185, 191-93, 202-07, 214-15). Indeed, Montague reports that his wife has actually *died* from grief—a possibility the play has raised metaphorically previously but which has now become a literal fact (5.3.210-11). Shakespeare chose, wisely, to keep her death off-stage and merely reported; actually showing her die from grief might have been too melodramatic. Instead, the play winds down slowly. No more traumas occur. Instead, events are carefully recounted, especially by the Friar, in ways that impose a final quietness and solemnity, both on the page and on the stage. The work began with potential trauma and then moved to various traumas in fact. It became, perhaps, most deeply traumatic and traumatizing during the scenes in which Juliet is abused by her father and then found apparently dead. These—especially the former—are the scenes (along with the deaths of Mercutio and Tybalt) that truly stick in the mind, leaving a traumatic impact difficult to forget or deny. The deaths within the tomb could almost have been predicted, but nothing quite prepares us for the sudden losses of the two young men or the full fury of Capulet's vicious attack on his own young daughter. In moments like these, Shakespeare achieves both deep tragedy and true trauma.

## Notes

1.   See, for instance, the books by Alexander, Balaev, Beulens, Caruth, and LaCapra. These amount to just the very top of the proverbial tip of the iceberg.

2.   For rare discussions of Shakespeare and trauma, see, for instance, Anderson, Brooks, Cahill, Davis, Silverstone, and Stark-Estes.

3.   For a few good studies of trauma (from among many others that might be cited), see, for instance, Alexander, Bicknell-Hentges and Lynch, Bisson, Charles and O'Loughlin, Ringell and Brandell, and especially Janoff-Bulman.

## Works Cited

Alexander, Jeffrey. *Trauma: A Social Theory*. Polity, 2012.

Anderson, Thomas Page. *Performing Early Modern Trauma from Shakespeare to Milton*. Ashgate, 2006.

Balaev, Michelle, editor. *Contemporary Approaches to Literary Trauma Theory*. Palgrave Macmillan, 2014.

Beulens, Gert, et al., editors. *The Future of Trauma Theory: Contemporary Literary and Cultural Criticism*. Routledge, 2014.

Bicknell-Hentges, Lindsay, and John J. Lynch. "Everything Counselors and Supervisors Need to Know about Treating Trauma." Paper based on a presentation at the American Counseling Association Annual Conference and Exposition, Charlotte, NC. 2009.

www.counseling.org/knowledge-center/vistas/by-year2/vistas-2009/docs/default-source/vistas/vistas_2009_bicknell-hentges-lynch/. Accessed 21 Feb. 2017.

Bisson Jonathan I. "In-Depth Review: Post Traumatic Stress Disorder." *Occupational Medicine*, vol. 57, 2007, pp. 399-403. occmed.oxfordjournals.org/content/57/6/399.full/. Accessed 22 Feb. 2017.

Brooks, Douglas A., Matthew Biberman, and Julia Reinhard Lupton, editors. "Shakespeare After 9/11: How a Social Trauma Reshapes Interpretation [Special Issue]." *Shakespeare Yearbook*, vol. 20, 2011, pp. 1-289.

Cahill, Patricia A. *Unto the Breach: Martial Formations, Historical Trauma, and the Early Modern Stage.* Oxford UP, 2009.

Caruth, Cathy. *Listening to Trauma: Conversations with Leaders in Theory and Treatment of Catastrophic Experience.* Johns Hopkins UP, 2014.

_____. *Unclaimed Experience: Trauma, Narrative and History.* Johns Hopkins UP, 1996.

Charles, Marilyn, and Michael O'Loughlin. "Fragments of Trauma: An Introduction." *Fragments of Trauma and the Social Production of Suffering: Trauma, History, and Memory*, edited by Marilyn Charles and Michael O'Loughlin, Rowman and Littlefield, 2015, pp. 3-24.

Davis, Stephen Michael. "'All Are Punished': Staging Romeo and Juliet in a Post 9/11 World." *Shakespeare Yearbook*, vol. 20, 2011, pp. 233-237.

Janoff-Bulman, Ronnie. *Shattered Assumptions: Toward a New Psychology of Trauma.* Free Press, 1992.

LaCapra, Dominick. *Writing History, Writing Trauma.* Johns Hopkins UP, 2001.

Ringel, Shoshana, and Jerrold R. Brandell. *Trauma: Contemporary Directions in Therapy, Practice, and Research.* SAGE, 2012.

Shakespeare, William. *Romeo and Juliet*, edited by René Weis, Bloomsbury, 2012. The Arden Shakespeare—Third Series.

Silverstone, Catherine. *Shakespeare, Trauma and Contemporary Performance.* Routledge, 2011.

Stark-Estes, Lisa S. *Violence, Trauma, and Virtus in Shakespeare's Roman Poems and Plays: Transforming Ovid.* Palgrave Macmillan, 2014.

# Chamber, Tomb, and Theater: Living in *Romeo and Juliet*'s Spaces of the Dead_____

Adam Rzepka

The Chorus that opens *Romeo and Juliet* informs us of its lovers' doom in the same sentence that introduces them as lovers: they are "death marked" before we meet them (Pro.9).[1] But didn't we already know this before we entered the theater? Some degree of familiarity with the play's iconic plot can be assumed at least since its immediate and extraordinary success in London's public theaters at the end of the sixteenth century. As the first quarto of the play announced on its title page in 1597, this is a tragedy that had already "been often (with great applause) plaid publiquely."[2] Even for its first audience, the story might have been familiar from Shakespeare's immediate source for the play, Arthur Brooke's 1562 poem, *The Tragicall History of Romeus and Juliet*, which depended in turn on its own Italian sources.[3] Certainly today it would be difficult to imagine many playgoers attending this most popular of Shakespeare's works without already knowing how it ends. As John Channing Briggs has argued, the play seems uniquely to inspire in audiences a "compulsion to repeat, to witness and undergo [its] delights and rigors . . . again and again" (see esp. 295). Seeing *Romeo and Juliet*, then, has been for a long time an act of remembrance. As we watch the play's events progress, we are recollecting precisely how the lovers meet the fate that they have met so many times before, in so many theaters.

One of the strangest and most compelling aspects of the play is that it seems to anticipate this reiterative aspect of its future performances by working the inevitability of its protagonists' tragic deaths into the drama that leads to them. Nowhere else in Shakespeare are dramatic ends woven so intimately into dramatic means, from the Chorus's opening reminder onwards. As the play unfolds, Shakespeare unleashes a blizzard of morbidity, including variations on the words "death" and "dead" alone (leaving aside references to "fate," "doom," the "end" of life, and an ever-expanding constellation of funereal terms like "bier," "tomb," "grave," and "shroud") 126 times—more than in any of his other plays. To note that love and death are closely related in *Romeo and Juliet* is, on its own, neither new nor particularly surprising, and some basic reasons for that relationship are easy to imagine (see, for example, Carroll). Romeo and Juliet know how extraordinarily dangerous their love is, given the bitter enmity between their families, and they are aware of the dire escalation of that danger once Romeo has killed Juliet's cousin Tybalt. It's also true that the fire of passionate, young love was frequently associated in the Renaissance with its impending self-immolation (in Friar Laurence's rendition, such "violent delights have violent ends / And in their triumph die, like fire and powder, / Which as they kiss consume" [2.6.9-11]). But these explanations, like the general observation that teenage passions in any era have often tended towards expression in dramatically dire terms, do not do justice to the peculiar thoroughness of Shakespeare's conjunction of death in love in this play. That thematic union is so insistent that it generates an uncanny sense that Romeo and Juliet are not simply hurtling towards death but already living it—that throughout the play, these electrifying young lovers are, in Mercutio's words, "already dead" (2.4.13). Mercutio's quip is meant to mock the pallid quality that has overcome Romeo in his unrequited love for Rosaline, Juliet's predecessor as the object of his overwhelming passion. That hopeless love has rendered him nearly inhuman to his friends, whom he avoids, like a condemned spirit, in favor of deep night, dark woods, and shuttered rooms. Yet once Juliet arrives, she seems only to magnify and focus the quality of living death that Mercutio notes. Later in the play, Juliet is herself described by Friar Laurence as a lover exhumed from a grave; she presents us with three increasingly immersive visions of either Romeo or herself entombed alive; she is the subject of a dream in which Romeo imagines himself to be a conscious corpse; and, of course, both she and Romeo find themselves alive inside an actual tomb in the play's final scene.

In this essay, I trace this escalation of what we might think of as Romeo and Juliet's self-mourning: the ways in which they seem not only to anticipate their violent end, but to be gradually recollecting and working through it with us. In particular, I am interested in the spaces of this self-mourning, from Romeo's melancholic haunts in the first Act to Juliet's terrifying visions of encryption and, finally, to the paradoxically dark, cloistered, vast, and illuminated Capulet tomb—"That dim monument," as Juliet calls it, where the tragedy finds its promised conclusion. As Ramie Targoff has shown, Shakespeare displays a distinctly Protestant sensibility in erasing from his source for the play any sense that the lovers will be reunited in the afterlife, and in suggesting instead that the best possible conclusion for mortal love is "posthumous intimacy in the tomb" (24). What neither Targoff nor other scholars have attended to is the way that both Romeo and Juliet have of placing themselves in the intimacy of tomblike spaces throughout the play. Ultimately, I will suggest that these spaces take on a metatheatrical cast, as they begin to echo the space shared by the play and its audience. The tomb finds a resonance in the theater, that enclosure where Romeo and Juliet are killed, reincorporated, and reanimated in performance after performance.

## Artificial night

A useful way to begin an exploration of *Romeo and Juliet*'s spaces of living death is to join Romeo's mother, as the play begins, in wondering where on earth he is. "O, where is Romeo?" Montague's Wife asks Benvolio; "Saw you him today?" (1.1.115). In the audience, we might ask the same question about the eponymous hero of the play we've come to see and share an equal interest in the two successive answers given to us by Romeo's friend Benvolio and by his father, Montague. Both answers present carefully etched portraits of the world as it is lived by Romeo in the profound melancholy of his unrequited love. Benvolio gives the first report:

Madam, an hour before the worshiped sun
Peered forth the golden window of the east,

A troubled mind drive me to walk abroad,
Where underneath the grove of sycamore
That westward rooteth from this city side,
So early walking did I see your son.
Towards him I made, but he was 'ware of me,
And stole into the covert of the wood. (1.1.120-27)

Benvolio's lyrical, visionary description introduces us to the world of the love-melancholic as a quest for secluded enclosure within a cosmic expanse of phantom light. His opening images of the rising sun recall the "rosy-fingered Dawn" of the Homeric epics so directly and with such precise verse that we might well forget that his sighting of Romeo takes place "an hour before" the sunrise. The common effect of vividly describing off-stage events is doubled here: Benvolio allows us to "see" what is no longer present, and also to see a sunrise that was not even present in the scene being described. Romeo flees the approach of his friend, but he also seeks refuge from this impending dawn (as his father's account a moment later makes clear). Stealing into the "covert of the wood" sequesters him from social contact and from a luminous beauty he knows is coming but cannot yet see. Both aversions were thought of as typical symptoms of melancholia in the Renaissance. As Robert Burton tells us in the *Anatomy of Melancholy*, melancholics display a predilection for solitude and specifically for "woods, orchards, gardens, rivers . . . dark walks and close" (262). The nature of Romeo's melancholy, though, is at the more extreme end of these symptoms. Benvolio's own "troubled mind" still welcomes the coming "worshiped sun," and walking "underneath" the sycamore grove is enough cover to suit his sadness. Romeo's particular melancholy requires a deeper darkness and a more secretive enclosure—a retreat from the pre-dawn grove into the lightless woods.

Romeo's father, Montague, rehearses the same visualized elements in his elaboration of Benvolio's observations, returning us to the pre-dawn hour and to Romeo's daily flight into enveloping darkness:

Many a morning hath he there been seen,
With tears augmenting the fresh morning's dew,
Adding to clouds more clouds with his deep sighs;
But all so soon as the all-cheering sun
Should in the farthest east begin to draw
The shady curtains from Aurora's bed,
Away from light steals home my heavy son
And private in his chamber pens himself,
Shuts up his windows, locks fair daylight out,
And makes himself an artificial night. (1.1.137-140)

Montague's account puts Romeo in a more direct relationship with the celestial and meteorological sweep of the wide world outside the walled city of Verona, but then plunges him into an even more profound entombment. We are brought back "there" to the sycamore grove at the city's edge, where Romeo's tears and sighs expand into the dew and mist of the early morning, and this time, he flees into darkness not an hour before the dawn but at first light. Yet Montague seems at pains to convey the degree of confinement that Romeo seeks in direct opposition to these vistas. His refuge is not only to be "private in his chamber," but shut up and locked in, enveloped in an "artificial night" that is, as Montague's grammar allows, not only self-made but "himself." One eye on the break of day in the "farthest east," Romeo constructs a hermetically sealed enclosure in which he embodies and preserves the night. This dialectic between expansive vision and enclosed solitude was also a fundamental property of early modern melancholia, captured precisely in Albrecht Dürer's widely influential 1514 engraving *Melencolia I* (Fig. 1).

Fig. 1. Albrecht Dürer, *Melencolia I*

In Dürer's portrait of melancholy, its emblematic sufferer is not simply removed from the living, social world and immobilized in "dark walks and close" or private chambers.[5] That confinement is balanced against a view of the outside world rendered as a vast, illuminated expanse—a "golden window" on a "worshiped sun." This paradoxical marriage of claustrophobic enclosure and cosmic scope will return first as the fantasy space of Romeo and Juliet's love, with its "vast shores" imagined from within the "mask of night" (2.2.83-85), and then as its literal and final destination in a tomb that is also "full of light" (5.1.86). But Romeo is already in love in that space, and in love with it, before Juliet arrives on the scene. Its lineaments here sketch the shape of fatal love in the rest of the play.

Benvolio's and Montague's parallel accounts of Romeo's transit between the poles of exterior and interior exile—the cloudy, sun-threatened grove and the covered wood or shuttered chamber—also note its curious furtiveness. Romeo does not flee headlong from his friend, or from the sun, but slips away from them. Benvolio tells us that he "stole" away from him, and Montague tells us that he "steals home." There is something in these descriptions that casts Romeo as ghostly, a visitation glimpsed only for a moment in the dead of night, who shuns humans and vanishes "all so soon" as day breaks. To think of Romeo's melancholy as a living death in this preternatural sense might seem odd at first, but it is supported both by parallel passages elsewhere in Shakespeare and by others later in *Romeo and Juliet*. Puck, for instance, in *A Midsummer Night's Dream*, uses the only other reference to "Aurora" in Shakespeare to invoke the pre-dawn star that drives the walking dead back to their graves: it is "Aurora's harbinger," he reminds Oberon, "At whose approach ghosts, wand'ring here and there, / Troop home to churchyards." Like Romeo, "They willfully exile themselves from light, / And must for aye consort with black-browed night" (3.2.380-87). Romeo might also remind us of another Shakespearean entity that walks abroad at night, that fails to respond to initial advances and that leaves at the approach of "morn in russet mantle clad": the ghost of Hamlet's father, "Doomed for a certain term to walk the night, / And for the day confined. . ." (1.1.166; 1.5.10-11).

The action of Act II of *Romeo and Juliet* begins with Romeo again walking the night, just after the Capulet feast. He is on stage for only two lines before turning to go back and seek out Juliet, so this time, it is the audience from whom he steals away almost as soon as he is seen. When Benvolio suggests that Mercutio call out for him, Mercutio instead proposes to "conjure" him, like a demon, or, when Romeo fails to respond, like the ghost of a dead man: "He heareth not, he stirreth not, he moveth not; / The ape is dead, and I must conjure him" (2.1.6-16). Benvolio's response to Mercutio's extended conjuration ends that particular joke, but only by returning us to the earlier account of the grove and the wood, this time in an even more sinister vein. "Come," he says to Mercutio," "He hath hid himself among these trees / To be consorted with the humorous night. / Blind is his love and best befits the dark" (2.1.33-35). This new explanation of Romeo's retreat orchestrates commonplace characterizations of love-melancholy as a humoral disorder and of love as a blind passion with something that sounds tantamount to the demonic. In the next Act, the Friar frames Romeo in terms that sound similarly threatening, similarly reminiscent of unnatural visitation: "Commend thee to thy lady, / And bid her hasten all the house to bed /. . . Romeo is coming" (3.3.165-68). This again echoes Puck's insistent sense of the fairies as leagued with the undead in *A Midsummer Night's Dream*, when, at the end of that play, he ushers them into Theseus's sleeping house:

> Now the hungry lion roars,
> And the wolf behowls the moon,
> Whilst the heavy plowman snores,
> All with weary task foredone.
> ....
> Now it is the time of night
> That the graves all gaping wide,
> Every one lets forth his sprite,
> In the churchway paths to glide:
> And we fairies, that do run
> By the triple Hecate's team,
> From the presence of the sun,
> Following darkness like a dream,
> Now are frolic . . . (5.1.363-74)

In contrast to other Shakespearean characters notably defined by their sadness, like Antonio in *The Merchant of Venice*, or like Hamlet,

Romeo is stricken with a melancholy that seems to redefine what sort of being he is. Whether he is pining for Rosaline or hastening back to Juliet, he is a creature of the night, subject to conjurations and haunting uneasily the spaces of friendship and family.

This ghostly quality is not lost on Romeo himself, though it takes the form of a dim suspicion rather than a conscious self-awareness. Although he seems oblivious to the sinister aspect that others apprehend in his melancholy, something dire is growing in Romeo and pressing on him from within. This object at first appears to him to be his love for Rosaline, but in this form it is formless, composed of nothing but maddening paradoxes—a "misshapen chaos of well-seeming forms, / Feather of lead, bright smoke, cold fire, sick health, / Still-waking sleep, that is not what it is!" (1.1.178-80). By the time the plan is afoot to attend the Capulet feast, however, the dim object taking shape in Romeo is his own death, as two of his objections to that plan suggest. After insisting repeatedly that he is too "heavy" to go and dance, Romeo simply says that "'tis no wit to go." "Why, may one ask?" replies Mercutio, and Romeo explains, "I dreamt a dream tonight" (1.4.49-50). But the contents of this foreboding dream are immediately covered over by the sprawling flight of folkloric fancy that is Mercutio's "Queen Mab" speech, which replaces Romeo's specific dream with an extensive survey of the legendary mechanisms of dreams in general. In Act V, however, Romeo has had a dream again, and this time, he tells us the specific content: "I dreamt my lady came and found me dead / (Strange dream that gives a dead man leave to think!)" (5.1.6-7). This does not mean, of course, that this is the only oneiric scenario of which Romeo is capable (and indeed in this second dream he is instantly resuscitated and made "an emperor"). Yet these are the only two dreams mentioned in the play, and as such, they cannot be disentangled. With the story of the first so grandiosely obscured, we are left with the story of the second: when Romeo dreams, he dreams of his living death.

The suggestion that the obscured object of Romeo's desire has begun to resolve into this "strange dream" of being a conscious corpse is reiterated and given a spatial dimension in the final, unsuccessful protest he offers at the end of the same debate. In reply to Benvolio's efforts to hurry everyone along to the Capulet house lest they "come too late," Romeo replies, "I fear, too early; for my mind misgives / Some consequence, yet hanging in the stars, / Shall bitterly begin his fearful date / With this night's revels and expire the term / Of a despisèd life, closed in my breast, / By some vile forfeit of untimely death" (1.4.105-111). These lines cannot be reduced to uneasiness at the prospect of a dangerous prank. They clearly look beyond the crashing of the party to a tragic ("untimely") end beyond it. They thus install in Romeo a semi-conscious awareness of the preordained fate that the Chorus has announced, opening character psychology to what would otherwise remain a dramatic irony that relies on what only the audience knows. Stranger still is the specification that the life that this looming fate will end is "closed within" Romeo, as if what he grieves when he "pens himself" in the "private . . . chamber" of his room is his own life, penned within himself. If the space of Romeo's sadness is fundamentally one of enclosure, here it is internally repeated, like the multiplied interiors of a set of nested dolls. Ensconced within a self in turn ensconced in darkness, Romeo's expired life is stirring.

## That dim monument

Once Romeo meets Juliet, these murky, proliferating enclosures snap fully into focus, gaining a concrete form: for Juliet, they are quite explicitly graves or crypts in which she is laid while still thrillingly, horribly, viscerally alive. Like Romeo, Juliet is sometimes referred to by other characters, more or less explicitly, as undead. The clearest instance is in Friar Laurence's initial assessment of Romeo's newfound love, "old desire," as the Act 2 Chorus has informed us, now lying in "his deathbed" (2.0.1):

> ROMEO: Thou chid'st me oft for loving Rosaline.
> FRIAR: For doting, not for loving, pupil mine.
> ROMEO: And bad'st me bury love.
> FRIAR: Not in a grave,
> To lay one in another out to have. (2.3.86-90)

This is yet another place in the play where Shakespeare steers the commonplace elements of a debate about love emphatically towards the macabre. In this case, the Friar's correction of Romeo—that he chided him for doting on Rosaline rather than for truly loving her—can stand on its own, and indeed it will be picked up again on its own terms three lines later. Yet Shakespeare takes a moment to interject the jarring image of Juliet being hauled out of the grave and replaced with Rosaline's corpse. As in earlier scenes, reanimation of the dead seems to be an explicit topic for some characters and a vague background notion for Romeo. The afterthought that launches the Friar's grim image of corpse-switching in this exchange is Romeo's shift to the general metaphor of buried love, and this directly recalls the Friar's precise philosophical observation, in the soliloquy that opens the scene, that "The earth, that's nature's mother, is her tomb. / What is her burying grave, that is her womb" (2.2.9-10).

The notion of Juliet waiting (or even gestating) in the grave is not the Friar's alone, however: it is increasingly a concern for Juliet. There are at least three moments in the second half of the play when Juliet is overwhelmed by images of graves and tombs, even if we set aside passing rhetorical figures like her plea to her mother either to delay her marriage to Paris or "make the bridal bed / In that dim monument where Tybalt lies" (3.5.213). The first of these moments occurs as Romeo is retreating from the balcony after their only night together and assuring Juliet that "all these woes shall serve / For sweet disclosures in our times to come" (3.5.52-53). Juliet is less certain, and her uncertainty is inscribed in the space between her window and Romeo's stage below:

> O God, I have an ill-divining soul!
> Methinks I see thee, now thou art so low,
> As one dead in the bottom of the tomb.
> Either my eyesight fails or thou lookest pale. (3.5.54-57)

Even for Juliet, there is something persistently deathly about Romeo. But here she takes this sense a step further: if Romeo's friends have a tendency to describe him as "already dead," Juliet sees him here as already entombed. This first of Juliet's visions of the tomb, though disturbing, is still directly linked to her love for Romeo: he is encrypted, while the lovers remain bound together in a mutual gaze so that Juliet's observation that he looks pale is immediately echoed by Romeo with "in my eye so do you" (3.5.58). After her initial entombment of Romeo, however, the pale figure in the tomb becomes Juliet herself. Having confessed the sin of despair to the Friar ("I long to die"; 4.1.67), Juliet proceeds to a list of the fates she would be willing to suffer in order to avoid marrying Paris and return to Romeo:

> O, bid me leap, rather than marry Paris,
> From the battlements of any tower,
> Or walk in thievish ways, or bid me lurk
> Where serpents are. Chain me with roaring bears,
> Or hide me nightly in a charnel house,
> O'ercovered quite with dead men's rattling bones,
> With reeky shanks and yellow chapless skulls.
> Or bid me go into a new-made grave
> And hide me with a dead man in his shroud—
> Things that, to hear them told, have made me tremble—
> I will do it without fear or doubt,
> To live an unstained wife to my sweet love. (4.1.78-89)[6]

Juliet names other traumatic alternatives in her speech, but the last two possibilities, of being enclosed alive in the spaces of the dead, clearly hold a special fascination for her even before the Friar lays out the plan that will require her to do exactly that. The crypt is imagined as a place of vivid sensation, the bones and shrouds of the dead pressing against her in what Matthew Spellberg has described as "the felt-closeness of dream"; even secondhand stories of live burials make her "tremble" (80). Yet the purpose of the imagined burial is her perfect, "unstained" preservation beneath this cover of mortal remains, as she waits to emerge into marriage. The fantasy is an exact and unusual one, in which virgin purity and the contamination of overwhelming feeling coincide. Like Romeo's immersion in "artificial night," the space in which Juliet secrets herself is not simply one of seclusion from life, but one of suspended animation.

Juliet's third and final vision of the crypt comes to her in her room, just as she is about to drink the Friar's "distilling liquor" (4.1.94). This episode is understandably more intense and sustained than either of the previous two, since now these have been matched with the plan actually to enter a sleep like death. As in the previous vision, Juliet passes through a number of grim scenarios relatively quickly—what if the potion simply kills her? What if she awakens early and suffocates?—before being gripped at much greater length by the prospect of remaining alive and conscious in the tomb:

> Or, if I live, is it not very like
> The horrible conceit of death and night,
> Together with the terror of the place—
> As in a vault, an ancient receptacle
> Where for this many hundred years the bones
> Of all my buried ancestors are packed;
> ….
> O, if I wake, shall I not be distraught,
> Environèd with all these hideous fears,
> And madly play with my forefathers' joints,
> And pluck the mangled Tybalt from his shroud,
> And, in this rage, with some great kinsman's bone,
> As with a club, dash out my desp'rate brains? (4.3.55-60)

Juliet returns to the "reeky shanks" and shroud from her second scenario of live entombment, but now the contrast between the filth of decay and the idyllic purity preserved within it has given way to active violation as the crypt erupts into time and motion. Juliet's body, previously chaste beneath the press of bones, is now in awful interaction with them, and these hallowed relics are themselves also disturbed. This shroud is not some hypothetical "dead man's" but specifically Tybalt's, and the bones are not anonymous "rattling bones" but those of Juliet's "forefathers," her "ancestors" who have lain here "this many hundred years" (4.3.40-41). In shifting from static preservation to active violation, Juliet's living death is now figured as impious, or even sacrilegious. Just as the corollary to Romeo's suspended animation is his haunting of the social world like a condemned spirit, the corollary to Juliet's is now the imagined desecration of the family's memorial space.

## A vault full of light

Just such a desecration is the subject of the first line Romeo speaks to Juliet, as he touches her hand with his: "If I profane with my unworthiest hand / This holiest shrine. . ." (1.5.94-95). When Juliet imagines her profanation of the Capulet tomb in Act 4, she picks up this theme and relays it ahead to the beginning of the climax in Act 5, when Romeo uses a "mattock and the wrenching iron" to force open that same "womb of death" (5.3.22, 45).[7] All of the play's enclosures, entombments, and encryptions lead here, to the moment when the "dim monument" containing the living Juliet is opened to the space of the theater. It is a matter of debate how this would have been staged in Shakespeare's time because it is unclear whether the "detestable maw" that Romeo pries open would have been a space beneath the stage accessed by a trapdoor; a free-standing platform on the stage; or an extension of the same curtained discovery space that served earlier as the bed upon which Juliet falls when she drinks the Friar's concoction.[8] In each of these possibilities, however, there is the additional problem of the larger architecture of the "monument" that stands in the churchyard. The tomb requires a space to be opened, but it also implies an above-ground memorial to open into. Romeo seems to gesture to this larger space as he discovers Juliet: "A grave? / O, no, a lantern, slaughtered youth, / For here lies Juliet, and her beauty makes / This vault a feasting presence full of light" (5.3.84-86). The language of illumination that Romeo uses to cast the crypt as shining with Juliet's beauty is also an architectural language that magnifies her dark enclosure. A "lantern" is not just a light but, as most editors of the play remind us, a windowed turret atop a cathedral dome that lets in a circle of light. The primary meaning of "presence" in these lines is the receiving room in a palace, where audiences with the sovereign would take place. "Vault" can indicate either an underground crypt or a ceiling overhead; Romeo's only other use of the term in the play describes the starry sky as "The vaulty heaven so high above our heads" (3.5.22). Romeo has proved adept before at uniting dark enclosure and cosmic scope, and here he finds within the crypt the open, attendant brightness that would have suffused the open theater around him, despite the "artificial night" in which the scene takes place. Each of the elements that define this larger space above the hidden "maw" or "womb" echoes the architecture of the theaters in which *Romeo and Juliet* would have been "plaid publiquely" in Shakespeare's day. The circle of the "lantern" evokes the circle of daylight above the walls of the open theater. As in the earlier reference to "vaulty heaven," the "vault" that is also a "feasting presence full of light" glances at the canopied "heavens" over the stage and takes in the audience arrayed around it, like celebratory guests in a royal receiving hall. In this sense the tomb joins the Capulet feast, where Romeo serves as a torchbearer casting a "circle of light," and the playhouse, which Julia Lupton describes as the play's twinned spaces of "hospitality" (see "Making Room"). As audience, we are being welcomed into the tomb.

The opening of the Capulet tomb into the theater may also rely on a more general symmetry between the architecture of tombs and playhouses in the period. Here we are on speculative ground, since we cannot know what Shakespeare had in mind when he imagined a Veronese tomb and do not know how he staged it. Scholars today agree that there is far too much unjustified specificity in assertions like Joseph Hunter's, in 1853, that "It is clear that Shakespeare, or some writer whom he followed, had in mind the churchyard of Saint Mary the Old [Santa Maria Antica] in Verona, and the monument of the Scaligers which stood in it" (see Furness 269). There is no solid evidence that Shakespeare knew that kind of local detail about Italy either through first-hand travel or through published accounts. Yet he is perfectly likely to have had a degree of acquaintance with Italian literature and culture, and neither Shakespeare nor his audience would have been strangers to the kind of memorial to which Hunter refers.[9] Tombs incorporating similar architectural elements had been part of the Catholic tradition in England and, in some cases, were still used. An important feature of monuments like the Scaliger tomb, and of some of the more elaborately constructed English tombs, is the vaulted roof, or baldachin, supported by forward poles, above the space of entombment (whether this was a subterranean crypt or a raised sarcophagus). The resulting structure has a strong visual parallel with the London stages on which *Romeo and Juliet* was first performed, with their sheltering and decorative heavens supported by pillars above the stage, a concealed space beneath the stage, and an open viewing area surrounding it (see Figs. 2-3).

Fig. 2. Tomb of Cangrande I, Santa Maria Antica, Verona.
Public domain photo.

Fig. 3. Shakespeare's Globe Theatre, London
[a modern reconstruction of the original].
Public domain photo.

This architectural symmetry speaks to the theatrical quality of memorial displays in the period as well as to the memorial appearance of Shakespeare's theater in this Act. Placed side by side, the tombs begin to look like little theaters, and the theater like an expansive tomb. When the stage becomes emphatically a "churchyard" (Shakespeare reminds us of this three times in the first forty lines of the scene), with Juliet's "poor living corpse" interred upon or beneath it, its pillars and heavens are recast as the outward elements of a monument to an undead dramatic heroine (5.2.29).

This hybrid theater-monument gathers up the play's determined exploration of its protagonists' vitally morbid enclosures into a figure for its own potential legacy as an enduring tragic drama. If the Chorus's opening reminder, the relentless references to living death, and the lovers' own intimations of that living death seem far in excess of anything we might call foreshadowing, one explanation may be that this play, more than any other in Shakespeare, has "untimely death" as a fundamental concern: not only death at the wrong time, but death in the unending, cyclical time of repeated performance.[10] We return to the unique enclosure of the theater to see Romeo and Juliet reincorporated and reanimated there, and to see them find their way back to the crypt where we last laid them to an uneasy rest. As an audience returning again and again to this "strange dream," we are invited each time to experience *Romeo and Juliet* as a memorial ritual and its theater as a memorial space.

## Notes

1. All quotations of Shakespeare are from the Orgel and Braunmuller edition unless otherwise noted.

2. William Shakespeare, *Romeo and Juliet (Q1)*. Reprint of *An excellent conceited tragedy of Romeo and Juliet*, John Danter, 1597. See Bevington. For an argument that "*Romeo and Juliet* was clearly becoming a fashionable currency" as early as 1598, see Cathcart, esp. 155.

3. For Brooke's poem, see Bullough 1:284–363. For a capsule survey of Brooke's Italian sources, see Young, esp. 181-92.

4. The unusually murderous Richard III comes closest to this total, at 121 instances, though that play is more than 600 lines longer than *Romeo and Juliet*. By way of comparison with other tragedies, "death" and "dead" occur in *Hamlet* sixty times and in *Macbeth* only thirty-six.

5. For a consideration of the powerful legacy of *Melencholia I* and its role as a "visual commonplace" in considerations of melancholy, see Daniel, 39-44.

6. To end line 86 with "shroud" is an innovation on the part of the Penguin editors, though it is one that suits my purposes. Q1 has "Or lay me in tombe with one new dead"; Q2 has "And hide me with a dead man in his," apparently referring back to the "grave" of the preceding line; and the Folio repeats the word, with "And hide me with a dead man in his grave" (see Bevington, *Internet Shakespeare Editions*).

7. The parallel is even stronger if we consider the Catholic tradition in which statues in saints' shrines sometimes also served as reliquaries, with a supposed physical relic of the saint's body entombed within the statue. For a consideration of such reliquary statues, see Belting, 297-310.

8. On the likely possibilities for staging the tomb in the Shakespearean theater, see Thompson.

9. On Shakespeare's knowledge of Italy, see, for instance, Levith, Marrapodi et al., and D'Amico.

10. On the metatheatrical relationship between the audience's sense of the time of performance and the lovers' concerns with passing time, see Kumamoto. "The stage becomes a potent and visible signifier," Kumamoto writes, "of the playgoers' tacit but profound understanding of . . . time's actions and human responses to them" (102).

## Works Cited

Belting, Hans. *Likeness and Presence: A History of the Image Before the Era of Art*. Translated by Edmund Jephcott, U of Chicago P, 1994.

Bevington, David, editor. *Internet Shakespeare Editions*, 2013. internetshakespeare.uvic.ca/doc/Rom_Q1/complete/. Accessed 22 Feb. 2017.

Briggs, John Channing. "*Romeo and Juliet* and the Cure of Souls." *Ben Jonson Journal*, vol. 16, 2009, 281-303.

Bullough, Geoffrey. *Narrative and Dramatic Sources of Shakespeare*. Routledge and Kegan Paul, 1957–75. 8 vols.

Burton, Robert. *The Anatomy of Melancholy*. New York Review of Books, 2001.

Carroll, William. "'We were born to die': *Romeo and Juliet*." *Comparative Drama*, vol. 15, Spring 1981, pp. 54-71.

Cathcart, Charles. "Romeo at the Rose in 1598." *Early Theatre*, vol. 13, 2013, pp. 149-62.

D'Amico, Jack. *Shakespeare and Italy: The City and the Stage*. U of Florida P, 1993.

Daniel, Drew. *The Melancholy Assemblage: Affect and Epistemology in the English Renaissance*. Fordham UP, 2013.

Furness, Howard, editor. *Romeo and Juliet*, Dover, 1963.

Kumamoto, Chikako D. "Time and Stage Directions in Quarto 1 and Quarto 2 of *Romeo and Juliet.*" *Journal of the Wooden O Symposium*, vol. 11, 2011, pp. 97-112.

Levith, Murray J. *Shakespeare's Italian Settings and Plays.* St. Martin's, 1989.

Lupton, Julia Reinhard. "Making Room, Affording Hospitality: Environments of Entertainment in *Romeo and Juliet.*" *Journal of Medieval and Early Modern Studies*, vol. 43, 2013, pp. 145-72.

Marrapodi, Michele, A. J. Hoenselaars, Marcello Cappuzzo, and L. Falzon Santucci, editors. *Shakespeare's Italy: Functions of Italian Locations in Renaissance Drama.* Manchester UP, 1993.

Shakespeare, William. *William Shakespeare: The Complete Works*, edited by Stephen Orgel and A. R. Braunmuller, Penguin, 2002.

Spellberg, Matthew. "Feeling Dreams in *Romeo and Juliet.*" *English Literary* Renaissance, vol. 43, 2013, pp. 62-83.

Targoff, Ramie. "'*Romeo and Juliet*' and the Practice of Joint Burial." *Representations*, vol. 120, 2012, pp. 17-38.

Thompson, Leslie. "'With Patient Ears Attend': 'Romeo and Juliet' on the Elizabethan Stage." *Studies in Philology*, vol. 92, 1995, pp. 230-47.

Young, Bruce. "'These Times of Woe': The Contraction and Dislocation of Time in Shakespeare's *Romeo and Juliet.*" *Shakespeare and the Italian Renaissance: Appropriation, Transformation, Opposition*, edited by Michele Marrapodi, Routledge, 2014, pp. 181-98.

# Flight and Spaceflight in *Romeo and Juliet*

Matthew Steggle

Approximately 1.7 billion miles from where you are sitting, Juliet is in orbit around a giant planet. She is an icy moon, about seventy miles in diameter, travelling fast and close to her parent. The sun is bright in the black sky, but tiny compared to how it appears from Earth. Instead, Juliet's heaven is dominated by the ice giant she orbits, which, thanks to the odd geometry of this planetary system, will be perpetually visible and perpetually at half phase. It will look something like our half-moon, except blue-green and permanent and nearly a hundred times larger in the sky. Far above Juliet— although "above" is tricky in this tilted frame of reference—lies Romeo, a hundred-mile crater across the frozen surface of the moon Oberon. Not too far away from them both, on the corrugated moon of Miranda, is their home town Verona in the form of Verona Rupes, three miles or more in height, the largest cliffs currently known to mankind.

None of the above is science fiction: rather, it is the stuff of textbooks describing the moons and their features around the planet Uranus (see Greeley and Batson, esp. 402). And the names are, on one level, a cultural artefact that can be described in terms of the history of Shakespeare's reception, the process by which a version of him assumed a central place in Western culture. Shakespeare was prestigious in mid-nineteenth-century Britain, where Sir John Herschel named the four known moons of Uranus after fairy characters from the British poets then regarded as the greatest, Shakespeare and Pope. Shakespeare was prestigious, too, in twentieth-century America, where first Gerard P. Kuiper in 1949, and then later scientists working on Voyager data, elected to adapt Herschel's naming system, extending it beyond fairies to encompass mortal characters and indeed Shakespearean locations (Kuiper 129). Nor is *Romeo and Juliet* the only Shakespeare play used for names in the Uranian system. Juliet is one of a group of small moonlets, the

Portia group, whose members include Desdemona, Cordelia, and Ophelia. And yet *Romeo and Juliet* seems a particularly resonant source of names for these objects, since the play speaks strangely well to modern imaginations of flight and spaceflight.[1]

The problem is that attempts to talk about this play's "cosmology" tend to run into the sand in a scholarly but quaint language of Ptolemaic spheres, epicycles, and astrology. Seventy years ago, E. M. W. Tillyard posited the existence of an "Elizabethan World Picture," in which both political systems and the physical universe itself were seen as hierarchical, just, and orderly, with God at the top. While we may finally have got out from under his shadow as regards Elizabethan ideas of politics, we still live in it when it comes to our perceptions of how the Elizabethans viewed the physical universe. In what follows, therefore, I propose that this play is far more subversive in its relationship to cosmology than has generally been recognized.

## *Romeo and Juliet* and Cosmology

In many respects, *Romeo and Juliet* looks like—and is often treated as—a textbook example of the Elizabethan understanding of an ordered universe.[2] The sun, moon, and stars are frequently described in ways that open up a series of conventional Renaissance discourses. Romeo and Juliet themselves are, famously, a "pair of star-crossed lovers," their fates seemingly sealed in advance by a deterministic astrology. Even the action of the play, as has long been noted, is framed by a series of very formal descriptions of time, mostly in the shape of sunrises and sunsets. Here, for instance, is Benvolio's description of dawn in 1.1:

> Madam, an hour before the worshipped sun
> Peered forth the golden window of the east,
> A troubled mind drove me to walk abroad. . . . (1.1.109-11)

To which Montague contributes his own description of dawn, again one framed in fairly static, conventionally mythological terms.

---

But all so soon as the all-cheering sun,
Should in the farthest east begin to draw
The shady curtains from Aurora's bed,
Away from light steals home my heavy son. . . . (1.1.125-26; see also
2.3.1-4)

These set-piece descriptions of time continue through the play,
suggesting a benevolent, predictable universe against which human
passions play out. The only serious scholarly debate has been around
whether the universe depicted is always geocentric, or whether
Shakespeare flirts with ideas of heliocentrism. But the proposition
that Shakespeare depicts astronomy as fundamentally ordered and
reassuring has not been in doubt.[3]

Right from the start, though, this universe of almost
overdetermined order is at odds with the lovers. Whereas these
opening descriptions describe the heavens as a sort of house, with
windows, curtained beds, and the like, Romeo turns this simile on
its head, using doors and curtains to interfere with the cosmology
and shutting out daylight to "[make] himself an artificial night"
(1.1.131). And in fact, the lovers repeatedly think in terms of altering
or destroying the usual rules and material furniture of the universe.

First of all, Romeo and Juliet have a distinctly unusual
relationship with gravity. To begin with, things seem conventional,
as when the pre-Juliet Romeo talks about his inability to fly:

ROMEO        I have a soul of lead
             So stakes me to the ground I cannot move.
MERCUTIO     You are a lover, borrow Cupid's wings,
             And soar with them above a common bound.
ROMEO        I am too sore enpiercèd with his shaft
             To soar with his light feathers. . . . (1.4.15-20)

In Act Two, however, once the lovers have met, flight becomes
extremely possible. Romeo begins the act by giving his companions
the slip, since according to Benvolio, "he leapt this orchard wall"
(2.1.5). Romeo himself describes this act in terms of having been
able to fly, in language that clearly picks up that used in the previous

---

act: "With love's light wings did I o'erperch these walls, / For stony limits cannot hold love out" (2.2.66-67). The detail is taken over from the source, Brooke's *Romeus* ("so light he wox, he lept the wall"), and made literal, if not in the action, then certainly in the dialogue.[4] It has proved problematic in performance—is the wall represented on stage and does Romeo actually carry out some spectacular leap?—but whether or not Romeo actually performs a stunt at this point, this is certainly a moment where he is described in terms of taking flight.[5]

Juliet, too, is imagined in the same scene as flying. Romeo says as much:

> O, speak again, bright angel, for thou art
> As glorious to this night, being o'er my head,
> As is a wingèd messenger of heaven
> Unto the white-upturnèd wond'ring eyes
> Of mortals that fall back to gaze on him,
> When he bestrides the lazy puffing clouds,
> And sails upon the bosom of the air. (2.2.26-32)

"O'er my head" is the critical phrase here. The poetic imagery of effortless flight, sailing upon the bosom of the air, chimes with her literal placement up in the air on her balcony. A third sort of flight is added later in the scene, when the lovers compare one another to birds of prey: a "tassel-gentle," a "nïesse" (2.2.159, 168). The bird imagery invites historicizing footnotes on the class associations of falconry, but it also links the lovers to the ability to fly.

That idea of flight continues, and is literalized further, in the Q1 version of the scene of their marriage:

> FRIAR   Youth's love is quick, swifter than swiftest speed.
>             *Enter Juliet somewhat fast, and embraceth Romeo.*
>                   See where she comes.
>             So light of foot ne'er hurts the trodden flower.[6]

The later quartos lose this exchange and the wonderful stage direction. But Juliet's apparent ability to float is still commented on

---

by the Friar in Q2. He comments of her gait: "A lover may bestride the gossamers / That idles in the wanton summer air, / and yet not fall, so light is vanity" (2.6.18-20), that last phrase recovering what Evans aptly calls "his momentarily lapsed didactic tone" (2.6.18-20 and Evans's commentary).

This imagery of the lovers as literally defying gravity explains, I think, some of the ways in which *Romeo and Juliet* turns up so frequently in language to do with twentieth-century spaceflight. We have already seen some examples of this at Uranus, and here are more.

In 1963, the Soviet Union put two spacecraft into orbit, spacecraft that approached at one point to within a couple of miles of each other. One was piloted by the cosmonaut Valery Bykovsky, the other by his colleague Valentina Tereshkova, who thus became the first woman in space. The American press, bewildered by how to describe a female spaceman, reached for Shakespeare: "Romanoff and Juliet are in a space duet" (Ellis 66). In 1969, the first manned landing on the moon required two spaceships: the Lunar Module, which Armstrong and Aldrin piloted to the surface, and Collins's Command and Service Module, with which they had to dock in space in order to make the journey back home. The ships ended up being called "Eagle" and "Columbia." But the three-man crew had considered many different names for this pair of spacecraft: among them, appropriately, "Romeo" and "Juliet" (Armstrong et al. 208). Romeo and Juliet, then, were nearly the spaceships that first took humankind to the moon.

As well as thinking (and acting) as if they can fly, the lovers repeatedly figure their activities in terms of altering, and indeed destroying, the heavens. Romeo's famous lines in the balcony scene are so well-known that we are in danger of not hearing what they say:

> But soft, what light through yonder window breaks?
> It is the east, and Juliet is the sun.
> Arise, fair sun, and kill the envious moon,
> Who is already sick and pale with grief. . . . (2.2.2-5)

---

The comparison between lover and sun is a staple of Petrarchan imagery, frequently invoked in Elizabethan love sonnets and indeed mocked by Shakespeare in Sonnet 130. But this image is given a surprising and destructive twist. She is a planet-killing sun, one that can get rid of the moon. Similarly, Romeo's next simile for his beloved is, again, one with a long Petrarchan heritage, which then takes an apocalyptic turn.

> Two of the fairest stars in all the heaven,
> Having some business, do entreat her eyes
> To twinkle in their spheres till they return. (2.2.15-17)[7]

Thus far, the comparison is conventional and Petrarchan: her eyes are so bright that they might be temporary substitutes for stars. But Romeo warms to his theme, reversing the simile. In the space of three lines, her eyes become far brighter than mere stars, burning with a supernova-like intensity that can turn night to day.

> What if her eyes were there, they in her head?
> The brightness of her cheek would shame those stars,
> As daylight doth a lamp; her eyes in heaven
> Would through the airy region stream so bright
> That birds would sing and think it were not night. (2.2.18-22)

"Supernova" sounds like an ahistorical term, but Shakespeare had of course experienced the very bright supernova of 1572, to which he is famously linked by James Joyce in *Ulysses* (201 and note; see also Falk 48-49). And the imagery of Juliet's light "streaming" through the heavens is very striking: René Weis observes that this is "perhaps a rhetorical reminiscence" of *Doctor Faustus*, where Christ's blood "streams in the firmament," and we shall return to this observation later. It could also fairly be said that this image is part of what G. Blakemore Evans calls the play's "special quality of light in darkness," its interest in confounding night and day: and also as programmatic for the argument here in its sense that the lovers can exceed the machinery of the universe.[8]

---

Juliet, so far, has been seen as usurping the sun and the stars and as threatening the moon. In the next scene, she herself proposes to rewrite the as-yet-unwritten laws of relativity: "love's heralds should be thoughts, / Which ten times faster glides than the sun's beams." Love, for Juliet, exceeds the celestial by an order of magnitude. Just as Romeo replaces the sun with her in 2.2, so she, in Q1's version of 2.6, gets rid of the sun in favor of him: seeing him, she observes, "I am (if I be day) / Come to my sun" (see Evans's apparatus on 2.6). And by 3.2, Juliet commandeers and rewrites the formula seen elsewhere in the play in which time indications are described in terms of formal mythological descriptions. For Juliet, it is not enough that night is coming at its usual speed, and she asks it to come quicker: "Gallop apace, you fiery-footed steeds, / Towards Phoebus' lodging. . ." (3.2.1-2). Here, once again, Juliet wants to overwind the clockwork of the cosmos.[9]

In this connection she also delivers one of the most famous images of the play. Once again, it is her turn to imagine Romeo as usurping a feature of the physical universe:

> Give me my Romeo, and when I shall die,
> Take him and cut him out in little stars,
> And he will make the face of heaven so fine
> That all the world will be in love with night,
> And pay no worship to the garish sun. (3.2.21-25)

This is, of course, wildly inconsistent with her own previous celestial imagery—or at least consistent only in its denigration of the existing furniture of the heavens.

The passage in question, incidentally, has been sent to the moon. After the death of the great planetary geologist Gene Shoemaker in 1998, and with the blessing of his wife and colleague Carolyn Shoemaker, colleagues at NASA put a small container of his cremated ashes inside the Lunar Prospector probe, about to launch at the time of his death. Wrapped around the capsule was this quotation, printed on brass foil (NASA, "Lunar"). The detail again speaks to this play's ongoing resonance for space scientists, in the interconnection of human love and flight.

Shoemaker's lunar journey is also bound up with the idea of physical interactions with celestial objects. In his youth, Shoemaker nearly made the Apollo astronaut training program but was debarred from flying in space because of a health problem. In the words of Shoemaker's colleague Carolyn Porco:

> Gene had always wanted to go to the moon. . . . He said only last year, "Not going to the moon and banging on it with my own hammer has been the biggest disappointment in life." I felt that this was Gene's last chance to get to the moon. (NASA, "Lunar")

In 1999, with the probe's propellant running out, scientists flew it into the moon in order to study the debris plume that the collision threw up. Thus, the aim of making an impact upon the moon was something that Shoemaker achieved in some style: the speed at impact was around 3,800 mph, and as a result there may not in fact be much left of the brass foil (NASA, "Creative"). Anachronistic though the comparison seems, it is all entirely in keeping with *Romeo and Juliet*. This complex of ideas—earthboundness and flight; love and loss; exchange between human bodies and celestial bodies; destruction, which is almost glorious—is very much to be found in the play.

Of course, as the play turns to tragedy, imagery of flight becomes increasingly entangled with imagery of death. Mercutio is the first to go: "That gallant spirit hath aspired the clouds, / Which too untimely here did scorn the earth" (3.1.108-09). Tybalt soon joins him: "Mercutio's soul / Is but a little way above our heads, / Staying for thine to keep him company" (3.1.117-19), says Romeo to Tybalt as he kills him. As the consequences spread Juliet contemplates suicide by falling: "O bid me leap, rather than marry Paris, / From off the battlements of any tower" (4.1.77-78)—a passage that one hopes was in the mind of those who named the cliffs at Verona Rupes. And in her supposed death, Juliet is said to finally to have achieved spaceflight: "she is advanced / Above the clouds, as high as heaven itself" (4.5.73-74). Flight, in short, becomes death. All this imagery of flight, coupled with the lovers' restless desire to reconfigure the physical universe, makes *Romeo and Juliet* sound strangely similar to a near-contemporary play to which it is rarely likened: Marlowe's *Doctor Faustus*.

### *Romeo and Juliet* and Marlowe's *Doctor Faustus*

Up until now, very little has been written on *Romeo and Juliet*'s relationship to *Doctor Faustus* in particular. What detailed work there has been on this play's reception of Marlowe has focused, perhaps understandably, on its relationship to *Hero and Leander*.[10] But this is a strange lacuna, since the immensely successful *Doctor Faustus* was one of the defining plays of the 1590s theatre for which *Romeo and Juliet* was written. Therefore, before considering the particular case of the flight imagery, one should consider how *Romeo and Juliet* might have looked to early audiences who knew *Doctor Faustus*.

First of all, *Romeo and Juliet* is working with the same type of story. Romeo and Juliet, like Faustus, are continental figures, well known from earlier print accounts in English, while possessing only a very vague claim to historicity. They are all three somewhat outside the usual run of tragic heroes, being neither royal nor military. Secondly, the opening is the same. In each play, the heroes' arc from aspiration to flight to fall is laid out in advance by a Chorus in the Prologue, in a way which—as critics of both plays have commented—seems to suggest that the action that follows is predestined. Both Faustus and Romeo have a coadjutor in the shape of a Franciscan friar, and both know a character named "Benvolio." Given that our only texts of *Dr Faustus* postdate 1597, it is hard to know exactly what to make of some of the smaller parallels—as, for instance, in 2.1.23-6, where Mercutio jokes about raising devils in circles, i.e., in women's vaginas, a passage that seems to recall Robin making the same joke in *Doctor Faustus*.[11]

What is more, there is a parallel between *Dr Faustus*'s Scene 19, and *Romeo and Juliet*'s 5.3, both scenes in which the hero sends away his allies as the nocturnal crisis approaches. Faustus warns the scholars, "what noise soever ye hear, come not unto me, for nothing can rescue me": the suicidal Romeo similarly warns Balthazar, "What e'er thou hear'st or seest, stand all aloof, / And do not interrupt me in my course." The similarity is clinched by Romeo's somewhat irrelevant threat to "tear [Balthazar] joint by joint" if he disobeys—which is not in Brooke and makes relatively little sense in context, but which may recall to auditors Faustus's fear of being torn "in pieces" for the same crime in the corresponding scene, and indeed his actual dismemberment at the end of the play.[12] Romeo might, at this moment, seem to his early viewers like a new Faustus.

But most strikingly of all, the imagery of flight and spaceflight is ubiquitous in both plays. As A. D. Nuttall has brilliantly observed, flight forms a repeating master-trope in Marlowe's play—flight attempted, flight achieved, and flight that fails: "Marlowe's *Dr Faustus* begins with the glittering image of Icarus who flew up towards the sun. Thereafter images of flight and ascent, mingled with images of rapid travel over the surface of the globe, recur with extraordinary power in the play" (26).[13]

Such images include Faustus's flight high into the atmosphere:

[S]itting in a chariot burning bright
Drawn by the strength of yoked dragons' necks,
He views the clouds, the planets and the stars. (Chorus I 5-7)

At a lower altitude, Helen's "lips suck forth [his] soul: see where it flies"; he imagines, in his last seconds, his body being drawn up "like a foggy mist" into the clouds (xviii 102 and xix 159). Such images of flight occur in *Romeo and Juliet*, too, as we have seen.

There are similarities, too, in the way that both sets of heroes want to break time and space. Faustus considers his magic powerful enough to threaten the fabric of the cosmos: he believes he has the power "To make the moon drop from her sphere," just as Romeo and Juliet consider their love as being able to kill the moon (*Dr. Faustus* iii 40). Juliet's desire to interfere with time is like Faustus's. As has often been noticed, Juliet's "Gallop apace" line remakes Ovid's *Lente, lente currite noctis equi* [run slowly, you horses of the night]. Less often noted is that this text is perhaps most famous, to the original audiences of Shakespeare's play, from Faustus's despairing quotation of it.[14]

Critical Insights

These links raise, then, the question of whether and how *Romeo and Juliet* may connect, like *Dr Faustus*, with ideas of Gnosticism, the heretical belief that the creator of the world is not in fact benevolent and should be opposed and fought against at every turn. Nuttall convincingly demonstrates the extent to which *Doctor Faustus* is saturated in second-hand Gnostic imagery, particularly around, once again, human flight, the master-trope of Gnosticism. In particular, Faustus himself recalls the figure of the early Gnostic sorcerer, Simon Magus, who claimed (among other things) that his lover was Helen of Troy reincarnated. At the heart of the myth of Simon Magus is the story of his death: how he leapt from a high tower and actually achieved flight before St. Peter broke his spell and caused him to crash fatally into the pavement of Rome. Faustus, Icarus, and Simon Magus: all overreachers who fly too high, but all (Nuttall argues) open to rereading as heroes in the morally different terms of Gnosticism (*The Alternative Trinity* 41-70, esp. 57).

The extent of Shakespeare's overall engagement with Gnosticism remains open to fuller investigation, although in recent years, writers including Nuttall himself (*Shakespeare*) and Harold Bloom ("Introduction") have suggested that there is indeed some engagement there to be considered. It would be a brave scholar who argued the case that the Gnostic texts known to Marlowe were also necessarily known to Shakespeare, or, in the case of this play, that Juliet's desire to leap from a tower is necessarily a direct reference back to the Apocryphal story of Simon Magus. But one could more reasonably argue that the lovers' fascination with flight, and with—metaphorically at least—wrecking the cosmos, links them to the Gnostic energies of *Doctor Faustus*. One final instance of this may help prove the point. In discussing how Marlowe's play relates to ideas of predestination, Nuttall quotes Calvin: "Man is so held captive by the yoke of sin that he can of his own nature neither aspire to good through resolve nor struggle after it through effort"—something that Nuttall contrasts with Gnostics' celebration of images of flight and liberation.[15] We don't have a yoke of sin in this play, but we do have a long-noted string of astrological references that invoke the idea that human fate is predetermined. This begins with the Prologue's "star-crossed lovers" (6) and continues with an allusion to "some consequence yet hanging in the stars" (1.4.107). And yet Romeo rejects this sense of destiny—"I defy you, stars"—before finally and climactically resolving to "shake the yoke of inauspicious stars / From this world-wearied flesh" (5.3.111-12)—although, alas, not to any material effect. Romeo and Juliet aspire to flight, aspire to overturn the order of the cosmos, destroying the moon, usurping the sun, and displacing the stars. Even though their ambition fails in the most earthy of earthbound locations, the Capulet family tomb, it still seems on some levels admirable. By the end of the play, in the last of the series of cosmological descriptions of time, even the clockwork universe seems temporarily damaged by the impression they have made upon it: "The sun for sorrow will not show his head" (5.3.306).

All this suggests a *Romeo and Juliet* that could almost be considered a companion piece to *Doctor Faustus*, except that its arc of flight and crash is powered, not by magic, but by love. It is a play that repeats and rephrases the questions of *Dr Faustus* about man's relationship to the physical universe, predestination, the Problem of Evil in a universe that may not, in fact, be reassuring and benevolent: questions, in fact, which are also at the heart of the Gnosticism on which *Dr Faustus* draws. It is not merely a love story, but through that love story a thought-experiment in cosmology. It is, therefore, appropriate that *Romeo and Juliet* should feature so often in the language of twentieth-century space exploration; that lines from it should be part of an impactor fired into Earth's moon; that Juliet, speeding through the strange and alien Uranian system, should be a planetary body in her own right.

### Notes

1.  This essay focuses on the reception of *Romeo and Juliet* in the fields of space science and spaceflight: the countless science-fiction adaptations of the story are too numerous even to consider here.
2.  See, for instance, Guthrie; Falk; and Chiari and Popelard. All three of these sources use quotations from *Romeo and Juliet* as evidence for early modern beliefs about the cosmos.

3. For starting-points on the critical history of the play, see Helfer's essay and others in the book edited by Lupton.

4. *Romeo and Juliet*, 2.1.5, 2.2.66-7; Brooke, *Romeus*, 830, cited here and hereafter from the appendix in Evans's edition of *Romeo and Juliet*.

5. See Evans, Introduction (30), who discusses the performance history. Similarly suggestive, and similarly debated but undetermined, is the question of how Romeo "*goeth down*" from the upper stage at 3.5.42SD: by the usual offstage route? by climbing down the rope ladder? or in some more adventurous way still?

6. Q1, cited from Evans's apparatus on 2.6 and silently modernized. There is of course a large scholarly debate about the exact status of Q1, omitted here.

7. René Weis makes the acute suggestion that the line is an implied stage direction, and that Juliet is looking up to the heavens at this point.

8. Evans, Introduction (19); Weis's note on 2.2.21 (Marlowe's line has also been read as a reference to the *aurora borealis*); Christopher Marlowe, *Doctor Faustus* (xix.146). The play is cited throughout from Jump's edition, which is based on the B-Text.

9. Cf. Philippa Berry's argument, from a very different methodological standpoint, that *Romeo and Juliet* is looking to challenge conventional ideas of time and temporality.

10. See, for example, Walley (on *Hero and Leander*). Logan, while offering much of interest about Shakespeare's famously problematic literary relationship to Marlowe, does not pursue this play. Interestingly, John Ford saw the two plays as compatible, mixing elements from both to make the dark Caroline tragedy *'Tis Pity She's a Whore*: see, for instance, Hoy. I owe this point – and much besides – to my colleague Lisa Hopkins.

11. *Dr Faustus*, A-Text (vii.1-6), cited from Jump's edition.

12. *Dr Faustus* (xix.72, 80-81); *Romeo and Juliet* (5.3.26-7, 35); Brooke's Romeo merely threatens to kill his man: "Romeus" (2619).

13. A. D. Nuttall, *The Alternative Trinity* (26); Borlik, who argues that the one of the things that was done in the 1602 revisions was probably augmentation of the flying effects, and, for a different consideration of flight on the early modern stage, see Booth.

14. See also Evans's Supplementary Note. The connection between Juliet's line and *Dr Faustus* has indeed been made before: e.g. Nuttall, *Shakespeare the Thinker* (114); for another cosmologically flavored moment when *Romeo and Juliet* has been seen as echoing *Dr Faustus*, see above.

15. Calvin, *Institutes of the Christian Religion*, qtd. in Nuttall, *Alternative* (28).

## Works Cited

Armstrong, Neil, et al. *First on the Moon: A Voyage with Neil Armstrong, Michael Collins [and] Edwin E. Aldrin, Jr.* Konecky and Konecky, n.d.

Berry, Philippa. "Between Idolatry and Astrology: Modes of Temporal Repetition in *Romeo and Juliet*." *Region, Religion and Patronage: Lancastrian Shakespeare*, edited by Richard Dutton, Alison Findlay, and Richard Wilson, Manchester UP, 2003, pp. 68-83.

Bloom, Harold. "Introduction." *William Shakespeare's Macbeth*, edited by Harold Bloom, new ed., Infobase, 2010, pp. 1-7.

Booth, Roy. "Witchcraft, Flight and the Early Modern English Stage." *Early Modern Literary Studies*, vol. 13, no. 1, May 2007, 3.1-37, purl.oclc.org/emls/13-1/bootwitc.htm. Accessed 21 Feb. 2017.

Borlik, Todd A. "Hellish Falls: Faustus's Dismemberment, Phaeton's Limbs and Other Renaissance Aviation Disasters—Part I." *English Studies*, volume 97, no. 3, 2016, pp. 254-276.

Chiari, Sophie, and Mickael Popelard. "'Shakespeare and Science': A Critical Assessment." Actes des congrès de la Société française Shakespeare, vol. 33, 2015, shakespeare.revues.org/3401/. Accessed 21 Feb. 2017.

Ellis, Thomas. "The Cosmonaut in the American Imagination: 1961-1975." M. Phil. thesis, University of Cambridge, 2012.

Falk, Dan. *The Science of Shakespeare: A New Look at the Playwright's Universe*. Thomas Dunne Books, 2014.

Greeley, Ronald, and Raymond Batson. *The Complete NASA Atlas of the Solar System* Cambridge UP, 1990.

Guthrie, W. G. "The Astronomy of Shakespeare." *Irish Astronomical Journal*, vol. 6, 1964, pp. 201-11.

Helfer, Rebecca. "The State of the Art." *"Romeo and Juliet": A Critical Reader*, edited by Julia Reinhard Lupton, Bloomsbury, 2016, pp. 79-100.

Hoy, Cyrus. "'Ignorance in Knowledge': Marlowe's Faustus and Ford's Giovanni." *Modern Philology*, volume 57, 1960, pp.145-154.

Joyce, James. *Ulysses*, edited by Jeri Johnson, Oxford World's Classics, 2011.

Kuiper, Gerard P. "The Fifth Satellite of Uranus." *Publications of the Astronomical Society of the Pacific*, vol. 61, 1949, p. 129.

Logan, Robert A. *Shakespeare's Marlowe: The Influence of Christopher Marlowe on Shakespeare's Artistry.* Ashgate, 2007.

Lupton, Julia Reinhard, editor. *"Romeo and Juliet": A Critical Reader*. Bloomsbury, 2016.

Marlowe, Christopher. *Doctor Faustus*, edited by John D. Jump. Revels, 1962.

NASA. "Creative Impact Experiment to mark end of Lunar Prospector." *NASA*, 28 July 1999. www.nasa.gov/centers/ames/news/releases/1999/99_47AR.html/. Accessed 21 Feb. 2017.

_____. "Lunar spacecraft carries ashes, special tribute to Shoemaker." *NASA*, 6 Jan.1998. www2.jpl.nasa.gov/sl9/news82.html/. Accessed 21 Feb. 2017.

Nuttall, A. D. *The Alternative Trinity: Gnostic Heresy in Marlowe, Milton, and Blake*. Clarendon, 1998.

_____. *Shakespeare the Thinker*. Yale UP, 2007.

Shakespeare, William. *Romeo and Juliet*, edited by G. Blakemore Evans. Cambridge UP, 1984.

Tillyard, E. M. W. *The Elizabethan World Picture*. Chatto and Windus, 1943.

Walley, H. R. "Shakespeare's Debt to Marlowe in *Romeo and Juliet*." *Philological Quarterly*, volume 21, 1942, pp. 257–67.

Weis, René, editor. *Romeo and Juliet*, by William Shakespeare. Arden, 2012.

# Pears and Statues

Lisa Hopkins

The most famous scene in *Romeo and Juliet* is set in an orchard. It contains the two passages that everyone can quote—"O Romeo, Romeo!—wherefore art thou Romeo?" (2.1.33) and "That which we call a rose / By any other word would smell as sweet" (2.1.43-44)— and the image of Juliet on the balcony and Romeo below has become both iconic and synecdochic of the play as a whole. However, these more celebrated elements of the scene have distracted attention from other features of interest, chief among them (it seems to this reader) the way it treats the relationship between house and garden and the way in which that relationship itself can be mapped onto a wider pattern within the play, which contrasts the natural world with the built environment. We do hear of the architectural detail for which Italy was famous in Renaissance England (particularly in the shape of balconies and walls), but bodies swarm over that architecture and cross its boundaries, first when Romeo scales the wall and climbs up to the balcony and then later when living bodies violate the funerary architecture of the Capulet tomb. (The Zeffirelli film does a particularly fine job of bringing out this contrast between static architecture and moving bodies.) House and garden are thus figured not as partners or as complementary to each other, but as in opposition. In this essay, I want to consider the way in which *Romeo and Juliet* pits against each other images of growth and life, particularly images of fruit and flowers, with images of death, which the play connects to man-made structures such as tombs and statues. There is a pattern there which conforms to the house/garden distinction but also goes beyond it because the images of life and the images of death both prove to contain within themselves something of their own opposites. This, I argue, helps explain why the effect of Romeo and Juliet's deaths is tragic not in the way that tragedies of state, such as *Hamlet*, *Macbeth* and *King Lear*, are but tragic in a way that audiences have typically found beautiful and that is, paradoxically, life-affirming.

## Tensions between Animate and Inanimate

The tension between animate and inanimate is established from the first scene of the play, which contains the following exchange:

> *Sampson.* Me they shall feel while I am able to stand; and 'tis known I am a pretty piece of flesh.
> *Gregory.* 'Tis well thou art not fish; if thou hadst, thou hadst been poor-John. Draw thy tool. Here comes of the house of Montagues.
> *Sampson.* My naked weapon is out. (1.1.27-32)

There is a persistent ambiguity here about whether we are talking about flesh or metal—is Sampson's 'tool' his penis or his sword?—and by implication about whether what we are seeing is private selves or social selves. This introduces an important element of the play, which is the conflict between personal and public identities, in the shape of either family relationships (for Romeo and Juliet) or public office, as for the Prince (a character whose role is too often neglected). These polarities can be seen as mirroring the distinction between outside and inside which is emblematized by the tension between house and garden, but they also introduce a play-world in which things which may seem to be opposites blur and bleed into each other. *Romeo and Juliet* trembles between comedy and tragedy, with the tonality not becoming definitively established until the death of Mercutio. The references to plants represent the green world through which comedy finds renewal, but here plants ultimately end up in bottles of poison.

The idea of plants is introduced early. In the first scene, Benvolio tells Romeo's parents that

> underneath the grove of sycamore
> That westward rooteth from this city side,
> So early walking did I see your son. (1.1.121-3)

It seems clear here that the sycamore grove is just outside the city rather than within its walls, and it is there that Romeo seeks solace in the same way as the hero of a comedy might. He does not find it though. In the first place, the sycamore is an inauspicious tree. John Bossewell in his 1572 *Workes of armorie* identified it with the wild fig tree climbed in the Bible by Zacheus to see Jesus (sig. D2r), but the only other time it appears in Shakespeare is ominous: it is in Desdemona's Willow Song, which begins "The poor soul sat sighing by a sycamore tree, / Sing all a green willow," and which tells a story of loss of love, despair, and death (4.3.38-9). In the second place, Romeo, Friar Laurence's pupil, may know about the medicinal properties of plants—he tells Benvolio "Your plantain leaf is excellent for that'"(1.2.51), alluding to the well-known use of plantain in the healing of wounds—but for him "There is no world without Verona walls" (3.3.17), and the only trees we hear of within the public spaces of the city are emblems of death, as we see when Paris says to the page "Under yond yew trees lay thee all along" (5.3.3). It is as though we are invited to be aware of the green world, but also to be aware that we are dangerously cut off from it.

## Juliet and Flowers; Romeo and Fruit

As the play unfolds, the green world continues to manifest itself, in two principal ways: references to flowers, which tend to accrue to Juliet, and references to fruit, which tend to accrue to Romeo. However, there is a strongly developed sense that when flowers are mentioned by or in connection with Juliet, they either do not carry signifying force at all or do not carry it in the way that might be expected. Juliet herself asks:

> What's in a name? That which we call a rose
> By any other word would smell as sweet. (2.2.43-4)

Here the idea of the rose is, in effect, dissolved as soon as it is created, since it is mentioned specifically to undo the sense that there is a correlation between word and thing. Later she tells Romeo,

---

This bud of love, by summer's ripening breath,
May prove a beauteous flower when next we meet. (2.2.121-2)

But she is, of course, wrong. Instead she herself will become a flower that, like the rose, belies its own nature; as her father tells Paris,

O son, the night before thy wedding day
Hath death lain with thy wife. There she lies,
Flower as she was, deflowèred by him. (4.5.35-7)

Capulet's bitter pun ostensibly relies solely on the term "to deflower" as meaning "to take a girl's virginity," but it also quietly mobilizes a more purely verbal conceit in which the word "flower" undoes itself as it is spoken in the same way as the name "rose" is dissociated from its meaning: Juliet was a flower, blooming and beautiful, but now she is robbed of that floral quality, destabilizing the whole idea of flowers. Along with this goes an insistent undercurrent of suggestion that what is verdant may be sinister or sickly rather than blooming. Romeo says of the moon "Her vestal livery is but sick and green" (2.2.8) and Juliet apostrophises "bloody Tybalt, yet but green in earth" (4.3.42) and fears "shrieks like mandrakes torn out of the earth" (4.3.47). In all these instances, greenness works in the same way as it sometimes does in modern movies, where a greenish glow connotes the unnatural or undead: the moon is green because she is sick ("greensickness" was a disease thought to afflict girls who were kept waiting too long to be married), and Tybalt is "green in earth" not because he is growing but because he is decaying.

Romeo, by contrast, is associated with fruit. I have already observed that the first time we hear of him is in connection with trees, and this becomes a *leitmotif*. Indeed his father figures Romeo himself as a tree when he observes that:

he, his own affections' counsellor,
Is to himself—I will not say how true—
But to himself so secret and so close,
So far from sounding and discovery,
As is the bud bit with an envious worm

Ere he can spread his sweet leaves to the air
Or dedicate his beauty to the sun. (1.1.147-53)

Romeo is however a tree that has been blighted, and his own first reference to trees—or at least to bushes—also registers unsatisfactoriness:

Is love a tender thing? It is too rough,
Too rude, too boisterous, and it pricks like thorn. (1.4.25-6)

Despite their dangers and their prickliness, though, trees continue to be his preferred habitat. After the Capulets' party, Benvolio says "Come, he hath hid himself among these trees / To be consorted with the humorous night" (2.1.30-1) and Mercutio says:

Now will he sit under a medlar tree
And wish his mistress were that kind of fruit
As maids call medlars when they laugh alone.
O, Romeo, that she were, O that she were
An open-arse and thou a poppering pear! (2.1.34-8)

Margaret Willes identifies "openarse" as the medlar, noting that "The fruit is picked in October or early November when the fruit is yet unripe, although Gerard recommended eating hard green medlars to 'stop the belly'", and also observes that:

John Parkinson described the popp'rin or popperin as a firm, dry pear, somewhat spotted and brownish on the outside. . . . It was a Flemish pear, probably named after Poperinge, in the marches of Calais, and therefore easily imported into England until the loss of the port in the reign of Mary Tudor (120, 122, 138-40).

One would not want to press this too far—audiences cannot carry etymologies in their heads throughout performances—but it might be suggestive that the name of the pear, which Mercutio mentions, should carry echoes of this story of separation, loss, and conflict.

More directly, though, the idea that Juliet might be a medlar (open and malleable) and Romeo a poppering pear (harder, and more phallic in shape) not only sexualises them but connects them both to ideas of fertility, abundance, and the seasonal reproductive cycle. Much Renaissance love poetry refers to the idea inherent in the Latin phrase "carpe diem," perhaps best translated as "pluck the fruit of the day"; it tropes women as ripe for plucking, but is not much interested in what happens to them after that. To figure both Romeo and Juliet as fruit, though, is to cast their relationship in a very different way. This is not about Romeo "taking" or "enjoying" Juliet: this is about seeing them as emblems of growth and seasonality and as emblematizing the perilousness and fragility of the transitional stage that is young adulthood.

Most notably, it is in an orchard that Romeo declares his love to Juliet. She establishes the setting for us when she says:

> The orchard walls are high and hard to climb,
> And the place death, considering who thou art,
> If any of my kinsmen find thee here. (2.2.63-5)

Again trees are marked as dangerous here—being found in the orchard could mean death for Romeo—but nevertheless, wanting to swear his love, the first thing he thinks of is trees:

> Lady, by yonder blessèd moon I vow,
> That tips with silver all these fruit-tree tops. (2.2.107-8)

It is, I think, significant that Romeo is not just among trees, but specifically among fruit trees. Fruit is rich in associations in Renaissance culture, and Shakespeare often makes use of these. Margaret Willes notes that Shakespeare used John Gerard's 1597 *The Herball or Generall Historie of Plantes* and that:

> In his writings, Shakespeare introduced all kinds of orchard fruits, as well as berries and nuts from the hedgerow. In *Richard II* he focuses on apricots. Brought to England in the early sixteenth century, they would in fact not have been known to the Plantagenet

king and his court, but Shakespeare's concern here is the role of the orchard. . . .The fig bookends the tragedy of *Antony and Cleopatra*. (6-7, 15, 89)

Shakespeare's references to fruit often convey meaning. Annaliese Connolly links the dewberries mentioned in *A Midsummer Night's Dream* to gooseberries, traditionally supposed to suppress menstruation (184-5). Willes notes that there is an additional significance in that "Ovid in his *Metamorphoses* described how the white fruit of the mulberry turned to red from the blood of Pyramus" (126). Hema Dahiya argues that in *Coriolanus* "the fruit of Mulberry becomes a metaphor for mildness, softness, or mellow nature" (37). Lawrence J. Ross notes the emblematic significance of the mention of strawberries in *Richard III* (229), and strawberries were also thought to be the food of children in Paradise, as in Martin Schongauer's *Madonna of the Rose Bush* in the church of the Dominicans in Colmar in northern France, making them particularly appropriate for a play in which two children are murdered.

In *Romeo and Juliet*, flowers are generally not particularized—they are just "flowers," with the exception of Mercutio's "Nay, I am the very pink of courtesy," which is retrospectively identified as a specific flower by Romeo when he says "Pink for flower" (2.4.56-7), and the possible exception of Angelica, the name of the nurse, but also the name of a tall, umbelliferous plant to the possible significance of which I shall return later. Fruit, however, is differentiated and given a name. Juliet says:

> It was the nightingale, and not the lark,
> That pierced the fearful hollow of thine ear.
> Nightly she sings on yond pomegranate tree. (3.4.2-4)

The particular choice of fruit here is striking. Rupindra-Guha Majumdar sees both the Masque of Ceres in *The Tempest* and the Hermione/Perdita strand of *The Winter's Tale* as glancing directly at the myth of Persephone, who was abducted by the god of the underworld (163-179). Her mother Demeter, goddess of fertility, came to rescue her, but Persephone had already committed herself by eating six seeds of a pomegranate and was therefore doomed to spend six months of every year underground; Demeter mourns for her throughout those six months, and that is why we have winter. I think the myth is being evoked here, too: halfway through the play, on the last occasion on which Romeo and Juliet see each other alive, the atmosphere is turning from the promise of warmth and summer to the cold and death of winter, and fruit, in the shape of the pomegranate, is being used to signal that. Life and death are set side by side again when the Nurse says "They call for dates and quinces in the pastry" (4.4.2). Willes notes that "quinces . . . had a particular connection with weddings. According to Plutarch, a decree handed down by Solon in Athens stipulated that a bride should eat a quince before lying with her husband, for it brought fertility. The tradition continued right through to the Renaissance" (28-30). They could not be eaten just as they were, though, for the

> consumption of raw fruit was regarded with much suspicion in Tudor times, as John Gerard makes clear in his herbal. Again and again he talks of how difficult it is to digest fruit, recommending instead that they be cooked and made into tarts, or marmalade. Apples and pears in particular were the subject of much concern, and were therefore baked long and hard in pastry cases, known as coffins, with sugar, spices and saffron added. (Willes 153)

Quinces may suggest fertility, but they are safe only if they have been put in a coffin.

If fruit must be put in a coffin, flowers, too, can suggest either birth or death. The Friar holds the balance between life and death:

> I must up-fill this osier cage of ours
> With baleful weeds and precious-juicèd flowers.
> The earth that's nature's mother is her tomb.
> What is her burying grave, that is her womb. (2.3.3-6)

The tomb/womb rhyme reinforces the paradox: life and death are intertwined. So far from being a contradiction, though, there is a continuum, for the cycle of seasonality means that death and birth must always follow each other and are, in a sense, two sides of the same coin. The same is true of the plants that grow from the tomb/ womb of the earth. The Friar knows that

> O mickle is the powerful grace that lies
> In plants, herbs, stones, and their true qualities. (2.3.11-12)

But he also knows that the reverse can be true: "Within the infant rind of this weak flower/ Poison hath residence, and medicine power" (2.3.19-20). Plants can cure, but they can also be distilled into poison, and two poisons in particular are suggestive. Willes argues that the potion Friar Laurence gives Juliet is deadly nightshade and that the drug Romeo uses to commit suicide is aconite because Shakespeare compares it to gunpowder, and in *Henry IV*, Part Two, he explicitly connects aconite to gunpowder (42, 83). Romeo asks the apothecary for

> A dram of poison, such soon-speeding gear
> As will disperse itself through all the veins,
> That the life-weary taker may fall dead
> And that the trunk may be discharged of breath
> As violently as hasty powder fired
> Doth hurry from the fatal cannon's womb. (5.1.59-65)

In *Henry IV*, Part Two, King Henry advises his son Thomas of Clarence to cultivate his brother, the Prince of Wales, so that the fraternal bond will be strong enough to withstand even what can be threatened by "aconitum or rash gunpowder" (4.3.48). Both aconite and nightshade have ironic resonance. The Latin name of deadly nightshade is *atropa belladonna*; "bella donna" means "beautiful lady," and that is, of course, what Juliet is, so once again, she is emblematized as a flower, but once again, it is in a way that dissolves the identification even as it is made. The name of aconite, meanwhile, is doubly suggestive. The plant's other names, as every reader of Harry Potter knows, are monkshood and wolfsbane. "Monkshood" chimes with the two friars, who, between them, have brought Romeo to this position; "wolfsbane" alerts us to an aspect of Romeo himself, for his name contains within itself that of the city of Rome, whose legendary founders Romulus and Remus were suckled by a she-wolf, and insofar as Romeo himself partakes of this lupine identity, the poison will indeed be bane to a wolf. Both the belladonna that brings Juliet to the tomb and the aconite that keeps Romeo there thus encapsulate and emblematize the identities of the lovers even in the moment that they put an end to them.

Aconite is also mentioned in John Ford's 1633 play *The Broken Heart*, and though this was written a generation after *Romeo and Juliet*, it is worth attending to because Ford's plays are so extensively engaged with Shakespeare's that he has some claim to be considered Shakespeare's first critic. In his most famous play, *'Tis Pity She's a Whore*, Ford offers an obvious reimagining of *Romeo and Juliet*, with two lovers, Annabella and Giovanni, who turn for advice to a nurse figure and a Friar respectively; the difference is that whereas Romeo and Juliet's families are too far apart from each other, Annabella's and Giovanni's are too close, for they are brother and sister. *The Broken Heart*, too, has elements of *Romeo and Juliet* in its plot: before the play began, Orgilus and Penthea were in love, but were forced apart by a family feud and now can only suffer and die. Orgilus refers to Ithocles, Penthea's brother and the man who separated them, as a "poisonous stalk / Of aconite" (1.1.36-7). Here though, the difference is that Ithocles is not Penthea's father but her brother and so her contemporary (indeed, he is repeatedly referred to as her twin), and this points up a contrast with *Romeo and Juliet* that reveals the extent to which it is a story of intergenerational conflict, with old and young at odds and mutually uncomprehending. The references to plants mirror and comment on this sense of a gap between generations. As buds, flowers are full of promise; ripened and distilled as poison, fully grown as aconite and deadly nightshade are, they kill.

Both the scenes in which we see the effects of poison also offer us a different sort of tension between proper and improper uses of things. In the first, Juliet's bedchamber, in which she has already consummated one marriage and is supposedly awaiting a next, becomes instead a chamber of death. In it, a body that should move lies still and apparently lifeless, and the flowers that should celebrate a marriage become instead emblems of death, which "lies on her like an untimely frost / Upon the sweetest flower of all the field" (4.5.28-9) so that "Our bridal flowers serve for a buried corse" (4.5.89). Rosemary in particular "was associated with weddings" (Willes 166), but now becomes a mark of death as Old Capulet says "Dry up your tears and stick your rosemary / On this fair corse" (4.5.79-80); Shakespeare seems to have noted how dramatically effective it was to have rosemary do double duty in this way, because he recurred to it in *Hamlet*, where the mad Ophelia says "There's rosemary, that's for remembrance—pray you, love, remember" (4.5.173-4), shortly before Gertrude comments that she had hoped to strew Ophelia's bride-bed but is instead decking her grave. In the second poison scene, conversely, a tomb comes alive as Juliet, supposedly still and composed in death, starts out into messy, unruly, emotional life and sheds hot red blood in the cold, dry abode of shrouds and bones. In this paradoxical environment, images of life and growth jostle with images of stillness and death. Paris commands his page "Give me those flowers" (5.3.9), Romeo's page declares that his master "came with flowers to strew his lady's grave" (5.3.281), and Paris laments,

> Sweet flower, with flowers thy bridal bed I strew—
>     O woe! thy canopy is dust and stones—
> Which with sweet water nightly will I dew;
>     Or, wanting that, with tears distilled by moans. (5.3.12-15)

The impression created here is of a false garden, planted in the dark and stony tomb where it cannot possibly grow, and watered by bitter tears.

## Fruits, Flowers, and Statues

As the fruits and flowers fail and die, all that is left are statues. Old Montague promises,

> I will raise her statue in pure gold,
> That whiles Verona by that name is known,

> There shall no figure at such rate be set
> As that of true and faithful Juliet. (5.3.299-302)

Moved, Old Capulet promises to do the same for Juliet; the quarrel between the two houses is thus mended, but only at the expense of the lovers' deaths. It is not quite as simple as that, however. These are the only statues in Shakespeare apart from the one in *The Winter's Tale*, and that is a statue that in fact proves to connote not death but life, as it apparently comes alive (it is of course not really a statue at all but the living Hermione masquerading as one). The statues of *Romeo and Juliet* will not come alive, but the fact that they are made of gold will keep them forever pure and uncorrupted and preserve their memories in perpetuity; it also means that their color is warm and glowing, giving them, in fact, something of the feel of fruit and connecting them to life. It does not even matter that those statues do not and did not exist because if they did, they would only disappoint: either Romeo or Juliet or probably both would be sure not to look as many readers had imagined them. *Romeo and Juliet* is a play of perfection and distillation, moving at an impossibly fast pace as Romeo passes both initiation rites of Renaissance manhood, killing a man and bedding a woman, on the same day; it is a play in which the standard Renaissance metaphor of orgasm as dying comes shudderingly alive as the consummation of the lovers' relationship is simultaneously its death-knell. It is of a piece with this impossible pitch and pace that it should be symbolized by statues we can never see, but it is important nevertheless that they are statues because Romeo and Juliet thus come to be symbolized by things standing above ground rather than below it, things which belong to the world of light and life.

It is perhaps also significant that of all the different kinds of fruit mentioned in the play, the name of apple never appears; the orchard contains pomegranates and pears, but not, so far as know, any apple trees and therefore has nothing to remind us of original sin or of the consequences thereof. There is a particularly suggestive contrast here with *Twelfth Night*, where Antonio declares, "An apple cleft in twain is not more twin / Than these two creatures"

(5.1.219-20). Antonio's image of the apple encodes difference as well as similarity, since it reminds us of the apple eaten by Eve and hence of the original sin, which weighs more heavily on women than on men; this shadows the play's supposedly happy ending and introduces a note of darkness and uncertainty in the same way as the Fool's bittersweet closing song does. It is true that Willes declares that Mercutio's "very bitter sweeting" refers to a kind of apple (43-44), but it is a very particular kind of apple. A sweeting is an apple that speaks of salvation rather than of sin because the medieval lyric "A Song of Love-Longing" addresses Jesus as "Jesus, Lord, my Sweeting" (Segar 13). It may also be significant that the full name of angelica is herba angelica and it is also known as "root of the Holy Ghost" (*Oxford English Dictionary*); it was believed to nullify the effects of poison. It does not do that in this play, but it does work in support of the general atmosphere of purity and holiness, in which Romeo's first conversation with Juliet is about saints and pilgrims. (This is something very nicely caught the use of religious iconography in the Baz Luhrmann film, not least by having Juliet come to the ball dressed as an angel.)

After *Twelfth Night*, Shakespeare never wrote comedy again, and in it, the comic mood is already showing signs of collapse. Paradoxical though it may seem, the vision of *Romeo and Juliet* is in some ways less tragic than that of *Twelfth Night*, and it is the use of fruit, which here *does* suggest rebirth but does *not* suggest guilt, that makes it so. Fruit and flowers may fade, but statues will give the lovers immortality. Moreover, even flowers, which speak of death, may bring some comfort. The Nurse tells Romeo that Juliet "hath the prettiest sententious of it, of you and rosemary, that it would do you good to hear it" (2.4.205-7). William R. West argues that although the play ends sadly, it also invites its audience to contemplate the possibility of happier resolutions: "Against, or besides, the completed vision of the lovers' tragedy, it sets the infinite potentiality of how things may turn out" (151), and Shaul Bassi notes that since at least the time of Lord Byron, the supposed tomb of Juliet has been a popular tourist attraction in Verona and that

Today, Juliet's Tomb is the site where many couples come from all over the world to crown their dream of love and get married in the place where Romeo and Juliet saw their hopes shattered. Clearly the bond of love that kept the two lovers together until the very end is stronger than any bad omen related to their violent death. (194-95)

*Romeo and Juliet* tells a sad story, but it is also a beautiful and a satisfying one with which young lovers continue to wish to be connected. Like fruit, there is something wholesome about it, and like fruit, any decay contains the seeds of new life.

## Works Cited

Bassi, Shaul. "The Names of the Rose: *Romeo and Juliet* in Italy." *Romeo and Juliet: A Critical Reader*, edited by Julia Reinhard Lupton, Bloomsbury Arden Shakespeare, 2016, pp. 177-198. pp. 194-5.

Bossewell, John. *Workes of armorie*. Richard Totell, 1572. sig. D2r.

Connolly, Annaliese. "Princes Set on Stages: Royal Iconography on the Early Modern Stage." Unpublished PhD thesis, Sheffield Hallam University, 2008, pp. 184-5.

Dahiya, Hema. "Shakespeare's Celebrated Tree: A Historical Study." *Journal of Drama Studies*, vol. 7, nos. 1-2 (January-July 2013), pp. 35-40.

Ford, John. *The Broken Heart*, edited by T. J. B. Spencer, Manchester UP, 1980.

Majumdar, Rupindra-Guha. "Many Persephones: Shakespeare's Heroines and Fading Memories of a Pomegranate." *Women in Shakespeare: A Post-Feminist Review*, edited by Bhim S. Dahiya, Viva Books, 2014.

Ross, Lawrence J. "The Meaning of Strawberries in Shakespeare," *Studies in the Renaissance*, vol. 7, 1960, pp. 225-240.

Segar, Mary Gertrude. *A Mediaeval Anthology: Being Lyrics and Other Short Poems, Chiefly Religious*. Longmans, 1915.

Shakespeare, William. *Hamlet*, edited by Harold Jenkins, Methuen, 1982.

_____. *Henry IV, Part 2*, edited by Peter Davison, Penguin, 1968.

_____. *Othello*, edited by Kenneth Muir, Penguin, 1968.

_____. *Romeo and Juliet*, edited by T. J. B. Spencer, Penguin, 1967.

_____. *Twelfth Night*, edited by Keir Elam, Cengage Learning, 2008.

West, William R. "*Romeo and Juliet*'s Understudies." *Romeo and Juliet: A Critical Reader*, edited by Julia Reinhard Lupton, Bloomsbury Arden Shakespeare, 2016, pp. 133-151.

Willes, Margaret. *A Shakespearean Botanical*. Bodleian Library, 2015.

# William Hawley Smith's Parody of *Romeo and Juliet* (and of *Hamlet*)

Robert C. Evans

Parodies of Shakespeare's writings were enormously popular in the Victorian period on both sides of the Atlantic. Richard W. Schoch, in his very helpful book *Not Shakespeare: Bardolatry and Burlesque in the Nineteenth Century*, focuses mostly on British examples, but evidence of American "travesties" of Shakespeare also abounds.[1] Schoch explores, in great detail, just why burlesquing Shakespeare was so popular among writers, readers, and playgoers during this period. Before focusing on one especially successful American parody, I want to review some of Schoch's claims and conclusions. Doing so can help us better understand why and how burlesques can reveal interesting things both about the works that inspired them and about the cultures that produced them and enjoyed them. After reviewing Schoch's arguments, I will concentrate on one particularly successful (but very little-studied) example of an American play that manages to parody not only *Romeo and Juliet* but also *Hamlet*. This play, titled *The New Hamlet* (1902), by William Hawley Smith, is an unusually successful parody that stands up very well today.[2] Unlike many other Victorian-era burlesques of Shakespeare, it is still often genuinely funny and reveals real literary and dramatic skill. It also nicely illustrates many of Schoch's claims about Shakespearean burlesques.

## Richard Schoch on Parodies of Shakespeare
Richard Schoch is careful to note that his book examines mostly British (not American) "travesties" of Shakespeare (3n). He suggests that many parodists justified their efforts by claiming that they wanted to rescue Shakespeare from the "respectable humbug" of Bardolatry—the rise of the whole academic Shakespeare industry and hothouse praise of Shakespeare that had turned him into a kind of literary god (3-4). Burlesques of Shakespeare were especially

popular on London stages between 1840 and 1890, with a brief hiatus in the 1860s (6). This popularity coincided with the ever-growing tendency to worship the Bard.

*Hamlet* alone generated more than a dozen burlesqued versions (Schoch10)—a fact relevant to Smith's *The New Hamlet*. Shakespeare's tragedies offered dramatists chances to treat lofty topics in low language (11), to set old plots in modern circumstances (12), and to burlesque particularly famous scenes and speeches (12). The burlesques Schoch discusses often abound in excruciating puns and specific allusions to modern life (12). They were appealing partly because of their topicality, novelty, and variety (13). Schoch argues that parodies of Shakespeare both built on and helped sustain Shakespeare's own continuing popularity (19). They resembled, in some ways, Shakespeare's own habit of drawing on earlier works for inspiration (22). Modern parodies could be read as rebukes to scholarly pedants, self-important literary critics, untalented performers, and pretentious modern theatrical productions (27, 34, 85). The parodies were in fact sometimes defended as affectionate tributes to their Shakespearean originals (57). Often they were designed to appeal to middle-class audiences, although Schoch cautions that the nineteenth-century British middle class was far from homogeneous (107, 113).

Just about every single one of the traits cited in the preceding paragraph applies to Smith's *New Hamlet*. Unlike many Victorian-era burlesques of Shakespeare, which can seem unfunny, strained, incomprehensible, and outdated today, Smith's parody is almost as easy to read, understand, and enjoy now as it was when it was first written and performed. As I will argue at the end of this essay, Smith's play avoids many of the pitfalls that make some parodies of Shakespeare seem much less successful in the twenty-first century than they apparently seemed to Britons and Americans of the Victorian period.

## William Hawley Smith's *The New Hamlet*
The fun provoked Smith's play begins with its elaborate title page: *THE NEW HAMLET / INTERMIXED AND INTERWOVEN*

*/ WITH / A REVISED VERSION OF ROMEO AND JULIET / THE COMBINATION BEING MODERNIZED, RE-WRITTEN AND WROUGHT OUT ON NEW-DISCOVERED LINES. AS INDICATED UNDER THE LIGHT OF THE HIGHER CRITICISM /* BY / WM. HAWLEY SMITH /AND / THE SMITH FAMILY, FARMERS / PRINTED FROM THE ORIGINAL MANUSCRIPT, WITH TEXT IN FULL. AND AS FIRST PRODUCED WHEN DONE IN ACTION BY THE SMITHS, THEIR OWN COMPANY. UNDER THE HAW TREE. ON THEIR FARM. AT THE THICKET. This phrasing already mocks the sort of academic pretentiousness especially associated with scholarship on the Bard, and such mockery continues throughout the text. Published in 1902 in Chicago, this printing was in fact labeled a "Second Edition," since an earlier printing (with a shorter title) had been done in Peoria, Illinois. Still another edition indicates that the play was first presented at the Smith family farm on June 17, 1902, where it was initially intended simply to entertain the family and (quite a few of) their friends.

In the "Preface to the Second edition," Smith immediately begins having fun, saying the play was at first "only a family affair," staged on the "veranda" of a "country house," with the audience "seated in chairs upon the lawn in front." That audience consisted of a mere "five hundred invited friends" (!). Each was given a privately printed copy of the text. The play soon became widely popular—itself an interesting historical fact that suggests much about Americans' widespread familiarity with Shakespeare at the turn of the century. "As time went on," Smith continues, people wanted to stage the play "in their own homes, or to use it for various 'literary' purposes— for school exhibitions, class day exercises, society entertainments, church sociables, and the like" (n.p.). Again, these facts suggest that numerous Americans were quite familiar with Shakespeare. But apparently many also enjoyed the idea of a humorous burlesque of his works. Probably the very academic stuffiness already mentioned made burlesques of Shakespeare especially appealing. In any case, Smith notes that his play's growing fame caused demands for more copies, which led to its publication.

Partly Smith seems to have wanted to have fun with contemporary audiences' widespread taste for happy endings. The preface says that if "the reading and playing of what is hereinafter set down shall in any way help, in these modern times, to make comedies out of tragedies," he will be pleased (n.p.). He then claims that if "Hamlet had married Juliet, and Romeo been wedded to Ophelia, all would have lived happily ever afterwards" (n.p.)—a statement that at first seems funny but also makes an odd kind of sense. Before the drama itself begins, however, Smith is careful to state, "at the outset, that Bacon did not write this play" (n.p.). He thus parodies the many claims that Shakespeare's works had actually been secretly composed by his prominent contemporary, Sir Francis Bacon. Bacon, of course, has been just one of numerous candidates nominated by people who think Shakespeare himself could not possibly have written "Shakespeare's" works. But the vogue for Bacon as the "real author" was especially strong in Smith's day. In the first of the text's many (excruciatingly, i.e., appealingly) bad puns, Smith says there "is no need of going into detail" about Bacon. After all (he notes), "Bacon is not located as far back as—'de-tail'" (n.p.). (Bacon, in other words, is cut from parts far from a pig's tail. [Groan]).

Smith then parodies the complicated arguments and tortured language popular then (and still today) among some scholars:

> However, let not the composition be despised if it should be shown that it is not the product of a sugar-cured author. It may turn out that it had an origin higher even than that.
>
> For, see: That which makes bacon is greater than the bacon it makes, and hence is greater than anything that the bacon it has made can make. This play was made by farmers. Farmers make bacon; and hence, even if their product had produced the play, by the stern laws of logic it could not have been as good as it is now. *Quod erat demonstrandum.* (n.p.)

After mocking the pretensions of New York "high society" and the ignorance of most modern theater-goers, Smith offers a proper Shakespearean prologue outlining his work's basic plot and the text's reason for being. Humorously mixing Elizabethan English with down-home, Midwestern American slang, the prologue promises the assembled "Gentles" that:

> We're not a-going to tell a tale of woe,
> Of awful tragedy, of death and pain.
> When Shakespeare wrote those doubly grewsome [*sic*] plays
> Of Hamlet, Romeo and Juliet,
> He wrote of things well suited to those days,
> But not to times like ours to-day, you bet.
> He made both outfits quarrel, slay and slug,
> And play to hard luck in a score of ways . . . .
> But modern thought declares these things all wrong.
> There is no need of such a waste of lives;
> Both men it would have marry and live long,
> Both women make the happiest of wives.
> To bring these things about[,] two mothers plan,
> Two wise old mothers, stronger far than Fate.
> See them get in their work, as mothers can,
> And bring these lovers strictly up to date. (n.p.)

Smith, then, both mocks and satisfies modern audiences' yearnings for romantic outcomes. Since tragedies are too depressing, Smith will turn two of the greatest tragedies ever written into a satisfying bit of comedy (and farce). This prologue, and the whole drama, together allow modern audiences to laugh at themselves as they laugh at the play and players. The joke is partly on modern persons, with their shallow tastes and preferences for unrealistically happy endings, but Smith also caters to those very tastes and preferences. In fact, Smith even notes that the probable "reason for [his play's] generous reception lies in the fact that we all of us very much prefer" happy outcomes (n.p.). (Any teacher who has ever had students ask why they are forced to read so much depressing literature will know what Smith means.) Smith's play allows audiences to enjoy, simultaneously, their familiarity with Shakespeare and their desire to see the Bard playfully burlesqued. Interestingly, he notes that the "publishers have kindly consented to permit schools, colleges, clubs, churches, social and charitable societies, to use this play" free of charge (n.p.). This largesse evidently made the work even more popular and more widely known and widely performed than it had been already.

## Act 1, Scene 1
The play itself opens at "Elsinore" in Denmark. Hamlet enters and begins speaking lines that sound fairly familiar except for all the modern slang:

> To do, or not to do, that is the question:—
> Whether 'tis nobler in the mind to bear
> The snubs a fellow gets—to cringe, and take
> Whatever comes along, or to take arms
> Against the mob, go up against 'em hard,
> And clean 'em out. That is what puzzles me.
> The king is dead, my uncle wears the crown;
> My mother's married to the carpet-bagger.
> So I'm done up! Between the two I'm left!
> Most beautifully left, slugged, scooped and squelched;
> Set down on hard! And now what's to be done?
> I give it up! The game's too tough for me! (13)

Smith's audiences must have enjoyed the sheer absurdity of hearing lofty Elizabethan diction mixed up with colloquial American lingo, and in fact part of the pleasure of burlesques like this, for American audiences, must have been the joy of having some fun at the expense of powerful (and, at that time, sometimes pretentious) transatlantic cousins. The United States could not boast either a literature or history as storied as England's. This was part of the reason English creative writers (especially Shakespeare) enjoyed such prominence and prestige in American culture. All the more reason, then, to occasionally let some air out of the balloon and have some fun with the greatest of all English authors. Teasing of this sort is almost always affectionate teasing—playing (around) with the very persons one loves.

In any case, almost as soon as Hamlet stops talking, Ophelia appears. Both seem depressed, so Hamlet asks, "Is not this life a suck and sell throughout?" Ophelia immediately agrees. Clearly these two are melancholy pessimists; as Ophelia memorably puts it, "all goes wrong, whichever way we go. / My doll is stuffed with sawdust, or with bran; / And who cares which?" Hamlet immediately responds, "'Tis even so, dear girl" (14). Any match between this pair would be a case of misery loving company, especially since both seem somewhat comically suicidal. After Ophelia departs, Hamlet proclaims, "Oh, that this too, too skinny flesh would all / Dry up and blow away, like Kansas dew!" (15), and so on. Fortunately, his mom arrives just in time to make things right.

When Hamlet starts insulting her for remarrying so soon, she wisely counsels "Now Hamlet, don't get gay, nor be too brash. / Just keep your underclothing on a while" (16). Otherwise, she will "box [his] ears." She tells him that "Because you've played at ping pong and bridge whist, / You think you know it all. You make me sick!" (17). She suspects he's upset only because he isn't king. She sagely reminds him that

> 'Tis a tough job to be a king! 'Twas that
> That killed your father, that I know. He died
> From nervous shock, caused by a quick decision
> Of the Supreme Court. He had thought't would take
> Them years to reach the sticking-point. But no!
> They made their guess of what was best to do . . .
> In just four hours! It took his breath away,
> And so he died! For who can live, sans breath? (18)

Throughout the drama, Gertrude displays this sort of impeccable logic. When Hamlet mentions seeing his father's ghost, she quickly retorts: "Oh, stuff! You are the victim of . . . / Those 'Smart Set' chums of yours" who "think if you were king, they would be in it" (18). She knows the ghost was just a fake because she "set the chief detective after him," who "ran him in last night, and he's in jail" (19). Smith, then, takes comic liberties not only with Shakespeare's language but with Shakespeare's plot. We laugh at such absurdities partly because they are completely unpredictable. We literally have no idea what literary offenses Smith will commit next. Shakespeare is completely at his mercy. Smith's play thus generates real suspense as we admire his sheer comic inventiveness.

Another reason Smith's farce gives so much pleasure is that he can do a reasonably tolerable imitation of Elizabethan English when he wants to, and he is also quite good at bringing in passages from other Shakespearean plays. His text is a pastiche not only of *Hamlet* and *Romeo and Juliet* but of various other works. His play is, in that sense, an intellectual challenge or game. It invites readers to see if they can "hear" all the varied bits of Shakespeare's phrasing he manages to echo. Smith pays tribute to Shakespeare even while mocking aspects of the Shakespeare cult.

One way Smith has fun with the Bard is by Americanizing and contemporizing plots originally set hundreds of years ago. Thus Gertrude, describing the dangers of being a king, tells Hamlet that

> . . . in that great new realm, United States,
> 'Tis most as bad just to be president.
> For, see my son, in less than forty years
> Three presidents have died unnatural deaths—
> Great Lincoln, Garfield wise, McKinley true. (20)

This, she explains, is why she married Claudius: to preserve Hamlet's sanity and life. Hamlet now sees her logic: "Oh, mother, you are wise; I never thought—" To which the queen replies, "Of course you never thought! You are not old / Enough to think" (21). (Surely this comes from a book of phrases mothers have been passing down from time immemorial. Part of Smith's humor results from having fun with family relations as well as with Shakespearean drama.)

Alluding to contemporary American politics, Gertrude explains that it's best to let Claudius be king for a while. When Claudius inevitably gets attacked, Hamlet can then take over when he's older and wiser. Gertrude says she learned her wisdom while visiting the United States:

> There is a party there they call Republican.
> They're old hands at the grindstone on such things.
> Whene'er their country gets all tangled up,

They let the Democrats come into power. . . .
Then, when the troublous times are at their worst
The Democrats get blamed for the whole thing;
The people rise, en masse, and turn them out.
Then the Republicans get back their jobs,
The skies all cleared, the seas all calm for sail. (23-24)

In the meantime (she suggests), Hamlet should "go abroad."
She has a friend living in Verona named Lady Montague; they're old
school chums. Gertrude suggests Hamlet should visit there, where he
may even find a wife. When Hamlet worries about ditching Ophelia,
his mother advises that they're both too nervous and melancholy to
make a good married couple. Their offspring "would be bluer far
than indigo; / Crosser than bears—in full, degenerates" (25). She
says she'll fix Hamlet up with a better mate.

### Enter Romeo and Juliet
At this point, Smith has some fun with *Romeo and Juliet*. Suddenly
we are in a garden in Verona. Juliet speaks:

O, Romeo, Romeo! Wherefore art thou, Romeo?
Or why not Edward Bok, or Elbert Hubbard,
Or some sweet soul my folks would like to see
Me wedded to? (26)

Romeo now enters and replies "Shall I hear more, or shall I speak at
this? / I'll try my luck."
Eventually, Juliet confesses her love: "To draw it mild, I'm
wholly mashed on thee!" (27). After many lines closely paralleling
phrasing from the original balcony scene, the lovers separate.
Romeo now addresses himself:

By all the gods at once, but she's a peach,
A plum, an apricot, a daisy, all!
And she's as stuck on me as I on her! (30)

Surely part of this play's fun came at the expense of absurd young love, especially *modern* young love. Old people could laugh, and laugh at memories of their own youthful foolishness, and young people could laugh at themselves. In any case, Romeo, startled, soon discovers his own mother walking home at night. She explains that she's returning from a meeting of her Women's Club and has overhead his exchange with Juliet. She now offers him some counsel:

> Romeo, to tell plain truth, you are a chump!
> You gush to Juliet, she giggles back to you.
> You rave, and she makes goo-goo eyes, that swim. (31-32)

Romeo's mother could not care less that Juliet is a Capulet; as she delicately puts it,

> . . . bogs may produce the fairest flowers,
> And rarest orchids grow on rotting trees.
> 'Tis not the stock I rail at, but the girl.
> She's just a spoony, foolish little thing . . . . (33)

Besides (she continues), Romeo is too young to marry; he doesn't even have his own place or an independent income:

> Who bought that necktie; paid for those new shoes?
> Your doublet and your hose; your hat and gloves?
> 'Twas papa paid it all, and still must pay.
> You've never earned a penny in your life.
> You've been to college, there learned how to play
> At foot-ball, and to smoke a cigarette.
> You've also graduated, in new clothes.
> And now, what next? (33-34)

As it turns out, Romeo's father is now bankrupt: "He's one of those who sold / Short on the West Pacific stock" (34). (Here, as in so many parodies of *Romeo and Juliet*, cold hard facts, often involving cold hard cash, intrude on the play's romantic tone and bring the whole plot very much down to earth.) Just as the play's *Hamlet* portion alludes to unsavory political realities, so this section alludes to disturbing financial facts. Smith reminds his audience that plays are often just that: plays. They temporarily take our minds off grim facts we'd rather forget. Fortunately, Lady Montague knows how Romeo can stir up some quick cash:

> Be a promoter, Romeo, son of mine!
> Exploit some scheme that's based on watered stock.
> For 'tis the alchemy of this great age
> To turn clear water into yellow gold.
> 'Twas once a miracle to make of water, wine;
> But men have passed that mark, in these last days.
> Nor will they stop or stay till they have turned
> Old Neptune's Ocean into paper stocks,
> And sold them all to lambs, who'll baa for more!
> Now, while the game is on, before it drops
> (For drop it must, ere many moons can pass),
> Get in your work, and make your fortune sure. (35)

The ironies here are plentiful and painful. A mother advises her son to become a shyster. She doesn't encourage him to make any genuine investments or take any personal risks. She knows quite well that his prosperity will come from others' suffering. The clear biblical allusions (water into wine; the "last days") help give the play an entirely new level of seriousness. We're reminded that there may literally be hell to pay if nominal Christians, like the Montagues, take advantage of other Christians, like the people Lady Montague plans to dupe. Suddenly the play becomes momentarily dark and disturbing. What began as farce now verges on real satire.

Romeo's mother has a simple plan: he will go to Denmark, enter "the first circles" there (36), sell bogus stocks, and basically swindle everyone. After all, she and Queen Gertrude are old pals: they were roommates at school; they "slept in one bed and ate / Our caramels from out one common sack" (phrasing typical of Smith's clever eye for convincing detail [36]). As Romeo departs, his mother seems pleased: "So! I've fixed him! Now let Miss Juliet go. / Do what she may, she'll ne'er catch Romeo" (36). In this play, the mothers are not motivated by long-time family feuds but by concern that their sons should marry compatible gals.

## Hamlet in Verona; Romeo in Denmark

In Act 2, Lady Montague receives a letter from Queen Gertrude introducing Hamlet. He's coming to Verona, and Gertrude asks her friend to treat him well. When Hamlet (typically depressed) arrives, Lady Montague tells him that a couple of sports named Mercutio and Benvolio can cheer him up. When Hamlet departs, she announces her plans to "work his lordship off on Juliet" (39). His melancholy will balance Juliet's giddiness. Their marriage can enslave the Capulets and bury old grudges all at once. Lady Montague will "kill two birds with a single stone" (40).

Meanwhile, in Denmark, Romeo is doing his best to sell Gertrude stocks. But she wisely asks him, "what assurance have we that this stock / Has any value past the parchment used?" He replies:

> Why, this, dear queen! This company of ours
> Is officered by men of rare repute.
> There's General Falstaff is the President;
> Sir Toby Belch the Grand Secretary;
> While Honest Iago is the Treasurer. (41)

How could this company possibly fail? Its officers have great experience in "boring for oil, or gas" (42). Besides, "this stock is fully guaranteed; Sir Andrew Augue [*sic*] Cheek is on the bond!" When Gertrude asks the price, Romeo replies, "We're selling now for fifteen cents the share. / The full face value of the same will soon / Be worth a hundred" (43). In passages like this, Smith shows his talent for imitating not only the romantic lingo of young lovers but the cynical lingo of shifty salesmen. His play indicts crass commercialism even while burlesquing Shakespearean tragedy. The idea of Romeo as a slick grafter is hilariously preposterous: so much for ideal young love!

But Gertrude's no fool. When Romeo leaves, she soliloquizes: "He takes me for a dunce. / . . . He thinks to sell me stock. Wait till he sees, / What I'll sell him without his agonies! / I'll wed him to Ophelia! What a pair!" (44). Interestingly, in Smith's play, it is the mothers, not the fathers, who are most cunning and conniving. Although Smith may have lived when women could not yet vote, he suggests how some women could exercise real power in other ways (as matriarchs, if not as suffragettes).

## Hamlet and Juliet; Romeo and Ophelia

Back in Verona, Hamlet and Juliet are walking a literally stony path. Hamlet admires Juliet's fearlessness: "strong and brave you are, sweet girl; / A quality most women lack, methinks." He confesses that his mom shielded him from most girls:

> My playmates all were ever boys and beasts.
> 'Twas held, in Denmark, to make weakling men,
> Should boys associate with the gentler sex.
> Indeed, we never heard of co-eds there . . . . (46)

Here and elsewhere, and in many different ways, Smith's drama tells us far more about the times in which *he* lived than about earlier eras. We particularly learn much about definitions of gender and actual gender relations. Juliet says her nurse has told her men are "horrid things" (47), but, as Hamlet courts her, Smith provides enough romance for anyone hoping to hear some of that. Juliet, startled by Hamlet's ardent affection, says "I never dreamed that you could love poor me. For I am but a simple, guileless girl" (48)—more burlesquing of romantic clichés just when the play seemed to be getting syrupy. Hamlet, impatient with Juliet's caution, urges her to love him, and she soon does. He is delighted:

> Now let the gods be thanked, the world be glad;
> The heart of Hamlet no more shall be sad.
> I'll sell my sables to the "ole clo'es" man,
> And laugh and sing, and dance the wild can-can! (49)

At this point, any hope for a fatal sword fight and gruesome poisoning must have seemed slim.

Meanwhile, in Denmark, things are also progressing smoothly. Romeo asks, "Oh, fair Ophelia, may I speak to your back hair?" She replies: "And why not to my bangs, I pray you, sir?" (49). (Smith's play must have been fun to stage as well as read.) Romeo explains: he's "seen and heard them say it, on the stage, / And there it's always said to the back hair" (49-50). Now Smith is burlesquing not only Shakespearean language but also theatrical conventions and their influence on "real" behavior. Romeo exclaims, "I swear I love thee! Wilt thou love in turn?" She, ever practical, replies, "How can I turn and still keep to thee my back hair?" (50). Eventually, they actually face each other and confess their love. In fact, love so transforms Romeo that he admits,

> I came to Denmark to exploit a scheme,
> To sell white paper for full pots of gold.
> By heaven, I'll prove my love for thee by this—
> I'll cut the whole sharp practice from my life;
> Throw every dollar to the whistling winds—

But Ophelia is ever practical:

> Oh, throw not dollars to the winds, my lord!
> What need have winds of dollars or of dimes?
> But men can use them, aye, and women too.
> So throw no gold away for me, I pray.
> Nay, and you love me, keep you all you have.
> We'll need it for some rainy day, perhaps. (51-52)

Romeo, realizing her intent to marry him, exclaims "How can I ever tell thee my delight? I'm glad mamma was late from club that night." He ends by announcing "The love of fair Ophelia and her Romeo" (52).

Act 4 opens in Verona, where Juliet is "seated with a baby in her lap" (53). Hamlet proclaims that the normal "winter of [his] discontent" has been "Made glorious summer by this son of ours. . . . For what boots honor, aye, or kingly crown, / Compared with fatherhood and its pure joys?" (53-54). His love of Juliet, and the fact that she's now a mom and he's a dad, has banished his earlier melancholy. They plan to party with the Capulets, now their friends, and "Friar Laurence will baptize the boy" (55), with Mercutio, Benvolio, and possibly even Tybalt as god-fathers. Smith must have been chuckling to himself and saying, "They want happy endings? *I'll* give them a happy ending!"

Cut to Denmark. Romeo hopes to prove that Claudius really did kill Hamlet's father. Then Hamlet can be king. With Ophelia's help, Romeo accomplishes this objective so quickly that we never actually *see* exactly how he did it. Claudius escapes death: he simply abdicates and is tossed out of town. Gertrude, thankful to be free of him, knights "Sir Romeo" (62). He, no longer a swindler, has become a perfectly courteous courtier. Hamlet soon returns, along with Juliet and Lady Montague, and pays heartfelt tribute to both older women. Romeo greets Juliet as an old friend (but nothing more). Conversely, Ophelia notes that Romeo (unlike Hamlet) "ne'er speaks to me of a nunnery!"—to which Hamlet responds, "A truce, Ophelia! Let the past be past" (67). After a final joke (an inside joke about a woman named Alice), the play concludes as all the characters head off to a banquet.

## Return to Schoch

Having recently read just about every nineteenth- and early twentieth-century parody of *Romeo and Juliet* I could find, I can honestly report that Smith's is one of the best. Some other examples fail to hold up well; many seem awfully dated, and some of them are actually painful to read. Occasionally a gem appears, but only occasionally. How, then, did Smith manage to produce a burlesque of the Bard that is so consistently funny even now, more than a century after it was written?

Several reasons suggest themselves. First, Smith was a widely published professional author who also spent much time (and traveled many miles) delivering literary lectures before popular audiences. He thus knew his trade and knew the people for whom he was writing. He was not a mere amateur who decided to produce a parody as a one-time joke; he knew what he was doing and was an old hand at successful authorship (one of his books sold over a million copies). But Smith also managed to avoid many of the errors outlined by Richard Schoch, who discusses numerous British burlesques of Shakespeare. Schoch reports that many of the texts he studied are tedious and fail to capture the on-stage liveliness that apparently made their staged productions popular (15-16). Smith's play, in contrast, is fun to read and would probably be even funnier if effectively staged. Schoch also notes that many Shakespearean parodies suffer from being *too* topical: jokes that would have made sense to the original audiences are often mystifying today (16, 19, 37-38). Smith, on the other hand, manages to deal with topical topics that have not lost their contemporary relevance (political chicanery, financial swindling, family relations, etc.). His play gives us the pleasure of taking us back into an earlier era without ever seeming merely of historical interest. Most people, for instance, have heard of Lincoln, Garfield, and McKinley, and Smith's jokes about Democrats and Republicans have not lost their edge or their relevance.

Schoch notes that many Victorian parodies of Shakespeare became uninteresting as soon as they no longer seemed new or fresh (16), but Smith's parody manages to seem fairly timeless. The characters he depicts are not only burlesques of Shakespeare's characters but are also themselves very familiar and archetypical. Unlike the phrasing in some of the plays Schoch discusses, which now seems stale and dated (37), Smith's language is readily accessible and readily understood; the meanings of the slang are easy to figure out if they are not already obvious. Some of the plays Schoch discusses seem to have been *designed* to be incomprehensible (42), but this never seems true of Smith's parody. He rarely if ever creates puns so complicated that they cannot be deciphered (Schoch 45). Nor does he, as some of Schoch's examples do (69), depart so far from Shakespeare that his play hardly seems Shakespearean at all. At the same time, he is not *so* faithful to Shakespeare that his play seems tediously unimaginative. Smith, in short, wrote what is arguably one of the best of all Shakespearean parodies—one that deserves to be revived not only through reading but also through staged performances.

## Notes

1. In addition to Schoch's book, see also the books by Levine, Teague, the Vaughans, and Wells.

2. Searches for "William Hawley Smith" in the MLA International Bibliography have turned up nothing. Searches of his name in connection with Shakespeare on Google Books and in the indexes of relevant books (such as those listed in my first note) have likewise turned up no substantial references to him in this connection in modern scholarship. However, there is plentiful evidence in Google Books about Smith's life and career, as well as evidence that Smith's parody was widely admired and performed in its own day.

## Works Cited

Levine, Lawrence. *Highbrow/Lowbrow: The Emergence of Cultural Hierarchy in America*. Harvard UP, 1988.

Schoch, Richard. *Not Shakespeare: Bardolatry and Burlesque in the Nineteenth Century*. Cambridge UP, 2002.

Smith, William Hawley. *The new Hamlet, intermixed and interwoven with a revised version of Romeo and Juliet; the combination being modernized, re-written and wrought out on new-discovered lines, as indicated under the light of the higher criticism*. J.W. Franks & Sons, 1902.

_____. *THE NEW HAMLET / INTERMIXED AND INTERWOVEN / WITH / A REVISED VERSION OF ROMEO AND JULIET / THE COMBINATION BEING MODERNIZED, RE-WRITTEN AND WROUGHT OUT ON NEW-DISCOVERED LINES. AS INDICATED UNDER THE LIGHT OF THE HIGHER CRITICISM / BY / WM. HAWLEY SMITH /AND / THE SMITH FAMILY, FARMERS / PRINTED FROM THE ORIGINAL MANUSCRIPT, WITH TEXT IN FULL. AND AS FIRST PRODUCED WHEN DONE IN ACTION BY THE SMITHS, THEIR OWN COMPANY. UNDER THE HAW TREE. ON THEIR FARM. AT THE THICKET.* Rand, McNally, 1902.

_____. *The new Hamlet, intermixed and interwoven with a revised version of Romeo and Juliet; the combination being modernized, rewritten and wrought out on new-discovered lines, as indicated under the light of the higher criticism by Wm. Hawley Smith and the Smith family, farmers. Printed from the original manuscript, with text in full, and as first produced when done in action by the Smiths, their own company, under the haw tree, on their farm, at the ticket* [sic], *June 17, 1902.* Rand, McNally, [1902].

Teague, Frances. *Shakespeare and the American Popular Stage.* Cambridge UP, 2006.

Vaughan, Alden T., and Virginia Mason Vaughan. *Shakespeare in America.* Oxford UP, 2012.

Wells, Stanley. *Nineteenth-Century Shakespeare Burlesques.* Glazier, 1978. 5 vols.

# Nineteenth- and Twentieth-Century American Newspaper Travesties of *Romeo and Juliet*_____

Sarah Fredericks

In the late nineteenth and early twentieth centuries, *Romeo and Juliet* was one of William Shakespeare's most often parodied and burlesqued plays. This drama—with its romantic plot, lofty language, and famously tragic outcome—readily lent itself to comic treatment. The play was often spoofed, both on the stage and even in newspaper articles of the time. The newspaper "travesties" (a popular term for this genre of parody) reveal much about American popular culture of the era. They suggest how Shakespeare's play could be appropriated for various uses, including uses that reflect the social, economic, political, gender, and even racial thinking of this period in American history. Rarely if ever were the parodies offered as serious works of art; almost always they were topical and ephemeral. For that very reason, however, they offer real insights into the ways the writers of the parodies thought about Shakespeare, about other people, and about the culture in which they lived.

## Poetical Parody and Rhyming Travesty

Some mid-nineteenth-century newspaper travesties of *Romeo and Juliet* parodied the play in verse. One example of such parody, "Romeo and Juliet—Bourcicaited by Joe Ragstock," appeared in the June 26, 1860 poetry section of the *Staunton Spectator* (Staunton, Virginia). The poem's rich diction, lowbrow renaming of characters, humorous rhymes, and deliberate undercutting of emotional moments all contrast with the play's serious nature, making the story seem utterly ridiculous—and the travesty a success.

The piece begins by establishing the setting and humorously renaming the feuding families: "It was in ancient Italy, a deadly hatred grew / Between old Caleb Capulet and Moses Montague" (Ragstock 1). The two lovers are similarly mocked when they are introduced:

Now Moses had an only son, a little dapper beau,
The pet of all the pretty girls, by name young Romeo;
And Caleb owned a female girl, just home from boarding school,
Miss Juliet was her Christian name—for short they called her Jule.
(Ragstock 1)

Romeo sneaks into Juliet's coming out party, a "ball at [Caleb Capulet's] plantation," and when Tybalt sees Romeo there "without an invitation," he starts to "growl and pout, / And watched an opportunity to put the fellow out" (Ragstock 1). As Romeo and Juliet spot each other, Ragstock uses a bit of humorously forced rhyme to describe their sudden attraction: "When Juliet saw Romeo his beauty his did enchant her; / And Romeo, he fell in love with Juliet instanter" (1).

The piece then moves quickly through a number of high-action scenes, skipping over the play's more emotionally rich or romantic episodes, such as that on Juliet's balcony. The couple's wedding is rather succinctly summarized: "Now, less their dads should spoil the fun, but little time was tarried— / Away to Squire Laurence sped, and secretly were married" (1). Romeo's altercation with Tybalt and subsequent banishment, however, receive a surprisingly substantial treatment:

Oh, cruel fate! that day the groom met Tybalt in the square;
And Tybalt being very drunk, at Romeo did swear.
Then Romeo his weapon drew (a knife of seven blades,)
And made a gap in Tibby's ribs that sent him to the shades.
The watchmen came; he took to flight, down alley street and square;
The Charlies ran, o'ertook their man, and took him 'fore the Mayor.
Then spake the worthy magistrate, (and savagely did frown,)
"Young man, you have to lose your head, or else vamose the town."
(Ragstock 1)

Faced with either exile or death, Romeo escapes to Mantua, leaving "his bride in solitude to pine" (1). With Romeo gone, Paris "comes to woo" Juliet, and her father warns her, "If you refuse the gentleman, I'll soundly wollop you" (Ragstock 1). Juliet seeks

Critical Insights

Squire Lawrence for counsel, and he advises her to "go to bed and take some laudanum," explaining that "'Twill make you sleep, and seem as dead; thus canst thou dodge this blow; / And humbugged man your pa will be—a blest one, Romeo" (1). Juliet agrees, and the next day, she is taken for dead and is buried.

In Mantua, Romeo learns that Juliet has "piped out," and he decides to return and commit suicide: "Quoth he, 'Of life I've had enough; I'll hire Bluffkin's mule. / Lay in a pint of baldface rum, and lie to-night with Jule'" (Ragstock 1). Romeo rides "to the sepulchre, 'mong dead folks, bats and creepers," and, settling himself beside her body, he "swallowed down the burning dose" when suddenly Juliet "ope'd her peepers!" (1). Confused as to whether she's a ghost or just "acting possum," Romeo commands her to identify herself, and Juliet responds that she is "Alive! . . . and kicking too" (1). Unaware that Romeo's poisoned himself, Juliet tells her husband that now they can "go home" since "pa's spite will have abated" (1). When he begins to stagger, she inquires, "Are you intoxicated?" (1). Romeo's reply and subsequent death are curiously deadpan: "'No, no, my duck, I took some stuff that caused a little fit.' / He struggled hard to tell her all—but couldn't—so he quit" (1). His cooling corpse is similarly described without emotion: "In shorter time than takes a lamb to wag his tail or jump, / Poor Romeo was stiff and pale as any whitewashed pump" (1). The travesty concludes with Juliet's suicide (and one of the most humorously deflating couplets of the entire poem): "Then Juliet seized that awful knife, and in her bosom stuck it; / Let out a most terrific yell, fell down, and 'kicked the bucket'" (1). Ragstock's parody shows that Shakespeare's work could be effectively burlesqued not only on stage but also in the pages of a small-town American newspaper. *Romeo and Juliet* was so well known (and loved) that it often inspired affectionate teasing.

## A Change of Scenery: Parodies Set on American Soil

As Ragstock's spoof shows, one characteristic typical of newspaper travesties involved setting the play's action in the United States and incorporating American cityscapes, language, technology, and economic situations into the parody. One travesty full of such

Americana is "Romeo and Juliet" by "The Fat Cootribtuor [*sic*]" published in "Our Shakesperian [*sic*] Gallery" in the July 31, 1868 issue of *The Pulaski Citizen* (Pulaski, Tennessee). In addition to containing vivid details that offer insight into the culture of this period, this travesty is notable for its puns and groaners, use of nicknames, comic absurdity, and humorous subversion of romantic clichés.

Rather than a city in Italy, the Verona of this travesty is a "small station on the New York Central Railroad" (The Fat Cootribtuor 1). The Montagues and Capulets, who live in Verona and have "backyards [fronting] on each other," have a longstanding feud "on account of a lawsuit that had long been pending between them, regarding a water privilege" (1). "Mr. Capulet, or 'Old Cap,' as he was familiarly known among the boys," hosts a masquerade ball in honor of young Juliet, who has just returned from boarding school. Although not invited, Romeo attends in disguise, wearing a Pilgrim's costume, "'just to see,' as he expressed it, 'what sort of a lay-out the old cuss had'" (1). Upon first seeing Juliet, Romeo falls in love with her; the narrator explains, "having been engaged fourteen times, he was naturally very susceptible" (1). In the following passage, the author creates multiple allusions—the first to the title of John Bunyan's famous Christian allegory, the second to Romeo's costume, and the third to dialogue from Act 1, Scene 5 (in which Romeo declares himself a pilgrim traveling to worship Juliet as though she were a saint). The author also plays with the dual meaning of "returning":

> In his disguise as a pilgrim [Romeo] made love to her at once, getting on very rapidly.—In fact, by the time the ball broke up, he had made such *pilgrim's progress* into her affections that Juliet was dead struck after him, even accepting a kiss at parting, which she immediately returned, however, it suddenly occurring to her that it wouldn't be right to keep it, he being almost a total stranger. (The Fat Cootribtuor 1)

Afterwards, Romeo is shocked to learn that Juliet is a Capulet; the news "sounded the death knell to his hopes, for," the narrator sarcastically informs the reader, "his intentions were strictly honorable" (The Fat Cootribtuor 1). Juliet was similarly distraught to discover that Romeo "was the son of her father's most detested enemy, John Jacob Montague!" (1). This name obviously alludes to John Jacob Astor IV, the famous American tycoon (1864–1912). The allusion is typical of many nineteenth-century Shakespeare parodies, which often mention famous persons and events, especially from contemporary economic or political contexts.

As with the location of Verona, the balcony of the Capulets' Italian villa is translated onto American soil, and Romeo must climb over a picket fence to get into the garden outside Juliet's window. This section of the travesty overflows with humorous subversions of what has become classic romantic imagery. Resting her gloved hand upon her cheek, Juliet looks out across the garden, singing a popular nineteenth-century love song, and Romeo wishes "that he was a boxing glove upon that hand that he might touch the largest possible amount of that cheek" (The Fat Cootribtuor 1). The narrator interjects, "Cheeky, wasn't it?" (1). Juliet's well-known meditation on Romeo's name gets similarly subverted: "Rummy! Oh, Rummy! Wherefore art thou, Rummy?" (1). Wanting to know "what's there in a name anyhow, unless it was good at the bank," Juliet declares that "a horse-shoe geraneum [*sic*] would emit as agreeable an odor called by any other name, or something to that effect" (1). The narrator concludes that "this is a question for botanists" (1). Romeo emerges from hiding in the bushes and does "some very pretty talking himself, showing a mastery of the English language rarely attained by one of his tender age" (1). The two quickly "plighted their respective troths then and there, and Romeo, who felt confident to take care of a family on account of the promise of a position in the Revenue Department, engaging to arrange as quickly as possible for their marriage, disappeared over the picket fence" (1).

The narration of the couple's marriage and subsequent schemes is filled with puns and details of American life and phrasing. Romeo seeks his friend, Friar Laurence, "to perform the marriage ceremony, having decided, to take it *fried*"—a pun on the homophones "friar" and "fryer" (The Fat Cootribtuor 1). Juliet sneaks out of the house by "pretending to her folks that she was going to the Rink to practice roller skating" (1). Following their wedding, which takes place in the Friar's "cell—a perpetual *sell* to many people, marriage is—they each went home to arrange for a wedding trip to Niagara Falls, if they could elude the old folks" (1). Alas, it seems "fate and Shakespeare stood in the way of their happiness." Returning home, Romeo gets "into a street fight" and stabs Tybalt with a "sword-cane" (1). Romeo is summarily "banished from Verona by the Board of Supervisors" (1). Romeo's last night in Verona, which he spends with Juliet in carnal pleasures, is delicately summarized as "an affecting interview with his wife," and in the morning, Romeo takes "a canal packet . . . for Mantua" (1). Unaware of Juliet's marriage and thinking that she is now "a grass-widow," the Capulets urge Juliet to marry "Count Paris, of Paris Hill," saying that "marriage with Paris would soothe her distress of mind—be as it were a plaster to her woe. / But, no; she didn't want any of it. No *Plaster of Paris* for her" (1). If she doesn't marry Paris, "Old Cap" says he'll support her no longer; she'll have to "support herself with her sewing machine" (1). Juliet, "being in a great *stew*," turns to Friar Laurence, who contrives "a plan to at once free her from the mated marriage [with Paris]—giving a 'grand *trip* to Paris,' as he facetiously called it—and uniting her and Romeo" (1). Juliet takes the sleeping potion and is entombed.

Friar Laurence telegraphs Romeo with news of their scheme, but Romeo never receives the dispatch. Instead, "picking up a morning paper," he reads "among the Associated Press dispatches" that "Juliet Dorothy, only daughter of our well-known citizen, William Henry Harrison Capulet, died very suddenly this morning" (The Fat Cootribtuor 1). Hastening back to Verona, Romeo "[purchases] a bottle of benzine of an apothecary," which he uses to kill Paris outside Juliet's tomb, for "[Paris] wasn't much used to liquor" (1). Romeo enters the tomb, "[drinks] the gallon of benzine," and dies, uttering "All right, old Cap!" with his dying breath. Juliet, awakening and seeing her husband's corpse, "[slays] herself with a dagger carelessly left in the tomb by 'the property man'" (1). The parody concludes with a surprisingly somber image of the simple inscription upon their shared tombstone: "Romeo and Juliet" (1). "The Fat Cootibutor" obviously had fun, made fun, and provoked

---

many laughs with his over-the-top spoof of Shakespeare's famous play. The very existence of his spoof suggests an appetite for all things Shakespearean in nineteenth-century American culture.

## Witty Narrators and Meta-Theatrical Musings

Some nineteenth-century American newspaper parodies capitalized on sassy and intelligent narrative commentary for their humor. Promoted as one of "Shakspeare's best known skits [written] in plain, intelligible blank verse," a travesty of *Romeo and Juliet*, composed by the otherwise unidentified "Cabriolet," was published in the January 7, 1888 issue of the *Springfield Daily Republic* (Springfield, Ohio). It offered readers witty running commentary on the actions of the play as well meta-theatrical analysis by discussing typical performance practices. Longer than other newspaper travesties, Cabriolet's spoof begins with a two-paragraph introduction in which the narrator reflects on his experience as an actor in an amateur production of *Romeo and Juliet*, what he calls "a sparkling little farce written by Shakspeare [*sic*] and composed by Bacon," a joking reference to a popular theory at the time that Sir Francis Bacon had authored Shakespeare's plays. *Romeo and Juliet*, Cabriolet asserts, features "passion, pathos and a second-floor porch," and "almost every minute or two somebody trips pleasantly out onto the stage and gets murdered quite a good deal" (1). Cabriolet emphasizes the veritable parade of characters getting killed onstage with "the assistance of some . . . huge bread-knife, sharpest on the handle" (1).

Cabriolet's travesty is accompanied by satirical narrative commentary and interjected explanations of Elizabethan culture. The Montagues and Capulets, Cabriolet explains, "had it in for each other on account of a trifling little muss away back before the war, which had been handed down or sent by mail from generation to generation, until it was a good deal soiled and mussed" (1). Because of this feud, the two families frequently now "cut [each other] full of assorted holes" and bite their thumbs at one another, which Cabriolet explains is "an old-time way of hollowing rats at anybody you didn't like, and raw thumbs in various stages of mastication were a common sight in those days" (1). One night, "Juliet's pa" gives "a little informal evening entertainment, with a six-handed game of indigestion and pickles, graham wafers and dancing" (1). Romeo sneaks in by pretending to be "a society reporter" and sees Juliet, who, Cabriolet explains, "Shakespeare made a maid of fourteen, but modern actresses impersonate an eighteen-year-old girl. But then Juliet was written up some time since and has naturally grown older" (1). Romeo and Juliet immediately "[fall] in love with each other at first sight, as slick as it could have been done at a choir meeting" (1). Romeo "makes a good, durable article of love to Juliet, telling her that she is the only girl in the room with a low-cut dress that doesn't give him the ennui" (1). Cabriolet cheekily explains that "Juliet is pretty well dressed in certain localities, but above the waist, doesn't seem to mind the climate at all. So Romeo saw considerable of her that evening and was much infatuated" (1). By the end of "her father's progressive euchre party," the two are "engaged to be married as soon as Romeo was promoted from the calico department to the ribbon counter" (1).

The balcony scene, "one of the best things in the skit," follows, with Juliet up on a balcony which "[looks] as if it might be a good place to watch a circus procession from" and Romeo "percolating around the yard" below (Cabriolet 1). Romeo "has it worse than ever and says considerable things of an amatory nature to indicate that he is dead gone on Juliet" (1). Seeing Juliet at the window, Romeo says, "But soft! What light through yonder window breaks? It is the east, and Juliet is the son" [sic] (1). "This remark," Cabriolet interjects, "doubles the interest of the audience, for up to this time it had been suspected that Juliet was the daughter" (1). Chiding Romeo for the risk he takes in visiting her, Cabriolet declares "that he doesn't care so long as nothing runs him—nothing like a dog. The dog and pants joke was alive and well even in those early days" (1). The lovers try to exchange "a lot of assorted taffies of different flavors," but in straining to reach one another, "Romeo's galluses [i.e., suspenders] have broken in several localities and a loud metallic snap has occurred about Juliet's waist, which everybody who has been out in society understands," and Juliet resorts to tossing down her "nubia," or woolen scarf (1). Romeo "kisses considerable of the dye out of it, and gets lint all over his chin because he has neglected to go that day to the barber and get his features peeled" (1). After Romeo tosses the nubia back to her, Juliet "kisses it all over and acts as if it was the best thing she ever tasted" (1). Unwilling to part, the lovers "indulge in one more passionate burst of consultation and call each other more pet names than a fond aunt could apply to a cross-eyed baby" (1). Finally, Juliet retires, and "the audience leans over and spits" (1).

"In the next act," Cabriolet narrates, "Romeo gets into a scrap with Tybalt and cuts his monogram on that party's liver with a sword. Tybalt dies from the effects of outraged modesty at having his bowels exposed to the public, and Romeo gets to be the rage in police circles" (1). Glossing over Romeo and Juliet's wedding, which Cabriolet asserts was kept secret "in order to keep [Romeo's] wages from being garnished," Cabriolet instead focuses on their wedding night. "Juliet," he says, "is prepared for bed and has only got on a yard or two more clothes than she wore at the party at which she met Romeo," but, of course, "the audience forgives her" (1). Remaining together in bed "till the milk wagons begin to rattle past" in the morning, the two tickle each other and playfully argue whether the bird singing outside is a lark or nightingale.

After her husband leaves, Juliet "falls clear to the bottom of a deep swoon, and rolls down a flight of stairs, greatly to the exhibition of her figure, which does not lie but rolls down" (Cabriolet 1). Juliet's father demands that Juliet marry Paris, who wears "green tights and [has] a large wholesale grocery and commission house—all bills payable as soon as due" (1). Arguments ensue, "during which Juliet's father calls her a list of names, and says she is no daughter of his—a statement at which Juliet's mother looks around in a puzzled way for the axe or something" (1).

"The rest of the play," Cabriolet informs the reader, "is quite sad and consists of death served in various styles" (1). In order to "escape being a bigamist and marrying Paris," Juliet swallows "a dose of do-good or something from Friar Laurence that kills her for a while, but allows her to return to life in time for her spring hat to be in style" (1). Juliet's death "annoys" Romeo, and he procures a "cough-mixture that will kill him for sure," for he's unaware that Juliet has a "codicil of resuscitation tacked on to her little tonic" (1).

Inside Juliet's tomb, Romeo gazes at "Juliet's alleged and fictitious remains [and] takes the Rough-on-Romeo" (1). When Juliet awakes shortly thereafter, the two get tangled up in one another's costumes. After the poison takes effect, "Romeo dies right there in public" (1). "[Hearing] the prompter in the files," Juliet "[swears] because she has forgotten her lines," and proceeds to kill herself (1). "At this point," Cabriolet concludes, "the curtain falls and the audience gets up and inquires of each other if it wasn't just too sweet" (1). "Cabriolet" (whoever he or she was) clearly enjoyed creating an especially absurd version of Shakespeare play. American readers could laugh at a spoof of one of the great monuments of English literature while also laughing at their own culture.

## American Culture in Travesties of the Balcony Scene

Rather than parodying *Romeo and Juliet* in its entirety, some newspaper travesties from the 1800s focused on a single scene. The balcony scene (Act 2, Scene 2) especially lent itself to parody for many reasons. One noteworthy parody of the balcony scene is "Romeo and Juliet—1878" by "Hawkeye" (otherwise unnamed), published in the March 21, 1878 issue of *The Daily Dispatch* (Richmond, Virginia). This piece, which is formatted like a real script, intermixes actual lines from the play with colloquial phrasing and slang, thus deflating the seriousness of the scene's emotions. Looking out from her balcony, Juliet remarks in a seemingly Southern voice, "goodness gracious me," and Romeo responds, "O, go on with the chin music," a term meaning idle talk or mindless prattle (Hawkeye 4). Trying to create a simile that compares Juliet to a majestic bird overhead, Romeo fumbles for words as though he's an actor who has forgotten his script. Juliet, in turn, meditates on the significance of Romeo's name, wondering if he could "get the legislature to change [his] last name" and whether he would be willing to "take all [of herself]" in turn (4). With shameless emphasis on the economic benefits of their union, Romeo asserts that he'll take her along with all her "goods, chattels, manors, rents. / Revenue, real and personal property, insurance, / Expectations, bank accounts, bonds, coupons, stamps, / Even nickels" (4).

Surprised by his audacity, Juliet calls him a "naughty man" and inquires as to how he managed to get into her garden (Hawkeye 4). Romeo boasts that he has "Come up the alley, poisoned the dog, / And climbed over the back fence," pointing to "the ashes on [his] boots . . . and coffee grounds /And eggshells on [his] trousers" as proof (4). "Look at this biceps muscle," he commands, "There is a goose egg for you" (4). Perhaps the best instance of anti-romantic, nineteenth-century language appears at the end of the piece, after Juliet has chided Romeo about swearing by the inconstant moon. Casting about for something else to swear by, Romeo utters a veritable catalogue of non-explicit nineteenth-century profanity:

> Romeo.  Well then, by Jimminy Pelt, by dad,
> By hokey, by the long armed spoon, by jocks,
> By thunder, Juliet; oh, by gosh—
> What shall I swear by?
> Juliet.  Do not swear at all;
> Or if thou wilt, swear by thy gracious self.
> Romeo.  Well, then, may I be did, dad, dug, dog-goned,
> Dad-binged to jude: Oh, may I be
> Teetotally cow-kicked over by a bullrush.
> Dad-slam the gaul-dinged dad-fisted
> Thing to thunder:—
> (Goes off after some new swears.) (Hawkeye 4)

Romeo's swearing runs the gamut of profanity: "Jimminy Pelt" and "jocks" are euphemisms for "Jesus"; "dad," "gosh," and "the long armed spoon" are euphemisms for "God"; "thunder" and "jude" are euphemisms for "hell"; "cow-kicked" and "dog-goned" are euphemisms for "damned"; and "dad-binged," "gaul-dinged," and "dad-fisted" are all euphemisms for "god-damned." The travesty's mockery of romantic overtures culminates in the abrupt termination of the lovers' interlude, not because of interrupting parents, but because Romeo must find some new profanity, further underscoring the ridiculousness of the encounter.

Although the contrast between lowbrow and highbrow makes some of these single-scene parodies interesting, not all satirical treatments of *Romeo and Juliet* are benign. Formatted like a script, "The Great Balcony Scene (As Montague Glass Might have Shakespeared It)" was published anonymously in the December 10, 1922 edition of *The Washington Times* (Washington, DC). It satirizes Jewish American language and culture and employs offensive stereotypes. One feature that this travesty particularly targets is the speech patterns of Jewish Americans, depicting both code-switching (in which Yiddish words are incorporated into English sentences) and code-mixing (in which English phrases and clauses are structured according to Yiddish syntactical patterns). Take, for example, Juliet's question to Romeo when she asks why he hasn't climbed up to her balcony: "Well, for why should you be standing down there in the damp grass, where you might be catchin' malaria, who knows? Gonif, ain't you got no feet for to climb up with?" (2E). Here, word order, verb tense and formation, and phrasing are all constructed to mimic the non-standard English stereotypically associated with some Jewish Americans. Juliet also uses the term "gonif," Yiddish slang for a rascal or disreputable person, which further stereotypically characterizes her speech as Jewish American.

In addition to unfavorably mimicking the language of Jews, this travesty offensively stereotypes them as greedy and miserly. Both Romeo and Juliet seem preoccupied with money. Looking at the moon, Juliet says it reminds her "more than nothing else of a $20 gold piece" (2E). When Romeo first greets Juliet, he asks her, "How's your old man?" and Juliet counters, "You ain't gone into the insurance business, have you? Why don't you ask how I was, maybe?" (2E). Juliet interprets Romeo's flippant inquiry into her father's health as interest in her inheritance rather than in herself. Later, Romeo invites Juliet to see the play "The Total Loss" at the Alhambra, and Juliet agrees—so long as she doesn't have to sit in the cheap seats in the balcony. Romeo tells her, "I ain't no dime-kisser, like your old man is" (2E). At the end of the piece, Romeo concludes their rendezvous by confessing that he has to return to his job and work overtime even though he is not getting paid for it. Furious, Juliet responds, "Yeah, you got a dame on your string, that's what you got, schlemiel what works overtime like he was paid for it. I ain't got nothin' more to do with you" (2E). Calling him a "schlemiel," or stupid person, for working without pay, Juliet cancels their impending date, perhaps unable to imagine herself with one who cares so little getting the money he should receive. Ultimately, both Romeo and Juliet are stereotyped in terms of their interest in money. It seems even *Romeo and Juliet* could be appropriated for post-World War I antisemitism. This parody reminds us that by the turn of the century, America had become a destination for millions of Jewish immigrants. Parodies of Shakespeare were often used to deal with topical political and social issues.

## A Play as a Backdrop: Parodies and Love Stories

Other newspaper parodies of the play used rehearsing and performing *Romeo and Juliet* as a backdrop for a love story. These adaptations frequently depict the characters performing the roles of Romeo and Juliet as quarreling lovers. Through farcical machinations and humorous mishaps in the production of the play, the characters eventually reconcile. Less humorous than other parodies, these adaptations tend to focus on scenes central to Juliet's emotional experience (and that of the actress performing the role), comparing both heroines' awakening passion while contrasting the arcs of their romances. Even as the play builds to its tragic climax, the story builds to a happy promise of marriage.

One such use of *Romeo and Juliet* appears in "An Old Play" by Dard Best, which was published in the February 3, 1876 issue of *The Cincinnati Daily Star* (Cincinnati, Ohio). The story begins at the end of a long estrangement between Ostrander, who has just completed college abroad, and the heroine Gathryn, who is staying at her Aunt's country house and secretly pining for her jilted Ostrander. Hearing of Ostrander's imminent return, Gathryn's cousin Erle insists that they put on a production of *Romeo and Juliet* as part of his own birthday party, and he enlists Gathryn to play the Juliet to his Romeo. Erle plots to reunite the two separated lovers by having Ostrander surreptitiously take his place as Romeo in the final performance. He further cements the relationship between the two by arranging for a real Justice of the Peace to perform the role of Friar Laurence; thus, after the play's wedding scene, Ostrander and Gathryn will be legally married. Initially, Gathryn is shocked at Ostrander's appearance onstage, but she quickly loses herself in her role of Juliet. Her lines are transformed into an earnest expression of Gathryn's affection for Ostrander. After the curtain falls at the play's end, Ostrander and Gathryn fully reconcile and agree to sign a marriage certificate, and the audience, having caught rumor of Erle's plot to marry the two, flood in to congratulate the couple and sign the certificate as witnesses (Best 2).

Best's adaptation overlays the classic arc of a Shakespearian comedy onto the performance of one of Shakespeare's most famous tragedies. Even as the Romeo and Juliet plot progresses towards a dramatic death scene, the Ostrander and Gathryn plot moves towards the happy formalizing of a marriage. Although it lacks the farce featured in other parodies, "An Old Play in Three Parts" has comedic moments. Erle, as an instigator of the plot to reconcile the couple, acts as a sort of Puck, and in the play's final scene in Juliet's tomb, Gathryn discovers that in his haste to see her, Ostrander has forgotten to put on his prop sword, and she is forced to stab herself with an imaginary blade.

Another adaption that similarly depicts a love story through the performance of the play is "Romeo and Juliet," anonymously published in the April 11, 1902 issue of the *Dakota Farmers' Leader* (Canton, South Dakota). The narrative begins during the East End Dramatic Club's rehearsal of *Romeo and Juliet*. Amy, the president of the club and the actress performing the role of Juliet, is dejected about the poor quality of their production: the performances lack emotion; the set's balcony was constructed too tall (so that as Juliet she has to stoop to keep from being hidden in the clouds); and her beau Jack, the actor playing Romeo, continually teases her about both her acting and her disposition. Despite early nerves, during the performance Amy fully identifies with the character of Juliet, and Jack responds amorously in turn. When she bends down to kiss "dead" Romeo in the tomb scene, Jack prevents her from drawing his dagger and pretending to deal her own deathblow until she promises to be his. "She had not counted," we are told, "on the revivifying effect her kiss might have on the stark Montague" (3). After a brief struggle and subsequent silent contemplation of his proposal, Amy relents, and with a happy cry, one not commensurate with the "tragic thrill she had so prided herself upon," she agrees, rushing through her final lines, so that, "forgetting to stab herself[,] she [falls] into his arms" (3).

One again, the humor in this form of parody is subtle. As with Best's adaptation, the solemnity of the play's performance is undercut by humorous mishaps: Mercutio's blade falls to pieces during his swordfight, and the "moon," a lantern held aloft by Amy's little brother who stands on a stepladder, shakes as the brother giggles at the actors. Another source of humor involves the narrator's sarcastic remarks on the characters' behavior and attitudes. Amy's pride and solemn self-importance are particularly attacked. The chief absurdity, however, comes from the final lines, in which the emotional crescendo of Romeo and Juliet's suicides is dramatically undercut by Amy and Jack's happy reconciliation, so that the final, tragic deathblow is entirely forgotten.

## Concluding Thoughts

Widespread familiarity with Shakespeare's works allowed his texts to be refashioned and parodied in numerous ways and for various ends. The story of star-crossed lovers could be adapted as a humorous conceit when relating cases from the local courthouse, as in "Romeo and Juliet Told is Prose Before the Court of Justice John" by "The Great Dispenser" published in the December 23, 1900 issue of *The Times* (Richmond, Virginia). Or it could even be used to subvert ideals of marital bliss, refiguring Romeo and Juliet as a bitter, bickering couple in Elizabethan England who only pretended to be in love when they knew they were being observed by Bill Shakespeare, as in "A Tabloid Tale" published in the May 30, 1919 issue of the *Richmond Times-Dispatch* (Richmond, Virginia). The very prestige of *Romeo and Juliet* as a work of "serious" literature made it a prime target for writers who wanted to be funny, and the cultural ubiquity of Shakespeare's plays ensured that Americans across social and economic classes could get in on the joke.

## Works Cited

Best, Dard. "An Old Play in Three Parts." *The Cincinnati Daily Star*, 03 February 1876, p. 2. *Chronicling America: Historic American Newspapers*. Library of Congress.

Cabriolet. "Romeo and Juliet." *Springfield Daily Republic* [Springfield, Ohio], 07 January 1888, p. 1. *Chronicling America: Historic American Newspapers*. Library of Congress.

The Fat Cootribtuor [*sic*]. "Romeo and Juliet." *The Pulaski Citizen* [Pulaski, Tennessee], 31 July 1868, p. 1. *Chronicling America: Historic American Newspapers*. Library of Congress.

"The Great Balcony Scene (As Montague Glass Might have Shakespeared It)." *The Washington times* [Washington, DC], 10 December 1922, p. 2E. *Chronicling America: Historic American Newspapers*. Library of Congress.

The Great Dispenser. "Romeo and Juliet Told is Prose Before the Court of Justice John." The *Times* [Richmond, Virginia], 23 December 1900, p. 5. *Chronicling America: Historic American Newspapers*. Library of Congress.

Hawkeye. "Romeo and Juliet—1878" *The Daily Dispatch* [Richmond, Virginia], 21 March 1878, p. 4. *Virginia Chronicle*. Library of Virginia.

Ragstock, Joe. "Romeo and Juliet." *Staunton Spectator* [Staunton, Virginia], 26 June 1860, p. 1. *Chronicling America: Historic American Newspapers*. Library of Congress.

"A Tabloid Tale." *Richmond Times-Dispatch* [Richmond, Virginia], 30 May 1919, p. 6. *Chronicling America: Historic American Newspapers*. Library of Congress.

# RESOURCES

# Chronology of William Shakespeare's Life_____

**1564**
William Shakespeare is born in Stratford-upon-Avon in April 1564. He is baptized in the local church on April 26. His date of birth is usually assumed to have been April 23. His parents are John and Mary Shakespeare. John is a successful glove-maker who, in the years preceding and following William's birth, is a respected member of the local government, although he later suffers financial and social reversals. In addition to giving birth to William, Mary bears seven other children. William almost certainly attends the local grammar school.

**1582**
William marries Anne Hathaway, daughter of a prominent local farmer. Anne is three months pregnant at the time of the wedding and eight years older than William. In 1583, Anne gives birth to a daughter (Susanna). In 1585, the couple has twins (Hamnet and Judith). Hamnet dies in 1596.

**1585-92**
Details of Shakespeare's life during this period are unclear and have been the subject of much speculation. One legend (now widely doubted) suggests that he had to leave Stratford to escape the law after he allegedly poached deer from the property of a prominent local landowner. Other writers have speculated that during his time in Stratford, Shakespeare may have worked for a lawyer and/or may have taught school. Some recent scholars have suggested that during part of this period, Shakespeare may have been living, teaching, and (as an amateur) acting while part of the household of a prominent Catholic family in Lancashire. Numerous other theories abound concerning these "lost years." The idea that Shakespeare taught in some capacity seems plausible to many.

| | |
|---|---|
| **1592** | An allusion this year by the London writer Robert Greene seems to mock Shakespeare as an "Upstart Crow" and implies that by this time, Shakespeare was living in London, acting in plays, and writing blank verse, presumably for the professional theaters that were increasingly being founded at this time. Greene's attack also alludes to one of Shakespeare's plays (now known as *Henry VI, Part Three*). Most scholars assume that by 1592, Shakespeare had already written a number of his earliest plays. |
| **1594** | In 1593, plague forces the closing of London's theaters. Shakespeare is often assumed to have written some of his most important nondramatic poems during the period when the theaters were closed. Partly these poems (especially the popular *Venus and Adonis*, which was followed by *The Rape of Lucrece*) seem to have been intended to attract the patronage of powerful persons. The earliest sonnets are also often dated to this period. Some scholars believe that Shakespeare was also writing plays during the time when the theaters were closed, with an eye either toward private performance, future public performance, or both. *Venus and Adonis, Lucrece*, and some of the sonnets were publicly praised in 1598, although the sonnets were not printed until 1609. In the period following the reopening of the theaters in 1594, Shakespeare's theatrical career once again flourished. He wrote plays, acted in them, and profited from the sales of tickets. These profits eventually made him a rich man. |
| **1594-99** | During this period, Shakespeare is productive as an actor; writer; and, in 1599, part owner of the newly constructed open-air, octagonal-shaped Globe Theater, one of the most important public theaters in history. He earns 10 percent of the profits of the new theater. He is a member of the so-called "Chamberlain's Men," an |

acting company sponsored by one of the most powerful political figures in the kingdom. By 1597, Shakespeare is able to purchase a substantial home in Stratford, where his wife and surviving children apparently still live, while he lives and works in London.

| | |
|---|---|
| **1603** | With the death of Queen Elizabeth in this year and the accession of King James I (who remained King James VI of Scotland), the name of Shakespeare's acting company is changed from "the Chamberlain's Men" to "the King's Men." Their patron is now the most important person in the entire now-united kingdoms. Both before and after Elizabeth's death, Shakespeare's plays are performed at the royal court. The actor/playwright is now both increasingly wealthy and increasingly well known. In 1602, he buys more property in Stratford, and in ensuing years, he makes further investments in his hometown. |
| **1608** | In this year, Shakespeare's company, in addition to performing at the Globe (in Southwark, across the River Thames and south of London), begins performing in a much smaller, more elite indoor theater inside the city of London itself. |
| **1611** | Shakespeare is often assumed to begin retiring from full-time involvement in the stage in this year, although some collaborative plays postdate this period. This is the year of his last great "romance" (a modern term), *The Tempest*, which is often seen as a valedictory work. |
| **1616** | Early in this year, Shakespeare amends his will, providing generously for his daughter, his sister, and the local poor and remembering various friends, including old theatrical colleagues. The will mentions his wife only briefly, which may or may not be significant. He dies on April 23 (that is, supposedly fifty-two years to |

the day of his supposed birth date). He is buried in the same local church where he had been baptized.

| | |
|---|---|
| **1623** | In this year, friends of Shakespeare oversee the publication of the famous "First Folio," the massive book that contains most of his works (although many of his writings had previously been individually published in small, cheap, "quarto" editions). |

**Note:** Much of the information cited here was helpfully assembled by Terry Gray and published on one of the many splendid pages of his generally splendid website "Mr. William Shakespeare and the Internet": http://web.archive.org/web/20111025081356/http://shakespeare.palomar.edu/life.htm. See, in particular: http://web.archive.org/web/20111007131108/http://shakespeare.palomar.edu/timeline/timeline.htm.

# Works by William Shakespeare_____

For an exceptionally detailed discussion of the chronology of Shakespeare's works (including discussion of the many disputes about this matter) see William *Shakespeare: A Textual Companion* by Stanley Wells and Gary Taylor (Norton, 1997), pp. 69-144. See also the similarly detailed discussion by David Bevington, editor, *The Complete Works of Shakespeare* (Longman, 1997), pp. A1-A21. Bevington helpfully gives the full titles of quarto (small format) printings and also makes their dates of publication quite clear.

Plays were usually first performed not long after they were written. In some cases, we have evidence of first (or at least early) performances; in some cases, we do not. Whereas dates of first printings are usually very solid, dates of first performances are often conjectural.

Even the best experts often disagree about the dates of probable composition of Shakespeare's works. In the listing below, Bevington's suggestions are cited alongside those of G. Blakemore Evans (in *The Riverside Shakespeare*, 2nd ed., Houghton Mifflin, 1997, pp. 77-87) and Wells and Taylor. The frequent variances will give some idea of how often even the best students of these issues can disagree.

*Love's Labor's Lost* (Bevington: ca. 1588–1597; G. B. Evans: 1594–95 ["revised 1597 for court performance"]; Wells and Taylor: 1593–95; comedy; first known printing, 1598).

*The Henry the Sixth Plays* (Bevington: ca. 1589–92; G. B. Evans: 1589–90 [revised 1594–95 for Part One; 1590–91 for Part Two; 1590–91 for Part Three]; Wells and Taylor: Part Three, 1590–92; Part Two: 1590–91; Part One: 1591–92 [with other authors]. Three history plays; the second part was first printed in 1594; the third part was first printed in 1595; the first part [perhaps the last written of the three] was first printed in 1623.

*Titus Andronicus* (Bevington: ca. 1589–1592; G. B. Evans: 1593–94; Wells and Taylor: 1590–91; tragedy; first known printing, 1594).

*The Comedy of Errors* (Bevington: ca. 1589–1594; G. B. Evans: 1592–94; Wells and Taylor: 1592–94; comedy; first known printing, 1623).

*The Two Gentlemen of Verona* (Bevington: ca. 1590–94; G. B. Evans: 1594; Wells and Taylor: 1589–93; comedy; first known printing, 1623).

*The Taming of the Shrew* (Bevington: ca. 1590–93; G. B. Evans: 1593–94; Wells and Taylor: 1590–93; comedy; first known printing, 1623).

*Venus and Adonis* (Bevington: 1592–93; G. B. Evans: 1592–93; Wells and Taylor: 1593; narrative poem; first known printing, 1593).

*Richard the Third* (Bevington: ca. 1592–94; G. B. Evans: 1592–93; Wells and Taylor: 1592–93; history play; first known printing, 1597).

*The Rape of Lucrece* (Bevington: 1593–94; G. B. Evans: 1593–94; Wells and Taylor: 1594; narrative poem; first known printing, 1594).

*The Sonnets* (Bevington: 1593–1603; G. B. Evans: 1593–1609; Wells and Taylor: 1598–1609; sonnet collection; first known printing, 1609).

*King John* (Bevington: ca. 1594–96; G. B. Evans: 1594–96; Wells and Taylor: 1594–96; history play; first known printing, 1623).

*Romeo and Juliet* (Bevington: 1594–96; G. B. Evans: 1595–96; Wells and Taylor: 1594–95; tragedy; first known printing, 1597).

*A Midsummer Night's Dream* (Bevington: ca. 1595; G. B. Evans: 1595–96; Wells and Taylor: 1594–95; comedy; first known printing, 1600).

*The Merchant of Venice* (Bevington: ca. 1596–97; G. B. Evans: 1596–97; Wells and Taylor: 1596–97; dark comedy; first known printing, 1600).

*Richard the Second* (Bevington: ca. 1595–96; G. B. Evans: 1595; Wells and Taylor: 1594–96; history play; first known printing, 1597).

*Henry the Fourth, Part I* (Bevington: 1596–97; G. B. Evans: 1596–97; Wells and Taylor: 1596–97; history play; first known printing, 1598).

*Henry the Fourth, Part II* (Bevington: 1597–98; G. B. Evans: 1598; Wells and Taylor: 1597–98; history play; first known printing, 1600).

*The Merry Wives of Windsor* (Bevington: 1597–1601; G. B. Evans: 1597 ["revised ca. 1600–1"]; Wells and Taylor: 1597; comedy; first known printing, 1602).

*Much Ado About Nothing* (Bevington: 1598–99; G. B. Evans: 1598–99; Wells and Taylor: 1598–99; comedy; first known printing, 1600).

*As You Like It* (Bevington: 1598–1600; G. B. Evans: 1599; Wells and Taylor: 1599–1600; comedy; first known printing, 1623).

*Henry the Fifth* (Bevington: 1599; G. B. Evans: 1599; Wells and Taylor: 1599; history play; first known printing, 1600).

*Julius Caesar* (Bevington: 1599; G. B. Evans: 1599; Wells and Taylor: 1599; tragedy; first known printing, 1623).

*The Phoenix and the Turtle* (Bevington: finished by 1601; G. B. Evans: ca. 1601; Wells and Taylor: 1601; allegorical poem; first known printing, 1601).

*Hamlet* (Bevington: ca. 1599–1601; G. B. Evans: 1600–1601; Wells and Taylor: 1600–1601; tragedy; first known printing, 1603).

*Twelfth Night* (Bevington: 1600–02; G. B. Evans: 1601–1602; Wells and Taylor: 1602–03; comedy; first known printing, 1623).

*Troilus and Cressida* (Bevington: ca. 1601–1602; G. B. Evans: 1601–1602; Wells and Taylor: 1602–03; "problem play?"; first known printing, 1609).

*A Lover's Complaint* (Bevington: ca. 1601–1605; G. B. Evans: 1602–1608; Wells and Taylor: 1598–1609; narrative poem; first known printing, 1609).

*All's Well That Ends Well* (Bevington: ca. 1601–1605; G. B. Evans: 1602–1603; Wells and Taylor: 1603–05; comedy; first known printing, 1623).

*Measure for Measure* (Bevington: 1603–04; G. B. Evans: 1604; Wells and Taylor: 1604; dark comedy; first known printing, 1623).

*Othello* (Bevington: 1603–1604; G. B. Evans: 1604; Wells and Taylor: 1603–04; tragedy; first known printing, 1622).

*King Lear* (Bevington: 1605–1606; G. B. Evans: 1605; Wells and Taylor: 1605–08; tragedy; first known printing, 1608).

*Timon of Athens* (Bevington: 1605–1608; G. B. Evans: 1607–1608; Wells and Taylor: 1604–07 [with Thomas Middleton]; tragedy; first known printing, 1623).

*Antony of Cleopatra* (Bevington: 1606–1607; G. B. Evans: 1606–1607; Wells and Taylor: 1606–07; tragedy; first known printing, 1623).

*Macbeth* (Bevington: 1606–1607; G. B. Evans: 1606; Wells and Taylor: 1606; tragedy; first known printing, 1623).

*Pericles* (Bevington: 1606–1608; G. B. Evans: 1607–1608; Wells and Taylor: 1608–09 [with George Wilkins]; comedy or "romance"; first known printing, 1609).

*Coriolanus* (Bevington: ca. 1608; G. B. Evans: 1607–1608; Wells and Taylor: 1608; tragedy; first known printing, 1623).

*Cymbeline* (Bevington: ca. 1608–1610; G. B. Evans: 1609–1610; Wells and Taylor: 1610–11; comedy or "romance"; first known printing, 1623).

*The Winter's Tale* (Bevington: ca. 1609–1611; G. B. Evans: 1610–1611; Wells and Taylor: 1609–10; comedy or "romance"; first known printing, 1623).

*The Tempest* (Bevington: ca. 1611; G. B. Evans: 1611; Wells and Taylor: 1610–11; comedy or "romance"; first known printing, 1623).

*King Henry the Eighth* (Bevington: 1613; G. B. Evans: 1612–1613; Wells and Taylor: 1613 [with John Fletcher]; history play; first known printing, 1623).

*The Two Noble Kinsmen* (Bevington: 1613–1614; G. B. Evans: 1613; Wells and Taylor: 1613–15 [with John Fletcher]; tragicomedy; cowritten with John Fletcher; first known printing, 1634).

The listing above follows Bevington's suggested order of possible composition; here, on the other hand, is the order suggested by G. B. Evans: *1 Henry VI*; *2 Henry VI*; *3 Henry VI*; *Richard III*; *Venus and Adonis*; *The Comedy of Errors*; *Sonnets*; *The Rape of Lucrece*; *Titus Andronicus*; *The Taming of the Shrew*; *The Two Gentlemen of Verona*; *Love's Labor's Lost*; *King John*; *Richard II*; *Romeo and Juliet*; *A Midsummer Night's Dream*; *The Merchant of Venice*; *1 Henry IV*; *The Merry Wives of Windsor*; *2 Henry IV*; *Much Ado about Nothing*; *Henry V*; *Julius Caesar*; *As You Like It*; *Hamlet*; *The Phoenix and the Turtle*; *Twelfth Night*; *Troilus and Cressida*; *A Lover's Complaint*; *All's Well That Ends Well*; *Measure for Measure*; *Othello*; *King Lear*; *Macbeth*; *Antony and Cleopatra*; *Coriolanus*; *Timon of Athens*; *Pericles*; *Cymbeline*; *The Winter's Tale*; *The Tempest*; *Henry VIII*; *The Two Noble Kinsmen*.

Here is the order of possible composition suggested by Taylor and Wells: *The Two Gentlemen of Verona*; *The Taming of the* Shrew; *3 Henry VI*; *2 Henry VI*; *Titus Andronicus*; *1 Henry VI* [with other authors]; *Richard III*; *The Comedy of Errors*; *Venus and Adonis*; *Sonnets*;

*The Rape of Lucrece; Love's Labor's Lost; The Rape of Lucrece; A Midsummer Night's Dream; Romeo and Juliet; Richard II; King John; The Merchant of Venice; 1 Henry IV; The Merry Wives of Windsor; 2 Henry IV; Much Ado about Nothing; Sonnets, A Lover's Complaint; The Passionate Pilgrim; Henry V; Julius Caesar; As You Like It; Hamlet; The Phoenix and the Turtle; Twelfth Night; Troilus and Cressida; Measure for Measure; Othello; All's Well That Ends Well; Timon of Athens; Othello; All's Well That Ends Well; King Lear; Macbeth; Antony and Cleopatra; Pericles; Coriolanus; The Winter's Tale; Cymbeline; The Tempest; Henry VIII; The Two Noble Kinsmen.*

# Recent Editions of *Romeo and Juliet*: A Selective Survey (1997–2017)

Scores and scores (if not hundreds) of editions of *Romeo and Juliet* exist, not to mention graphic novels, comic books, video versions, modernized "translations," and audio performances (to cite only a few of the most prominent of various genres). Which edition(s) should a reader, teacher, researcher choose, and why? The list below is simply designed to bring together, in one place, descriptions of the main features of recent competing texts. These descriptions should give readers a sense of the various options and methods open to editors, readers, and performances of this play and others by Shakespeare. [*R.C.E.*]

**2016**. SERIES: MACMILLAN COLLECTOR'S LIBRARY. No editor listed. 192 pp.

PUBLISHER'S DESCRIPTION: "Illustrated throughout by Sir John Gilbert (1817–1897), famous for his depictions of historical scenes. . . .With an Introduction by Ned Halley. * . . . Bound in real cloth, printed on high quality paper, and featuring ribbon markers and gilt edges, Macmillan Collector's Library are books to love and treasure."

**2016**. SERIES: NORTON CRITICAL EDITIONS. Edited by Gordan McMullan. Norton. 448 pp; illustrations.

CONTENTS: Introduction * A Note on the Text * The *Text of Romeo and Juliet* * Textual Variants * Sources, Contexts, and Early Rewritings: *A Tale about Two Noble Lovers* (ca. 1530), by Luigi Da Porto * *The Unfortunate Death of Two Most Wretched Lovers* (1554), by Matteo Bandello * *Of Two Lovers* (1559), by Pierre Boaistuau * *Romeus and Juliet* (1562), by Arthur Brooke * *The Goodly History of the True and Constant Love between Rhomeo and Julietta* (1567), by William Painter * "*Romio und Julieta*: A Case Study of an Early German Shakespeare Adaptation," by Kareen Seidler * From *Romio und Julieta* (ca. 1680) * From *The History and Fall of Caius Marius* (1680), by Thomas Otway * "Criticism and Later Rewritings: The Challenges of *Romeo and Juliet*," by Stanley Wells * "Pre-Twentieth-

Century Responses: [On *Romeo and Juliet*]," by Samuel Johnson *
From *Characters of Shakespear[e]'s Plays*, by William Hazlitt * [On
*Romeo and Juliet*], by Samuel Taylor Coleridge * From *On Some of
Shakespeare's Female Characters*, by Helena Faucit * "Twentieth-
and Twenty-First-Century Responses: *Romeo and Juliet*," by Harley
Granville-Barker * "*Romeo and Juliet*: Comedy into Tragedy," by
Susan Snyder * "The Sonnet's Body and the Body Sonnetized in
*Romeo and Juliet*," by Gayle Whittier * "The Definition of Love:
Shakespeare's Phrasing in *Romeo and Juliet*," by Jill L. Levenson *
"'Death-Marked Love': Desire and Presence in *Romeo and Juliet*,"
by Lloyd Davis * "De-generation: Editions, Offspring, and *Romeo
and Juliet*," by Wendy Wall * "Shakespeare's Mercutio," by Joseph
A. Porter * "The Ideology of Romantic Love: The Case of *Romeo
and Juliet*," by Dympna C. Callaghan * "Constructing Identities,"
by Sasha Roberts * "Juliet in *Romeo and Juliet*," by Niamh Cusack
* "Romeo in *Romeo and Juliet*," by David Tennant * "Shakespeare
with a View: Zeffirelli's *Romeo and Juliet*," by Courtney Lehmann *
From "*William Shakespeare's Romeo + Juliet*, by Baz Luhrmann," by
Craig Pearce * "*William Shakespeare's Romeo + Juliet*: Everything's
Nice in America?" by Barbara Hodgdon * "*Romeo and Juliet* in
Baghdad (and in Stratford and London and Qatar)," by Susan Bennett
* Selected Bibliography.

---

**2016**. SERIES: PELICAN SHAKESPEARE. Edited by Stephen Orgel
and A. R. Braunmuller. Penguin. 132 pp.

PUBLISHER'S DESCRIPTION: "Each book [in the Pelican Shakespeare]
includes an essay on the theatrical world of Shakespeare's time,
an introduction to the individual play, and a detailed note on the
text used. Updated by general editors Stephen Orgel and A. R.
Braunmuller, these easy-to-read editions incorporate over thirty years
of Shakespeare scholarship undertaken since the original series, edited
by Alfred Harbage, appeared between 1956 and 1967."

---

**2016**. SERIES: PLAYS AT THE GARRICK. Edited by Kenneth Branagh.
Nick Hern Books.

---

PUBLISHER'S DESCRIPTION: This production, "co-directed by Rob Ashford and Kenneth Branagh," was "performed as part of the Plays at the Garrick Season in 2016, starring Derek Jacobi as Mercutio, Meera Syal as the Nurse, and Lily James and Richard Madden as the star-crossed lovers. This official tie-in edition features the version of Shakespeare's text performed in the production as well as exclusive additional material," including interviews with the actors, photos of the sets, drawings of costume designs, and so on.

**2016**. SERIES: RSC [ROYAL SHAKESPEARE COMPANY] SCHOOL SHAKESPEARE. No editor listed. Oxford UP. 272 pp. With separate teacher's guide.

PUBLISHER'S DESCRIPTION: "These full-colour editions include the RSC's active approaches to exploring the text, vibrant RSC performance photographs, page summaries, glosses, contextual information and much more."

**2013.** SERIES: SHAKESPEARE MADE IN CANADA. Edited by Gilbert Sky and Jill L. Levenson. Oxford UP Canada. 184 pp.

PUBLISHER'S DESCRIPTION: "Canadians have enjoyed a long history of encounters with Shakespeare, from the visual arts to creative new adaptations, from traditional and nontraditional interpretations to distinguished critical scholarship. We have in over two centuries remade Shakespeare in ways that are distinctly Canadian. The series offers a unique vantage on these histories of production and encounter with attention to accessibility and presentation. These editions explore how a given country can inform the interpretation and pedagogy associated with individual plays. . . . The Canadian Adaptations of Shakespeare project at the University of Guelph has created a multimedia database of hundreds of adaptations, developed from Guelph's world-class theatre archives and a host of independent sources that reflect on a long tradition—from pre-Confederation times and heading vibrantly into the future—of playing Shakespeare in Canada. These are the first editions of the plays of William Shakespeare to place key insights from the world's best scholarship alongside the specific contexts associated with a dynamic Canadian tradition of productions and adaptations. Specially research[ed] images, never printed before, from a range of Canadian productions of Shakespeare will be featured in every play."

CONTENTS: Ten Tips for Reading Shakespeare * "Wherefore Art Thou, Masculinity?" by Sky Gilbert * "'Dear Account': The Romeo and Juliet Story from Myth to the National Ballet of Canada," by Jill L. Levenson * *The Tragedy of Romeo and Juliet* * Editorial Principles and Works Cited

---

**2013**. WITH A SCREENPLAY BY JULIAN FELLOWES. Ember, 2013.

PUBLISHER'S DESCRIPTION: "The new dazzling *Romeo and Juliet* screenplay, adapted by Julian Fellowes (*Downton Abbey*, *Gosford Park*), is paired with [Shakespeare's play] . . . in this omnibus edition. . . . Includes full-color photos" of the stars of the 2013 film directed by Carlo Carlei).

---

**2012**. SERIES: ARDEN SHAKESPEARE, THIRD SERIES. Edited by René Weis. 454 pp. 20; b + w illustrations.

CONTENTS: Introduction * "Writing love" * "All the daughters of my father's house" * "Love's young sweet song: 'an excellent conceited tragedy'" * "Love and literary form" * "Time's winged chariot" * "The dates of first performance and publication" * "Lord Hunsdon's servants and Will Kemp at the Curtain (1596–7?)" * "Earth tremors and thirteen-year-old children" * Nashe's *Have With You to Saffron Walden* (1596) and Romeo and Juliet" * *A Midsummer Night's Dream* * "Sources" * Brooke's *Tragical History of Romeus and Juliet*" * "Tybalt, Mercutio and Paris" * "Performing love" * "From London (ca. 1596) and Cambridge (ca. 1598–1601) to Douai (1694–5)" * "From Garrick (1748) to Berlioz (1839) and Cushman (1845)" * "From Gounod (1867) and Tchaikovsky (1870/80) to Gielgud and Prokofiev (1935)" * From *West Side Story* (1957) to Old Pronunciation Shakespeare (2004)" * "The age of Zeffirelli (1960–8)" * "Bogdanov and Luhrmann: from Alfa Romeo to *Clockwork Orange Shakespeare* and beyond (1986–)" * "The texts: Q1 (1597) and Q2 (1599)" * "Nurse's italics and Capulet's Wife's speech prefixes" * "Shakespeare's handwriting and what it has left us" * "Second thoughts: Queen Mab

---

and others" * "From Q1 to Q2" * "Q1's stage directions: a record of performance or 'literary' ornaments?" * "Editorial procedures" * *Romeo and Juliet* * Appendices * "Q1 and Q4 readings" * "Q1 *Romeo and Juliet*" * "Rhyme" * "Casting and doubling" * "Abbreviations and references" * "Abbreviations used in notes" * "Works by and partly by Shakespeare" * "Editions of Shakespeare collated" * "Other works cited or used" * Index.

**2012**. SERIES: SIGNATURE SHAKESPEARE. Edited by Mario DiGangi. Illustrated by Kevin Stanton. 396 pp.

PUBLISHER'S DESCRIPTION: "Featuring remarkable laser-cut paper designs throughout, this new series offers stunning presentations of Shakespeare's plays, complete with scholarship, commentary, notes, and illustrated essays about Shakespeare's language and performances of the play. . . . * Illustration: Original paper-cuts, in the form of laser tip-ins and scans, beautifully illustrate each play. Paintings and photographs add depth to front and back matter. * Scholarship: Premier scholars introduce each play with contemporary scholarship. An essay on editing the text provides an in-depth look at the quartos and folios used . . . * Context: Essays on Shakespeare's England, language, and life, along with essays on performing Shakespeare and significant performances . . . . * A look at the lasting influence of the play on music, art, film, and dance creates an interdisciplinary framework . . . . * Notes: Through one-word margin definitions, facing-page glosses, and longer end notes after each play, the series' approach to notes pulls readers away from the text fewer times . . . . * Further Reading—An annotated bibliography . . . takes readers beyond the edition for further reading. . . . [This edition] includes contextualizing essays and timelines by scholar Mario DiGangi, in collaboration with . . . David Scott Kastan of Columbia University."

CONTENTS: Introduction to *Romeo and Juliet* * "Shakespeare and His England" * "William Shakespeare: A Chronology" * "Words, Words, Words: Understanding Shakespeare's Language" * "Key to the Play Text" * *Romeo and Juliet* * 43 (2) "List of Roles" * "Longer Notes" * "Editing *Romeo and Juliet*" * "*Romeo and Juliet* on the Early Stage"

* "Significant Performances" * "Inspired by *Romeo and Juliet*" "For Further Reading."

---

**2011.** COLLINS CLASSICS. No editor listed. Collins. 320 pp; black and white illustrations.

CONTENTS: "The Theatre in Shakespeare's Day" * "Shakespeare: A Timeline" * "Life & Times" * "Money in Shakespeare's Day" * "Introduction" * "List of Characters * "Text" * "Summing Up" * "Theme Index" * "Shakespeare: Words and Phrases."

---

**2010.** FRANKLY ANNOTATED SHAKESPEARE. *The tragedie of Romeo and Juliet : a frankly annotated first folio edition.* Edited by Demitra Papadinis. McFarland, 2010.

PUBLISHER'S DESCRIPTION: "This annotated edition of *The Tragedie of Romeo and Juliet* . . . restores the language of Shakespeare to that of the First Folio of 1623, with its idiosyncratic and illuminating spelling, capitalization, and punctuation. It also provides footnotes and annotations that are candid and plainspoken in their accounting of Shakespeare's themes, including his oft-overlooked and under-appreciated adult themes."

CONTENTS: "Introduction: Of Forthright Footnotes (or, putting the 'count' back in 'country' * "Filthy Plaies and Enterluds" * "Why the First Folio?" * "What's Wrong with Editing?" * "The Importance of Spelling" * "The Importance of Punctuation" * "Notes on the Annotation" * "Abbreviations of Key Reference Works" * "*The Tragedie of Romeo and Juliet*: First Folio Play-script with Accompanying Annotation" * "Textual Preparation" * "Appendix I (Typographical Errors Corrected)" * "Appendix II (Stage Directions, Entrances and Exits Emended)" * "Appendix III (Lineation Emended)" * "Appendix IV (Character Tags Emended)" * "Bibliography."

---

**2009.** THE CAMBRIDGE DOVER WILSON SHAKESPEARE. Edited by John Dover Wilson, assisted by George Ian Duthie. Cambridge UP. 308 pp.; b + w illustrations.

---

PUBLISHER'S DESCRIPTION: "John Dover Wilson's New Shakespeare, published between 1921 and 1966, became the classic Cambridge edition of Shakespeare's plays and poems until the 1980s. The series, long since out-of-print, is now reissued. Each work is available both individually and as a set, and each contains a lengthy and lively introduction, main text, and substantial notes and glossary printed at the back. The edition . . . put into practice the techniques and theories that had evolved under the 'New Bibliography.' . . . As the volumes took shape, many of Dover Wilson's textual methods acquired general acceptance and became an established part of later editorial practice, for example in the Arden and New Cambridge Shakespeares."

CONTENTS: "Prefatory Note" * "Introduction" * "The Stage History" * "To the Reader" "Title-Page of the Second Quarto" * "*Romeo and Juliet*" * "The Copy for *Romeo and Juliet*, 1599" * "Notes" * "Glossary."

---

**2009**. SERIES: CAMBRIDGE SCHOOL SHAKESPEARE. Edited by Rex Gibson. 4th revised edition. Cambridge UP. 248 pp.

CONTENTS: "Introduction" * "Photo gallery" * *Romeo and Juliet* * "List of characters" * "Text of the play" * "The story of Romeo and Juliet" * "Characters" * "Perspectives and themes" * "Why did Romeo and Juliet die?" * "The language of *Romeo and Juliet*" * "*Romeo and Juliet* in performance" * "Writing about Shakespeare" * "Writing about *Romeo and Juliet*" * "Timeline."

---

**2009**. DOVER THRIFT EDITION. No editor listed. Dover. 176 pp.

PUBLISHER'S DESCRIPTION: "Includes the unabridged text . . . plus a complete study guide that features scene-by-scene summaries, explanations and discussions of the plot, question-and-answer sections, author biography, historical background, and more."

---

**2009**. HARPER TEEN EDITION. No editor listed. Harper Teen. 384 pp.; illustrations.

PUBLISHER'S DESCRIPTION: "Before Bella and Edward [of the *Twilight* novels], Romeo and Juliet were the original star-crossed lovers. . . . Presents Shakespeare's tragic tale of star-crossed lovers and feuding families along with a retelling of the play from Juliet's perspective."

**2009**. SERIES: OXFORD SCHOOL SHAKESPEARE. Edited by Roma Gill. Oxford UP. 176 pp.

CONTENTS: "Introduction" * "About the Play" * "Leading Characters in the Play" * "Synopsis" * *"Romeo and Juliet*: Commentary" * "Shakespeare's Verse" * "Source, Text, and Date" * "Characters in the Play" * *"Romeo and Juliet* "* "Extracts from *Romeus and Juliet*" * "Background" * "England in 1597" * "Government" * "Religion" * "Education" * "Language" * "Drama" * "Theatre" * "William Shakespeare, 1564–1616" * "Approximate Dates of Composition of Shakespeare's Works" * "Exploring *Romeo and Juliet* in the classroom" * "Ways into the Play" * "Setting the Scene" * "Keeping Track of the Action" * "Characters" * "Themes" * "Shakespeare's Language" * "Exploring with Drama" * "Writing about *Romeo and Juliet*" * "Further Reading and Resources."

**2009**. RSC [ROYAL SHAKESPEARE COMPANY] SHAKESPEARE. Edited by Eric Rasmussen and Jonathan Bate. Palgrave Macmillan. 216 pp; illustrations.

PUBLISHER'S DESCRIPTION: "THIS EDITION INCLUDES: * An illuminating introduction to *Romeo and Juliet* by . . . Jonathan Bate * The play—with clear and authoritative explanatory notes on each page * A helpful scene-by-scene analysis and key facts about the play * An introduction to Shakespeare's career and the Elizabethan theatre * A rich exploration of approaches to staging the play featuring photographs of key productions."

CONTENTS: "Introduction About the Text" * "Key Facts" * *"Romeo and Juliet*" * "Textual Notes" * "Scene-by-scene Analysis" * *"Romeo and Juliet* in Performance: the RSC and Beyond" * "Four Centuries of *Romeo and Juliet*" "An Overview At the RSC" * "The Director's Cut: Interview with Michael Attenborough" * "David Tennant on playing Romeo" * "Alexandra Gilbreath on playing Juliet" * "Shakespeare's

Career in the Theatre" * "Shakespeare's Works: a Chronology" * "Further Reading and Viewing" * "References."

**2008**. BRITISH LIBRARY: SHAKESPEARE'S FIRST FOLIO. No editor listed. British Library, 2008. 48 pp.; illustrations.

PUBLISHER'S DESCRIPTION: "'Shakespeare's First Folio' is a modern term applied by scholars to one of the world's most famous books, *Mr. William Shakespeares Comedies, Histories, & Tragedies*, the collected edition of Shakespeare's plays . . . . Published in folio form seven years after the playwright's death by Isaac Iaggard and Edward Blount, and overseen by Shakespeare's fellow actors John Heminge and Henry Condell, the First Folio contains the text of thirty-six plays, half of which had not been previously published during the Bard's lifetime. At last, readers had the plays as they were actually performed, 'where before,' the editors wrote, 'you were abused with diverse, stolen and surreptitious copies, maimed and deformed by the frauds and stealths of injurious imposters. . . .'"

**2008.** OXFORD WORLD CLASSICS. Edited by Jill L. Levenson. Oxford UP. 464 pp.; "numerous black and white plates."

PUBLISHER'S DESCRIPTION: "This innovative edition . . . offers modernized texts not only of the 1599 quarto but also of the short, or 'bad' quarto of 1597, regarding each as witness to a 'mobile text' which changed in composition as Shakespeare wrote it and which has continued to evolve throughout its richly varied history, both in the theatre and in film, television, opera, and ballet. The more familiar 1599 text is accompanied by a detailed explanatory commentary. The Introduction traces the Romeo and Juliet narrative from its origins in myth through its adaptation in the novella, and shows how Shakespeare's transmutation of the story reflects contemporary concerns with love, death, adolescence, and patriarchism."

**2007**. SERIES: ALEXANDER SHAKESPEARE. Edited by Peter Alexander. Collins Educational. 296 pp; illustrations.

PUBLISHER'S DESCRIPTION: "This edition . . . contains the full text, extensive notes and supplementary material written especially for school use. / The Theatre in Shakespeare's Day / Shakespeare's Life and Times / Introduction / Summing Up / Theme Index."

---

**2007**. SERIES: THE EARLY QUARTOS. *The first quarto of Romeo and Juliet*, edited by Lukas Erne. Cambridge UP, 2007. xvii + 192 pp; facsimiles.

PUBLISHER'S DESCRIPTION: "Two different versions of Romeo and Juliet were published during Shakespeare's lifetime: the second quarto of 1599, on which modern editions are usually based, and the first quarto of 1597. The latter version was long denigrated as a 'bad' quarto, but recent scholarship sees in it a crucial witness for the theatrical practices of Shakespeare and his company. The shorter of the two versions by about one quarter, the first quarto has high-paced action, fuller stage directions than the second quarto, and fascinating alternatives to the famous speeches in the longer version. The introduction to this edition provides a full discussion of the origins of the first quarto, before analysing its distinguishing features and presenting a concise history of the 1597 version. The text is provided with a full collation and commentary which alert the reader to crucial differences between the first and the second quartos."

CONTENTS: "Preface" * "Abbreviations and conventions" * "Introduction: 1. Textual provenance: A century of 'bad quartos'" * "Past thinking about Q1 Romeo and Juliet" * "The early draft / revision theory" * "Memorial reporters?" * "Stage abridgement, not memorial reconstruction?" * "Evidence of memorial agency" * "Alternatives to the traditional narrative—A version for the provinces?" * "Theatrical abridgement" * "Textual provenance: conclusion" * 2. "Dramatic specificities: Pace and action" * "Stage directions" * "The betrothal scene" * "Characterization" * "Inconsistent time references" * 3. "Publication and printing: The First Quarto in 1597" * "The First Quarto after 1597" * "Note on the text" * "List of characters" * "THE PLAY" * "Textual notes" * "Appendix A. Scene division" * "Appendix B. Casting and doubling" * "Appendix C. *Belvedere*

(1600)" * "Appendix D. Q1 in eighteenth-century editions of *Romeo and Juliet*" * "Bibliography."

---

**2007**. SERIES: NEW KITTREDGE SHAKESPEARE. Edited by James H. Lake, Laury Magnus, and Bernice W. Kliman. Focus/Pullins. 180 pp.; "photos from major productions."

PUBLISHER'S DESCRIPTION: "George Lyman Kittredge's insightful editions of Shakespeare have endured in part because of his eclecticism, his diversity of interests, and his wide-ranging accomplishments, all of which are reflected in the valuable notes in each volume."

Features of each edition include: * The original introduction to the Kittredge Edition * Editor's Introduction to the Focus Edition. An overview on major themes of the plays, and sections on the play's performance history on stage and screen. * Explanatory Notes. The explanatory notes either expand on Kittredge's superb glosses, or, in the case of plays for which he did not write notes, give the needed explanations for Shakespeare's sometimes demanding language. * Performance notes. These appear separately and immediately below the textual footnotes and include discussions of noteworthy stagings of the plays, issues of interpretation, and film and stage choices. * How to read the play as Performance Section. A discussion of the written play vs. the play as performed and the various ways in which Shakespeare's words allow the reader to envision the work 'off the page.' * Comprehensive Timeline. Covering major historical events (with brief annotations) as well as relevant details from Shakespeare's life. Some of the Chronologies include time chronologies within the plays. * Topics for Discussion and Further Study Section. * Critical Issues: Dealing with the text in a larger context and considerations of character, genre, language, and interpretative problems. * Performance Issues: Problems and intricacies of staging the play connected to chief issues discussed in the Focus Editions' Introduction. * Select Bibliography & Filmography. * Each New Kittredge edition also includes screen grabs from major productions, for comparison and scene study.

TABLE OF CONTENTS: "Preface" * "Introduction to the Kittredge Edition" * "Introduction to the Focus Edition" * "Some Other Where:

---

*Romeo and Juliet* as Ballet, as Musical" by Barbara M. Fisher * "*The Tragedy of Romeo and Juliet*" * "Reading *Romeo and Juliet* as Performance" * "Timeline" * "Topics for Discussion and Further Study" * "Bibliography" * "Filmography."

**2007**. PARALLEL QUARTO TEXTS. Edited by Jay L. Halio. U of Delaware P. 175 pp.; illustrations.

PUBLISHER'S DESCRIPTION: "Using this edition, the reader may see at once how Shakespeare's manuscript of the play, upon which the second quarto (Q2) is based, was adapted for the Elizabethan stage by the author and/or his colleagues. Q1 is considerably shorter than Q2. While many long speeches are cut, abbreviated, or revised, the structure of the play remains essentially as Shakespeare originally conceived it. . . . While both of these early quartos were once believed to be memorial reconstructions, and thus 'Bad' quartos, the theory of memorial reconstructions has now been seriously disputed. One of the essays appended to Halio's edition, "Handy-Dandy: Q1/Q2 Romeo and Juliet," discusses this issue and brings fresh evidence to bear to show that Q1 Romeo is not truly a 'Bad' quarto, as A. W. Pollard long maintained. In another essay, Halio offers a brief stage history of 'Romeo and Juliet.' Many non-authorial changes in the texts of Shakespeare's play were common in the eighteenth century. For example, Garrick introduced Juliet's spectacular funeral procession at the end of act 4, along with many new songs. Later, the American actress Charlotte Cushman removed many of these interpolations and restored much of Shakespeare's original text. Modern-dress productions of the play have often been staged, which introduced a good deal of modern technology into the action."

**2006.** SERIES: AUDIO EDUCATION STUDY GUIDES. Edited by Simon Potter. Smartpass. CD-Audio, MP3 format.

PUBLISHER'S DESCRIPTION: "Introduction to the guide, Shakespeare's world, Drama with commentary, Introduction to themes, Fate and destiny, Power and Authority, Youth and Age, Children and parents, Love and hate, Darkness and light—why it is not a theme, The individual and society, Close. The disc includes read-along scripts to view or print."

---

**2006**. SERIES: SHAKESPEARE ON THE DOUBLE. "Translated by Mary Ellen Snodgrass." John Wiley. 240 pp; illustrations (chiefly color).

PUBLISHER'S DESCRIPTION: "This modern translation and aids . . . make understanding the play quick and painless: * A brief synopsis of the plot and action * A comprehensive character list that describes the characteristics, motivations, and actions of each major player * A visual character map that shows the relationships of major characters * A cycle-of-death graphic that pinpoints the sequence of deaths and includes who dies, how they die, and why * Reflective questions that help you understand the themes of the play."

---

**2006**. SERIES: SIGNET CLASSICS. Edited by J. A. Bryant. Chamberlain Brothers. 224 pp. Mixed media product: softback and DVD Audio.

PUBLISHER'S DESCRIPTION: "Beautifully packaged with a DVD of the BBC production; unique features of this Signet Classics edition include an overview of Shakespeare's life, a special introduction to the play, the source from which Shakespeare derived Romeo and Juliet—Arthur Brooke's *The Tragicall Historye of Romeus and Juliet*—dramatic criticism from the past and present, a comprehensive stage and screen history, and up-to-date recommended readings."

---

**2006**. SERIES: SOURCEBOOKS SHAKESPEARE. Edited by Peter Holland, Barbara Gaines, and David Bevington. Sourcebooks. Mixed media product; 256 pages; photographs; contains paperback and CD-Audio.

PUBLISHER'S DESCRIPTION: "The Sourcebooks Shakespeare brings the Shakespeare page to life. . . . This dynamic book includes an integrated audio CD that showcases key scenes from great performances past and present. . . . Each book offers: * The full play, with line notes and a concurrent glossary * Scholars and theatre producers discussing the play and popular culture * Comments from every cast member of a current production. * This is also a very visual text, including: * Photographs from great performances * Costume designs and set renderings from different productions * Production notes that take you inside the stage experience. . . . Hear: * Ellen Terry from 1911 * The Renaissance Theatre production with Kenneth Branagh, Sir Jon Gielgud and Dame Judi Dench * Modern scenes with Kate Beckinsale and Joseph Fiennes * Read: * About the 1811 production in Covent Garden, London * And see how the Chicago Shakespeare Theater's 2005 cast approaches the play * Page facsimiles from the Garrick-Kemble text from the late 1700s * Costume designs and set renderings from Sir John Gielgud's 1935 production * Photographs from *Romeo + Juliet* directed by Baz Luhrmann * Narrated by: Sir Derek Jacobi."

---

**2004**. SERIES: NEW FOLGER SHAKESPEARE. Edited by Barbara A. Mowat and Paul Werstine.

CONTENTS: "Editors' Preface" * "Shakespeare's *Romeo and Juliet*" * "Reading Shakespeare's Language" * "Shakespeare's Life" * "Shakespeare's Theater" * "The Publication of Shakespeare's Plays" * "An Introduction to This Text" * "*The Tragedy of Romeo and Juliet*: Text of the Play with Commentary" * "Textual Notes" * "*Romeo and Juliet*: A Modern Perspective," by Gail Kern Paster * "Further Reading" * "Key to Famous Lines and Phrases." [For a free electronic version, see www.folgerdigitaltexts.org/html/Rom.html/.

---

**2003**. SERIES: BEDFORD SHAKESPEARE. Edited by Dympna Callaghan. Bedford. 475 pp.; illustrations.

PUBLISHER'S DESCRIPTION: "This edition . . . reprints the Bevington [text] accompanied by six sets of thematically arranged primary documents and illustrations . . . . The texts include travel accounts, poetry, excerpts from early modern fencing manuals, royal proclamations and statutes, tables and prognostications from an early modern almanac, and orders for religious ceremonies from The Book of Common Prayer. Unique to this edition, too, is the inclusion of numerous unpublished manuscript letters of the Bagot family and some poignantly moving passages from the diary of Lady Anne

---

Clifford. The documents contextualize the social relationships among men in Shakespeare's time, violence in Elizabethan society, views of love and the Petrarchan paradigm, spiritual life, family in Elizabethan society, and ideas about astrology, medicine, and death."

**2003**. SERIES: UPDATED CAMBRIDGE EDITION. Edited by G. Blakemore Evans. Cambridge UP. xii + 266 pp.; illustrations.

PUBLISHER'S DESCRIPTION: "Professor Evans helps the reader to visualise the stage action of *Romeo and Juliet* . . . . The history of the play in the theatre is accompanied by illustrations of notable productions from the eighteenth century onwards. A lucid commentary alerts the reader to the difficulties of language, thought and staging. For this updated edition Thomas Moisan has added a new section to the Introduction which takes account of the number of important professional theatre productions and the large output of scholarly criticism on the play which have appeared in recent years. The Reading List has also been revised and augmented."

CONTENTS: "Introduction, with new section on recent developments in criticism and production" by Thomas Moisan * "Note on the text" * "List of characters" * "The play" * "Supplementary notes" * "Textual analysis" * "Appendix: Brooke's *Romeus*" * "Reading list."

**2002**. SERIES: SHAKESPEARE IN PRODUCTION. Edited by James N. Loehlin. Cambridge UP. 270 pp.; illustration.

PUBLISHER'S DESCRIPTION: "This edition provides a detailed, thorough and readable account of the play in production. The introduction examines shifts in interpretation, textual adaptations and staging innovations over four centuries of theatrical production. The commentary gives detailed examples of how different performers, from Henry Irving and Ellen Terry to Leonardo DiCaprio and Claire Danes, have brought life and death to Shakespeare's star-crossed lovers."

**1998**. SERIES: REVISED SIGNET CLASSICS. Edited by J. A. Bryant. Penguin. 224 pp.

PUBLISHER'S DESCRIPTION: "Our Signet Classic Shakespeare Series was extensively revised in 1998. We offer the best of everything— [including] . . . comprehensive notes on the text, an essay on Shakespeare's life and times, source material, critical commentaries, extensive bibliographies, and footnotes. And there's more . . . including both historical and thoroughly contemporary critical commentary on such issues as feminist, political, and theatrical interpretations of the plays—with recent full-length essays by . . . Frank Kermode, Carolyn Heilbrun, Michael Goldman, Linda Bamber, and many others. [Includes an essay] on the Performance or Stage History of each play, written by Sylvan Barnet. —Revised bibliography."

**1997**. ARDEN SHAKESPEARE, SECOND SERIES. Edited by Brian Gibbons. Thomas Nelson Publishers.

CONTENTS: "Introduction" * "William Shakespeare, 1564–1616" * "Shakespeare's Theater" * "The Sound of Shakespeare" * "Publishing Shakespeare" * *Romeo and Juliet* * "Introduction to the Play" * *Romeo and Juliet*'s Sources" * "The Text of *Romeo and Juliet*" * "The Play" * "The Characters" * "Act I" * "Pre-Act Notes" * "Text of Act I and Modern Version" * "Post-Act Activities" * [Repeated for all five acts] * "Additional Resources."

# Bibliography

## Editions

Andrews, John F., editor. *Romeo and Juliet*. Everyman, 1993. Everyman Shakespeare.

Bate, Jonathan, and Eric Rasmussen, editors. *Romeo and Juliet*. Modern Library, 2009.

Bevington, David, et al., editors. *Romeo and Juliet*. Foreword by Joseph Papp. Bantam, 1988.

Brown, John Russell, editor. *Romeo and Juliet*. Applause, 2001.

Bryant, J. A., Jr., editor. *Romeo and Juliet*. 1964, 1986. Signet Classic, 1998. Signet Classics.

Callaghan, Dymphna, editor. *"Romeo and Juliet": Texts and Contexts*. Bedford / St. Martins, 2003. Bedford Shakespeare.

DiGangi, Mario, editor. *Romeo and Juliet*. Sterling Signature, 2012. Signature Shakespeare.

Erne, Lukas, editor. *The First Quarto of Romeo and Juliet*. Cambridge UP, 2011.

Evans, G. B., editor. *Romeo and Juliet*. 1984. Cambridge UP, 2003. New Cambridge Shakespeare.

Furness, Horace Howard, editor. *Romeo and Juliet*. Dover, 1963. New Variorum Shakespeare.

Gibbons, Brian, editor. *Romeo and Juliet*. Methuen, 1980. New Arden edition.

Gibson, Rex, editor. *Romeo and Juliet*. Cambridge UP, 2006. Cambridge School Shakespeare.

Gill, Roma, editor. *Romeo and Juliet*. 1982. Oxford UP, 2008. Oxford School Shakespeare.

Halio, Jay, editor. *Romeo and Juliet: Parallel Texts of Quarto 1 (1597) and Quarto 2 (1599)*. U of Delaware P, 2008.

Holland, Peter, editor. *Romeo and Juliet*. 2000. Penguin, 2016. Pelican Shakespeare.

Hosley, Richard, editor. *Romeo and Juliet*. Yale UP, 1954.

Houghton, Ralph E. C., editor. *Romeo and Juliet*. Clarendon, 1975.

Kastan, David Scott, and Mario DiGangi, editors. *Romeo and Juliet*. Barnes and Noble, 2007. Barnes and Noble Shakespeare.

Kittredge, G. L., editor. *Romeo and Juliet*. Ginn, 1940.

Levenson, Jill, editor. *Romeo and Juliet*. Manchester UP, 1988.

_____, editor. *Romeo and Juliet*. Oxford UP, 2000.

Mcmullan, Gordon, editor. *Romeo and Juliet*. Norton, 2016. Norton Critical Edition.

Mowat, Barbara, and Paul Werstine, editors. *Romeo and Juliet*. 1992. Simon and Schuster, 2011. Folger Shakespeare.

Pearce, Joseph, editor. *Romeo and Juliet*. Ignatius, 2011. Ignatius Critical Editions.

Raffell, Burton, editor. *Romeo and Juliet*. Yale UP, 2004.

Spencer, T. J. B., editor. *Romeo and Juliet*. 1981. Penguin, 1996. New Penguin Shakespeare.

Trussler, Simon, editor. *Romeo and Juliet*. Methuen, 1989. Royal Shakespeare Company.

Turner, Frederick, editor. *Romeo and Juliet*. U of London P, 1974.

Weis, René, editor. *Romeo and Juliet*. Bloomsbury, 2012. Third Arden Shakespeare.

Williams, George Walton, editor. *Romeo and Juliet*. Duke UP, 1964.

**Commentary**

Andrews John F., editor. *"Romeo and Juliet": Critical Essays*. Garland, 1993.

Belsey, Catherine. *"Romeo and Juliet": Language and Writing*. Bloomsbury, 2014.

Bigliazzi, Silvia, and Lisanna Calvi, editors. *Shakespeare, "Romeo and Juliet," and Civic Life: The Boundaries of Civic Space*. Routledge, 2016.

Bloom, Harold, editor. *William Shakespeare's "Romeo and Juliet."* Chelsea House, 2002.

_____. *William Shakespeare's "Romeo and Juliet."* Bloom's Literary Criticism, 2009.

Cole, Douglas, editor. *Twentieth Century Interpretations of "Romeo and Juliet."* Prentice-Hall, 1970.

Cookson, Linda, and Bryan Loughrey, editors. *"Romeo and Juliet": William Shakespeare.* Longman, 1991.

Evans, Robert O. *The Osier Cage: Rhetorical Devices in Romeo and Juliet.* U of Kentucky P, 1966.

Halio, Jay L. *"Romeo and Juliet": A Guide to the Play.* Greenwood, 1998.

_____, editor. *Shakespeare's "Romeo and Juliet": Texts, Contexts, and Interpretation.* U of Delaware P, 1995.

Holderness, Graham. *William Shakespeare: "Romeo and Juliet."* Penguin, 1990.

Holding, Peter. *Romeo and Juliet.* Macmillan, 1992.

Hoppe, Harry. *The Bad Quarto of "Romeo and Juliet."* Cornell UP, 1948.

Hunter, Lynette. *Negotiating Shakespeare's Language in "Romeo and Juliet": Reading Strategies from Criticism, Editing and the Theatre.* Ashgate, 2009.

Jackson, Russell. *"Romeo and Juliet." Shakespeare at Stratford.* Arden, 2003.

Johnson, Vernon Elso, editor. *Coming of Age in William Shakespeare's "Romeo and Juliet."* Greenhaven, 2009.

Lehmann, Courtney. *"Romeo and Juliet": A Close Study of the Relationship between Text and Film.* Methuen Drama, 2010.

Levenson, Jill. *Shakespeare in Performance: "Romeo and Juliet."* Manchester UP, 1987.

Loehlin, James N. *"Romeo and Juliet": Shakespeare in Production.* Cambridge UP, 2002.

Lupton, Julia Reinhard, editor. *"Romeo and Juliet": A Critical Reader.* Bloomsbury Arden, 2016.

Moore, Olin H. *The Legend of "Romeo and Juliet."* Ohio State UP, 1950.

Porter, Joseph A., editor. *Critical Essays on Shakespeare's "Romeo and Juliet."* G. K. Hall, 1997.

_____. *Shakespeare's Mercutio: His History and Drama.* U of North Carolina P, 1988.

Prunster, Nicole, editor and translator. *"Romeo and Juliet" before Shakespeare: Four Early Stories of Star-Crossed Love.* Centre for Reformation & Renaissance Studies, 2000.

Roberts, Sasha. *William Shakespeare, "Romeo and Juliet."* British Council, 1998.

Seward, James H. *Tragic Vision in "Romeo and Juliet."* Consortium Press, 1973.

Stavig, Mark. *The Forms of Things Unknown: Renaissance Metaphor in "Romeo and Juliet" and A Midsummer Night's Dream.* Duquesne UP, 1995.

Watts, Cedric. *Romeo and Juliet.* Twayne, 1991.

Wells Stanley, editor. "*Romeo and Juliet* and Its Afterlife." Special volume of *Shakespeare Survey*, vol. 49, 1946.

White, R. S., editor. *New Casebooks: "Romeo and Juliet."* Palgrave: 2001.

Wright Katherine L. *Shakespeare's "Romeo and Juliet" in Performance: Traditions and Departures.* Mellen, 1997.

# About the Editor

**Robert C. Evans** is I. B. Young Professor of English at Auburn University at Montgomery, where he has taught since 1982. In 1984, he received his PhD from Princeton University, where he held Weaver and Whiting fellowships as well as a university fellowship. In later years, his research was supported by fellowships from the Newberry Library, the American Council of Learned Societies, the Folger Shakespeare Library, the Mellon Foundation, the Huntington Library, the National Endowment for the Humanities, the American Philosophical Society, and the UCLA Center for Medieval and Renaissance Studies.

In 1982, he was awarded the G. E. Bentley Prize and in 1989 was selected Professor of the Year for Alabama by the Council for the Advancement and Support of Education. At AUM, he has received the Faculty Excellence Award and has been named Distinguished Research Professor, Distinguished Teaching Professor, and University Alumni Professor. Most recently he was named Professor of the Year by the South Atlantic Association of Departments of English.

He is one of three editors of the *Ben Jonson Journal* and is a contributing editor to the John Donne *Variorum Edition*.

He is the author or editor of over thirty-five books (on such topics as Ben Jonson, Martha Moulsworth, Kate Chopin, John Donne, Frank O'Connor, Brian Friel, Ambrose Bierce, Amy Tan, Philip Larkin, early modern women writers, pluralist literary theory, literary criticism, twentieth-century American writers, American novelists, Shakespeare, and seventeenth-century English literature. He is also the author of roughly three hundred published or forthcoming essays or notes (in print and online) on a variety of topics, especially dealing with Renaissance literature, critical theory, women writers, short fiction, and literature of the nineteenth and twentieth centuries.

# Contributors_____

**Christopher Baker** is professor of English at Armstrong State University, a former president of the South Central Renaissance Conference, and a past fellow of the American Council on Education. He is author of *Religion in the Age of Shakespeare* (2007), editor of *Absolutism and the Scientific Revolution 1600–1720: A Biographical Dictionary* (2002), and an assistant editor of the forthcoming MLA Variorum edition of *Cymbeline*. His essays have appeared in *Milton Studies, Ben Jonson Journal, Comparative Drama, Studia Neophilologica, Journal of Modern Literature, John Donne Journal, The Arthur Miller Journal*, and elsewhere.

**Bruce Boehrer** is Bertram H. Davis Professor of Renaissance literature in the Department of English at Florida State University. He is the author or editor of seven books, most recently *Environmental Degradation in Jacobean Drama* (Cambridge University Press). Since 2001 he has served first as founding editor and later as co-editor of the *Journal for Early Modern Cultural Studies*.

**Sarah Fredericks** is finishing her doctorate at the University of Arizona. She has published on such authors as Mark Twain, Herman Melville, Kate Chopin, and Maya Angelou and has contributed to books on the American novel and on LGBTQ literature.

**Richard Harp**, Barrick Distinguished Scholar at the University of Nevada, Las Vegas, has been Chair of the English Department as well as Director of Graduate Studies. Along with the late Stanley Stewart, he was a founding coeditor of the *Ben Jonson Journal* (Edinburgh University Press). With Professor Stewart, he coedited the *Cambridge Companion to Ben Jonson*. In addition to publications on Renaissance literature, he has also published on modern Irish literature and on composition. A recent essay reviewed the history of scholarship on Shakespeare's *Othello*.

**James Hirsh** is Professor of English at Georgia State University. He is the author of *The Structure of Shakespearean Scenes* (Yale University Press); *Shakespeare and the History of Soliloquies* (which won the 2004

South Atlantic Modern Language Association Book Award); and articles published in *Shakespeare Survey, Shakespeare Quarterly, Shakespeare Newsletter, Shakespeare, Medieval and Renaissance Drama in England, Modern Language Quarterly, Papers of the Bibliographical Society of America,* and elsewhere. He edited *New Perspectives on Ben Jonson* and an issue of *Studies in the Literary Imagination* on the topic "English Renaissance Drama and Audience Response." Dr. Hirsh has served as a scholar in residence at the Oregon Shakespearean Festival and is a recipient of the Georgia State University Distinguished Honors Professor Award.

**Lisa Hopkins** is Professor of English at Sheffield Hallam University. She coedits *Shakespeare,* the journal of the British Shakespeare Assocation, the Arden Early Modern Drama Guides, and Arden Studies in Early Modern Drama. She also co-organizes the annual *Othello's Island* conference in Cyprus. She has published extensively on Marlowe, Shakespeare, and Ford, including most recently *Shakespearean Allusion in Crime Fiction: DCI Shakespeare* (Palgrave, 2016) and *Renaissance Drama on the Edge* (Ashgate, 2014). She is currently completing *From the Romans to the Normans on the English Renaissance Stage* for ARC Humanities Press.

**Maurice Hunt** is Research Professor in the Baylor University Department of English, where he teaches undergraduate and graduate courses on different aspects of Shakespeare's work. He has published one or more book chapters or articles on each of Shakespeare's plays over the course of a forty-one-year career. He also teaches a late medieval/Elizabethan survey course and graduate courses in Edmund Spenser's *Faerie Queene* and Sir Philip Sidney's *Arcadia.* Recent books are *Shakespeare's "As You Like It": Late Elizabethan Culture and Literary Representation* (2008); *Shakespeare's Speculative Art* (2011); and *The Divine Face in Four Writers: Shakespeare, Dostoyevsky, Hesse, and C. S. Lewis* (2016).

**Adam Rzepka** is Assistant Professor of English at Montclair State University, where he teaches Shakespeare and other early modern drama, early modern poetry, and critical theory. He has published book chapters on Lucretian poetics and Renaissance systems of artificial memory. An article in the fall 2015 issue of *Shakespeare Quarterly*, titled "'How easy is a bush supposed a bear?': Differentiating Imaginative Production in *A Midsummer Night's Dream*," tracks the multiple functions of the imagination as a faculty of the soul in the play. His book in progress is on the field and function of "experience" in early modern discourse and Shakespearean drama.

**Matthew Steggle** is Professor of English at Sheffield Hallam University. He has published four books on early modern drama and worked as a contributing editor to scholarly editions including *The Cambridge Works of Ben Jonson* (2012) and the *Norton Shakespeare*, third edition (2015). He is coeditor, with Roslyn L. Knutson and David McInnis, of the Lost Plays Database (www.lostplays.org), and he is coeditor of the ejournal *Early Modern Literary Studies*. In 2015, he won the Hoffman Prize for Distinguished Publication on Marlowe. He is co-general editor, with Martin Butler, of the AHRC-funded *The Complete Works of John Marston*, forthcoming from Oxford University Press.

**Eric J. Sterling** earned his PhD in English, with a minor in drama and theatre, in 1992 from Indiana University. He is Professor of English at Auburn University at Montgomery, where he has taught since 1994. He has published four books, including *The Movement Towards Subversion: The English History Play from Skelton to Shakespeare* and *Life in the Ghettos during the Holocaust*. His areas of interest include drama, Shakespeare, the Old Testament, the Holocaust, and Gay and Lesbian literature.

**Frances Teague** is Meigs Professor and University Professor at the University of Georgia, where she holds a joint appointment in the Departments of English and of Theatre and Film Studies. Her research is on Renaissance drama performance history and theory and on early modern women writers. Recent books include *Shakespeare and the American Popular Theatre* (Cambridge, 2006) and with Margaret Ezell, *Educating English Daughters: Bathsua Makin and Mary More* (University of Toronto, 2016).

**Benedict J. Whalen** is Assistant Professor of English at Hillsdale College, where he teaches courses on Shakespeare, Renaissance tragedy, metaphysical poetry, and the tradition of the liberal arts. His research interests include the intersection of Reformation theological debates and early modern drama, and he is currently working on a monograph examining the relationship between penance and community on the early modern stage.

---

---